THE RA MATERIAL

The Law of One
BOOK I

The Law of One
Book I

AN ANCIENT ASTRONAUT SPEAKS

DON ELKINS ⚶ CARLA RUECKERT
JAMES ALLEN McCARTY

REDFeather™
MIND | BODY | SPIRIT
4880 Lower Valley Road, Atglen, PA 19310

INTRODUCTION

DON ELKINS: This book is an exact transcript from tape recordings of twenty-six sessions of an experiment designed to communicate with an extraterrestrial being. We started the experiment in 1962 and refined the process for nineteen years. In 1981 the experimental results of our efforts changed profoundly in quality and precision. This book is simply a report of the beginning of this latter phase of our work.

Since our experimental work began, and even before we officially formed a research group, there was considerable confusion about the nature of our research. I would like to state that I consider my point of view to be purely scientific. Many readers of this material have used as a basis for its evaluation a previously assumed philosophical bias, which has ranged from what I would call objectively scientific to subjectively theological. It is not the purpose of our research group to attempt to do anything other than make experimental data available. Each reader will undoubtedly reach his own unique conclusion about the meaning of this body of data.

In recent years there has been much controversy about phenomena that were apparently incompatible with accepted methods of scientific research. This included such things as UFOs, mental metal bending, psychic surgery, and many other seemingly miraculous happenings.

To prove or disprove any of these alleged phenomena is certainly not properly the task of the casual observer. However, most of the public opinion that has been generated with respect to these events seems to be the product of quick and superficial investigation. After almost thirty years of research and experimentation in the area of so-called paranormal phenomena, I must recommend extreme caution in reaching a conclusion. If it is possible to make money, gain notoriety, or have fun from perpetrating a hoax, then someone usually does it. Consequently, paranormal or psychic areas are prime targets for the trickster, and the careful researcher usually has to observe copious amounts of "garbage" data in order to find a possible imbedded gem of truth. This is especially true of Philippine psychic surgery and the large area of spirit communication in general.

It seems to me that the presently accepted scientific paradigm is less than adequate. It is my opinion that our present natural philosophy is a very special case of a much more general case yet to be unveiled. It is my hope that our research is in the direction of this discovery. After assimilating several million words of alleged extraterrestrial communication, it is also my opinion that this book and the subsequent volumes of the Ra material contain the most useful information that I have discovered. As a result of all of this delving into the rather confusing subjects of UFOlogy and parapsychology, I, of course, have formed my current opinion of how things "really are." This opinion may change at any time as I become aware of future information. This book is not intended to be a treatise of my opinion, so I will not attempt to defend its validity. The following is the best guess I can make about what we think we are doing. Only time will tell as to the accuracy of this guess.

Our research group uses what I prefer to call "tuned trance telepathy" to communicate with an extraterrestrial race called Ra. We use the English language because it is known by Ra. In fact, Ra knows more of it than I do.

Ra landed on Earth about 11,000 years ago as a sort of extraterrestrial missionary with the objective of helping Earthman with his mental evolution. Failing in this attempt, Ra retreated from the Earth's surface but continued to monitor activities closely on this planet. For this reason, Ra is highly informed about our history, languages, etc.

Probably the most difficult thing to understand about Ra is its nature. Ra is a sixth-density social memory complex. Since Earth is near the end of the third-density cycle of evolution, this means that Ra is three evolutionary cycles ahead of us. In other words, Ra's present state of evolution is millions of years in advance of Earthman's. It is not surprising that Ra had difficulty communicating with Earthman 11,000 years ago. The same problem still exists in our present "enlightened" time.

At this writing we have completed over 100 sessions of experimental communications with Ra. This approximately 300,000 words of information has suggested to me a possibly more adequate scientific paradigm. Only time and future experience will serve to validate and expand this paradigm.

UFOlogy is a large subject. A reasonable amount of background material would swell this introduction to book length. Therefore, the remainder of this introduction does not attempt to cover every portion of this diverse and growing field of study but is instead an accounting of some of the pertinent parts of our research from our beginnings to the present day and the Ra contact. I've asked my longtime research associate, Carla L. Rueckert, to tell our story.

CARLA L. RUECKERT: I first met Don Elkins in **1962**. To me he was a fascinating character, an unusual combination of a college professor and psychic researcher. He had done well over **200** hypnotic age regressions, probing past the birth experience and investigating the possibility that reincarnation might not be just possible but the way things really are.

In 1962, I joined an experiment that Don had created in order to start to test a hypothesis that he had developed with the help of Harold Price, an engineer for Ford Motor Company. Price had acquainted Don with some information that Don found quite interesting. Its source was allegedly extraterrestrial. Its content was largely metaphysical and seemed to be in line with all that Don had learned up to that point. Within this material, instructions were given for creating the means whereby to generate further material from this same source without the necessity of actual physical contact with extraterrestrials.

Don's hypothesis was that this phenomenon might be reproducible, so he invited a dozen of his engineering students to join in an experiment with the objective of achieving some sort of telepathic contact with a source similar to that of the Detroit group's. I was the thirteenth member, having become interested in the project through a friend of mine. In those early days of contact attempts, with Don attempting strenuously to keep the situation controlled, months went by with what seemed to be remarkable but puzzling results. As we sat "meditating," according to the instructions, everyone in the group except me began to make strange noises with their mouths. For my part, my main difficulty during those first six months was keeping a straight face and not laughing as the sessions gradually became a raucous symphony of guttural clicks, slurps, and tongue flops.

The nature of the experiment changed drastically when the group was visited by a contactee from Detroit. The contactee sat down with the group and almost immediately was contacted apparently by telepathic impression, saying: "Why don't you speak the thoughts that are on your minds? We are attempting to use you as instruments of communication, but you are all blocked through fear that you will not be speaking the proper words." Through this instrument, Walter Rogers of Detroit, Michigan, the group was instructed to refrain from analysis, to speak the thoughts and to analyze the communication only after it had been completed.

After that night, a month had not gone by before half the group had begun to produce information. By the time a year had passed, all in the group except me were able to receive transmissions. The speech was slow and difficult at first because each individual wanted a precise impression of each and every word and, in many cases, wanted to be completely controlled for fear of making an error in transmission. Nevertheless, this was an exciting time for the original group of students who began this strange experiment.

In January of 1970, I left my position as school librarian of a thirteen-grade private school here in Louisville and went to work for Don full time. By this time he was convinced that the great mystery of being could best be investigated by research into techniques for contacting extraterrestrial intelligences, and was determined to intensify his efforts in this area.

During this period, Don worked on many peripheral areas of UFO research, always trying to "put the puzzle pieces together." One of the great puzzle pieces for us was the question of how UFOs could materialize and dematerialize. The phenomenon seemed to posit a physics that we had not yet grasped and a being capable of using this physics. Don had gone to many séances by himself before I joined him in his research and had very systematically crossed each name off his list. He was looking for a materialization manifestation, not one he could prove to anyone else, but one that he, himself, could believe. It was his feeling that the materializations that séances manifest were perhaps of the same or similar nature as the materializations of UFOs. Therefore, his reasoning went, viewing personally the mechanism of a materialization and a dematerialization in a séance would enable him to hypothesize more accurately concerning UFOs.

In 1971, after I had been on several fruitless materialization medium searches with Don, we went to a séance held by the Reverend James Tingley of Toledo, a minister of the Spiritualist Church.

We went to see Reverend Tingley's demonstrations four times. Before the first time, Don had casually examined Reverend Tingley's modest meeting place inside and out. It was built of concrete blocks, like a garage. There were no gadgets either inside or outside the building. I did not know that Don was doing this. I merely sat and waited for the demonstration to begin.

This last point is an important one when talking about psychic research of any kind. Don has always said that one of my assets as a research associate is my great gullibility. Almost anyone can play a joke on me because I do not catch on quickly. I have a way of taking things as they come and accepting them at face value and only afterwards analyzing what has occurred. This gullibility is a vital factor in obtaining good results in paranormal research. A desire for proof will inevitably lead to null results and voided experiments. An open mind, one willing to be gullible, leads its possessor to a kind of subjective and personal certainty that does not equal proof, as it cannot be systematically reproduced in others. However, this subjective knowing is a central part of the spiritual evolution to which Ra speaks so compellingly in this volume and that we have researched for many years now.

The séance began, as do all the séances I have attended, with the repetition of the Lord's Prayer and the singing of hymns such as "Rock of Ages" and "I Walked in the Garden." There were approximately twenty-six people in this bare room, sitting on straight chairs in an oval circle. Reverend Tingley had retired behind a simple curtain and was also seated on a folding chair. Of the occurrences of the first séance, perhaps the most interesting to me was the appearance of a rather solid ghost known as "Sister." She wished to speak to me and to thank me for helping Don. Since I had never had a close friend that was a nun, I was quite puzzled. It was not until much later, when Don was flying us home, that he jogged my memory, and I realized that his mother, who had died before I met her, was known in the family as "Sister."

Both in that séance and in the following séance, when Don and I were called up, we could see the ghostlike figures of the materialized spirits quite clearly. I, with impaired night vision, could still make out features, but Don could see even the strands of hair on each entity.

During the second séance, an especially inspiring "Master" appeared suddenly and the room grew very cold. He gave us an inspirational message and then told us that he would touch us so that we would know that he was real. He did so, with enough force to bruise my arm. Then he told us that he would walk through us so that we would know that he was not of this density. This he did, and it is certainly an interesting sensation to watch this occur. Lifting his arms, he blessed all those in the room, walked back through us, and pooled down in a small pool on the floor and was gone.

In 1974, Don decided that it was time for me to become a more serious student of the art of channeling. He argued that twelve years of sitting and listening to inspirational messages were enough, and that it was time for me to take some responsibility for those "cosmic sermonettes," as Brad Steiger has called them, that I so enjoyed. We began a series of daily meetings designed to work intensively on my mental tuning. Many of those who were coming to our meditations on Sunday nights heard about the daily meetings and also came, and within three months we generated about a dozen new telepathic receivers.

During the process of these intensive meditations we instituted our long-standing habit of keeping the tape recorder going whenever we started a session. Using some of the large body of material that our own group had collected, I put together an unpublished manuscript, *Voices of the Gods*, which systematically offered the extraterrestrial viewpoint as recorded by our group meetings. In 1976, when Don and I began to write *Secrets of the UFO* (published by a private printing and available by mail), this unpublished manuscript was of great help.

During this period one other thing occurred that was synchronistic. Don and I, who had officially gone into partnership as L/L Research in 1970, had written an unpublished book titled *The Crucifixion of Esmeralda Sweetwater* in 1968.

In 1974, Andrija Puharich published a book with Doubleday titled *Uri*. The book is the narrative of Dr. Puharich's investigation of Uri Geller and their unexpected communication with extraterrestrial intelligences. The form of contact was quite novel in that, first, some object like an ashtray would levitate, signaling Dr. Puharich to load his cassette tape recorder. The recorder's buttons would then be depressed by some invisible force and the machine would record. On playback, a message from an extraterrestrial source would be present. Don was impressed by the large number of correlations between these messages and our own research.

The book is fascinating in its own right, but it was especially fascinating to us because of the incredible number of distinct and compelling similarities between the characters in the real-life journal of Dr. Puharich's work with Uri and the supposedly fictional characters in our book. We went to New York to meet Andrija after phoning him, sharing our long-standing research with him and comparing notes. As our genial host came out onto his front veranda to welcome us, I stopped, amazed, to look at the house. Even the house in which he lived in the country north of New York City was a dead ringer for the house his fictional counterpart had owned in our book. The identity was so close that I could not help but ask, "Andrija, what happened to your peonies? When I wrote about your house I saw your driveway circled with peony bushes." Puharich laughed, "Oh, those. I had those cut down three years ago."

In 1976, we determined to attempt an introduction to the whole spectrum of paranormal phenomena that are involved in the so-called UFO contactee phenomenon. This phenomenon is not a simple one. Rather, it demands a fairly comprehensive understanding and awareness of several different fields of inquiry. Since *The Ra Material* is a direct outgrowth of our continuous research with "alleged" extraterrestrial entities, it seems appropriate here to review some of the concepts put forward in that book in order that the reader may have the proper introduction to the "mindset," which is most helpful for an understanding of this work.

The first thing to say about the UFO phenomenon is that it is extraordinarily strange. The serious researcher, as he reads more and more and does more and more field research, finds himself less and less able to talk about the UFO phenomenon in a sensible and "down to Earth" way. Well over half the people in the United States have said in nationwide polls that they believe that UFOs are real, and television series and motion pictures reflect the widespread interest in this subject. Yet, there are few researchers who would pretend to be able to understand the phenomenon completely. Dr. J. Allen Hynek has called this quality of the research the "high strangeness" factor and has linked the amount of high strangeness with the probable validity of the case.

Some of the people who see UFOs have the experience of being unable to account for a period of time after the encounter. The UFO is seen and then the witness continues on with his or her daily routine. At some point, it is noticed that a certain amount of time has been lost that cannot be explained. Very often these same people report a type of eye irritation, or conjunctivitis, and sometimes skin problems. In extreme cases, a person who has lost time and seen a UFO will develop a change of personality and find it necessary to contact the aid of a psychologist or a psychiatrist for counseling. Dr. R. Leo Sprinkle, professor of psychology at the University of Wyoming, has been conducting yearly meetings of people who have experienced this type and other types of "Close Encounters."

It was in psychiatric therapy that one of the more famous of the UFO contact cases, that of Betty and Barney Hill, was researched. The Hills had seen a UFO and had lost some time but managed to reduce the significance of these events in their minds enough to get on with their daily lives. However, both of them, over a period of months, began experiencing nightmares and attacks of anxiety.

The psychiatrist to whom they went for help was one who often used regressive hypnosis for therapeutic work. He worked with each of the couple separately and found, to his amazement, that when asked to go back to the source of their distress, both Mr. and Mrs. Hill related the story of being taken onboard a UFO while on a drive, medically examined, and returned to their car.

Don and I have, through the years, investigated quite a few interesting cases, but perhaps a description of one will suffice to show some of the more outstanding strangenesses that are quite commonly associated with what Dr. Hynek calls "Close Encounters of the Third Kind." In January 1977, merely eighteen or so hours after our witness's UFO experience, we were called by a friend of ours, hypnotist Lawrence Allison. Lawrence had been contacted by the witness's mother, who was extraordinarily concerned about her boy. We made an appointment with the witness, a nineteen-year-old high school graduate employed as a truck driver.

He had seen a craft about 40 feet long and 10 feet tall, which was the color of the setting sun, at very low altitude, approximately 100 to 150 feet. The craft was so bright that it hurt his eyes, yet he could not remove his gaze from it. He experienced a good deal of fear and lost all sense of actually driving his car. When he was directly underneath the UFO, it suddenly sped away and disappeared. When the boy arrived home, his mother was alarmed because his eyes were entirely bloodshot. He was able to pinpoint his time loss since he had left precisely when a television program ended and since he noticed the time of his arrival home. He had lost thirty-eight minutes of his life.

The young man wished to try regressive hypnosis to "find" his lost time. We agreed, and after a fairly lengthy hypnotic induction, the proper state of concentration was achieved and the witness was moved back to the point at which he was directly underneath the UFO. Suddenly he was inside the ship in a circular room, which seemed at least twice as high as the entire ship had seemed from the outside. He saw three objects, none of which looked human. One was black, one was red, and one was white. All looked like some sort of machine. Each entity seemed to have a personality, although none spoke to the boy, and he endured a kind of physical examination. After the examination was finished, the machines merged into one and then disappeared. The ship bounced and rocked briefly, and then the witness was back in his car.

If you are interested in reading a full account of this case, it was published in the *A.P.R.O. Bulletin*, in *Flying Saucer Review*, in the *International UFO Reporter*, and in the *MUFON UFO News*.

One of the most familiar aspects of close encounters is the experience that our witness had of seemingly understanding what aliens were thinking and feeling without any speech having taken place. Telepathic communication has long been the subject of much experimentation, and, although there is much interesting research, there has never been a definitive study proving good telepathic communication. Consequently, the field of research into telepathy is still definitely a fringe area of psychic research. However, anyone who has ever known that the phone was going to ring, or has experienced the knowledge of what someone was going to say before it was said, has experienced at least a mild example of telepathy. Don states that telepathic experiments between himself and Uri Geller have been totally successful. However, since they were deliberately not performed under rigorous scientific control, they could not be included in any orthodox report. It is, in fact, our opinion that the rigorous controls have a dampening effect on the outcome of any experiment of this type.

L/L Research, which, since 1980, has been a subsidiary of the Rock Creek Research and Development Labs, to this day holds weekly meetings open to anyone who has read our books. We still tend to insert the word "alleged" before the words "telepathic communications from extraterrestrials" because we know full well that there is no way of proving this basic concept. However, the phenomenon certainly exists—millions of words in our own files and many millions of words in other groups' files attest to this fact.

Regardless of the more than occasional frustrations involved in paranormal research, the serious researcher of the UFO phenomenon needs to be persistent in his investigation of related phenomena, such as mental metal bending. The physics that Ra discusses, having to do with the true nature of reality, posits the possibility of action at a distance as a function of mind, specifically the will. Uri Geller has been tested in several places around the world, including the Stanford Research Laboratories, and an impressive list of publications concerning the results of those tests exists, most notably *The Geller Papers* and, as an offshoot of this metal-bending phenomenon, *The Iceland Papers*.

One example that shows the close connection between UFOs and mental metal bending happened to us in July of 1977, after our book, *Secrets of the UFO*, was published. We had been interviewed on a local program, and a woman in a nearby town had heard the broadcast and was very interested in what we had to say, since her son, a normal fourteen-year-old boy, had had a UFO encounter. He had been awakened by a whistling sound, went to the door, and saw a light so bright that it temporarily blinded him. Again, as is often the case, it was the same night that people nearby also saw lights in the sky. The woman wrote us a letter, and Don immediately called and asked her permission to speak to her son. After questioning the young man to Don's satisfaction, Don asked him to take a piece of silverware and tell it to bend without touching it in any firm or forceful way. The fourteen-year-old picked up a fork and did as Don suggested, and the fork immediately bent nearly double.

The boy was so startled that he would not come back to the phone, and his mother was unable to convince him that there was any value in going further with the experiments. She had enough foresight to realize that in the small town in which he lived, any publicity that might come to him on the subject of metal bending would be to his detriment, since the people of his small town would react in a most predictable way.

Nevertheless, the link is there quite plainly. John Taylor, professor of mathematics at Kings College, London, offered his book *Superminds* to make his careful experimentations on metal bending available to the world. Taylor used only children, about fifty of them, and for a great portion of his experiment he used metal and plastic objects sealed in glass cylinders that had been closed by a glass blower, so that the children could not actually touch the objects without breaking the glass.

Under this controlled circumstance the children were still able to bend and break multitudinous objects. As you read *The Ra Material* you will begin to discover why it is mostly children that are able to do these things, and what the ability to do this has to do with the rest of the UFO message.

Since I am not a scientist, at this point I will turn the narrative back to Don, whose background is more suited to this discussion.

DON: A persistent question when considering psychic demonstrations is: how does the paranormal event happen? The answer may well lie in the area of occult theory, which is concerned with the existence of various "planes."

After death, an individual finds himself at one of these levels of existence spoken of in connection with occult philosophy, the level of being dependent on the spiritual nature or development of the person at the time of his death. The cliché that covers this theory is a heavenly "birds of a feather flock together." When a ghost materializes into our reality, it is from one of these levels that he usually comes for his Earthly visit. In general, it is theorized that a planet is a sort of spiritual distillery, with reincarnation taking place into the physical world until the individual is sufficiently developed in the spiritual sense that he can reach the higher planes of existence and is no longer in need of this planet's developmental lessons.

Most of this theory was developed as a result of reported contact and communication with the inhabitants of these supposedly separate realities. I have come to believe that these levels interpenetrate with our physical space and mutually coexist, though with very little awareness of each other. A simple analogy, to which I've referred before, is to consider the actors in two different TV shows, both receivable on the same set, but each show being exclusive of the other. This seems to be what we experience in our daily lives: one channel or density of existence being totally unaware of the myriad entities occupying other frequencies of our physical space. The point of all this is that our reality is not ultimate or singular; it is, in fact, our reality only at the present.

Many of the UFO reports display ample evidence that the object sighted has its origin in one of these other realities or densities, just as do the materialized ghosts. I would like to emphasize that this does not in any way imply their unreality; rather, it displaces the UFOs' reality from ours. I'm saying the equivalent of: channel 4 on the TV is equivalent to but displaced from channel 3 on the same TV.

If you were told to build a scale model of any atom, using something the size of a pea for the nucleus, it would be necessary to have an area the size of a football stadium to contain even the innermost orbital electrons. If the pea were placed at the center of the 50-yard line, a small cotton ball on the uppermost seat in the stands could represent an electron of the atom. There is very little actual matter in physical matter. When you look at the stars in the night sky, you would probably see something quite similar to what you would see if you could stand on the nucleus of any atom of "solid" material and look outward toward our environment. To demonstrate an electron to you, a physicist will probably show you a curved trace of one on a photographic plate. What he probably does not tell you is that this is secondhand evidence. The electron itself has never been seen; only its effect on a dense medium can be recorded. It is possible, of course, to make accurate mathematical calculations about what we call an electron. For such work we must know some data on magnetic field strength, electron charge, and velocity. But since a magnetic field is caused by moving charges, which in turn are empirically observed phenomena, we find that the entire mathematical camouflage obscures the fact that all we really know is that charged particles have effects on each other. We still don't know what charged particles are, or why they create an action-at-a-distance effect.

Senior scientists would be the first to agree that there is no such thing as an absolute scientific explanation of anything. Science is, rather, a method or tool of prediction, relating one or more observations to each other. In physics, this is usually done through the language of mathematics. Our scientific learning is a learning by observation and analysis of this observation. In the sense of penetrating the fundamental essences of things, we really do not understand anything at all.

A magnetic field is nothing but a mathematical method of expressing the relative motion between electrical fields. Electrical fields are complex mathematical interpretations of a totally empirical observation stated as Coulomb's law. In other words, our forest of scientific knowledge and explanations is made up of trees about which we understand nothing except their effect, their existence.

To a person unfamiliar with the inner workings of modern science, it may seem that modern man has his environment nicely under control and totally figured out. Nothing could be further from the truth. The leaders of science who are researching the frontiers of modern theory argue among themselves continually. As soon as a theory begins to receive wide acceptance as being a valid representation of physical laws, someone finds a discrepancy, and the theory has to be either modified or abandoned entirely. Perhaps the most well-known example of this is Newton's "F=MA." This attained the status of a physical law before being found to be in error. It is not that this equation has not proven extremely useful: we have used it to design everything from a moon rocket to the television picture tube, but its accuracy fails when applied to atomic particle accelerators like the cyclotron. To make accurate predictions of particle trajectories, it is necessary to make the relativistic correction formulated by Einstein. It is interesting to note that this correction is based on the fact that the speed of light is totally independent of the speed of its source.

If Newton had penetrated more deeply into the laws of motion, he might have made this relativistic correction himself and then stated that the velocity correction would always be of no consequence, since the velocity of light was so much greater than any speed attainable by man. This was very true in Newton's day but is definitely not the case now. We still tend to think of the velocity of light as a fantastic and unattainable speed, but with the advent of space flight, a new order of velocities has arrived. We have to change our thinking from our normal terrestrial concepts of velocities. Instead of thinking of the speed of light in terms of miles per second, think of it in terms of Earth diameters per second. The almost unimaginable 186,000 miles per second becomes an entirely thinkable twenty-three Earth diameters per second, or we could think of the speed of light in terms of our solar system's diameter and say that light would speed at about two diameters per day.

Einstein's assertion that everything is relative is so apt that it has become a cliché of our culture. Let us continue being relativistic in considering the size of natural phenomena by considering the size of our galaxy. If you look up at the sky on a clear night, nearly all of the visible stars are in our own galaxy. Each of these stars is a sun like our own. A calculation of the ratio of the number of suns in our galaxy to the number of people on planet Earth discovers that there are sixty suns for each living person on Earth today. It takes light over four years to get from Earth to even the nearest of these stars. To reach the most distant star in our own galaxy would take 100,000 light years.

These calculations are made using the assumption that light has a speed. This may be an erroneous assumption in the face of new theory, but its apparent speed is a useful measuring tool, so we use it anyway.

So we have a creation in which we find ourselves that is so big that at a speed of twenty-three Earth diameters a second we must travel 100,000 years to cross our immediate backyard. That is a big backyard, and it would seem ample for even the most ambitious of celestial architects, but in truth this entire galaxy of over 200 billion stars is just one grain of sand on a very big beach. There are uncounted trillions of galaxies like ours, each with its own billions of stars, spread throughout what seems to be infinite space.

When you think of the mind-boggling expanse of our creation and the infantile state of our knowledge in relation to it, you begin to see the necessity for considering the strong probability that our present scientific approach to investigating these expanses is as primitive as the dugout canoe.

The most perplexing problem of science has always been finding a satisfactory explanation of what is called action at a distance. In other words, everyone knows that if you drop something it will fall, but no one knows precisely why. Many people know that electric charges push or pull on each other even if separated in a vacuum, but again no one knows why. Although the phenomena are quite different, the equations that describe the force of interaction are quite similar:

For gravitation: $F=GmmVr2$. For electrostatic interaction: $F=KqqVr2$. The attractive force between our planet and our sun is described by the gravitational equation. The attractive force between orbiting electrons and the atomic nucleus is described by the electrostatic interaction equation. Now each of these equations was determined experimentally. They are not apparently related in any way, and yet they both describe a situation in which attractive force falls off with the square of the distance of separation.

A mathematical representation of an action-at-a-distance effect is called a field, such as a gravitational or electric field. It was Albert Einstein's foremost hope to find a single relation that would express the effect of both electric and gravitational phenomena; in fact, a theory that would unify the whole of physics, a unified field theory. Einstein believed that this was a creation of total order and that all physical phenomena were evolved from a single source.

This unified field theory, describing matter as pure field, has been accomplished now. It seems that the entire situation was analogous to the solution of a ponderously complex Chinese puzzle. If you can find that the right key turns among so many wrong ones, the puzzle easily falls apart. Dewey B. Larson found the solution to this problem, and the puzzle not only fell apart but revealed an elegantly adequate unified field theory rich in practical results; like a good Chinese puzzle, the solution was not complex, just unexpected. Instead of assuming five dimensions, Larson assumed six, and properly labeled them as the three dimensions of space and the three dimensions of time. He assumed that there is a three-dimensional coordinate time analogous to our observed three-dimensional space.

The result of this approach is that one can now calculate from the basic postulate of Larson's theory any physical value within our physical universe, from subatomic to stellar. This long-sought-after unified field theory is different because we are accustomed to thinking of time as one dimensional, as a stream moving in one direction. Yet once you get the hang of it, coordinate time is mathematically a more comfortable concept with which to deal. Professor Frank Meyer of the Department of Physics at the University of Wisconsin currently distributes a quarterly newsletter to scientists interested in Larson's new theory, which explores perplexing questions in physical theory by using Larson's approach. I was interested in testing Larson's theory and made extensive calculations using his postulate. I became convinced that his theory is indeed a workable unified field theory.

I had been pondering several interesting statements communicated through contactees by the alleged UFO source prior to discovering Larson's work in the early sixties. Although the people who had received these communications knew nothing of the problems of modern physics, they were getting information that apparently was quite central to physical theory: first, they suggested that the problem with our science was that it did not recognize enough dimensions. Second, they stated that light does not move; light is. Larson's theory posits six dimensions instead of the customary four and finds the pure field, which Einstein believed would represent matter, to move outward from all points in space at unit velocity, or the velocity of light. Photons are created due to a vibratory displacement in space-time, the fabric of the field. Furthermore, the contactees were saying that consciousness creates vibration, this vibration being light. The vibratory displacements of space-time in Larson's theory are the first physical manifestation, which is the photon or light. According to the UFO contactees, the UFOs lower their vibrations in order to enter our skies. The entire physical universe postulated by Larson is dependent on the rate of vibration and quantized rotations of the pure field of space-time.

The contactees were suggesting that time was not what we think it is. Larson suggests the same thing. The UFOs were said to move in time as we move in space. This would be entirely normal in Larson's time/space portion of the universe.

Lastly, and perhaps most importantly, the contactees were receiving the message that the creation is simple, all one thing. Larson's theory is a mathematical statement of this unity.

For more information about Larsonian physics, contact the International Society of Unified Science, a group of scientists and philosophers currently promoting Larson's theory. Their address is: International Society of Unified Science, Frank H. Meyer, President, 1103 15th Ave., SE, Minneapolis, MN 55414.

What physicists have never before considered worth investigating is now increasing at a very rapid rate. Action at a distance, apparently as a result of some type of mental activity, seems repeatedly the observed effect. When Uri Geller performs on TV, mentally bending metal and fixing clocks, there are often many kids who try to duplicate Uri's "tricks." Sometimes the kids succeed. The number of children that can cause bends and breaks in metal and other materials just by wanting the break or bend to occur is increasing daily. As previously mentioned, John

Taylor, professor of mathematics at Kings College, reports in his excellent book *Superminds* on the extensive tests run in England on several of these gifted children. If the Gellerizing children continue to increase in numbers and ability, the 1980s will see such fantasies of TV as *My Favorite Martian*, *I Dream of Jeannie*, and *Bewitched* becoming a part of reality.

With controlled, repeatable experiments like those conducted by Taylor and by the Stanford Research Institute in the United States, we begin to have good solid data available for study. Gradually we are moving into a position from which we can begin to create a science of "magic," for that which has been called magic through the ages is now being performed at an ever-increasing rate, primarily by children. In the future, we may even find this "magic" added to the curriculum of the sciences at universities. In point of fact, the present disciplines of chemistry, physics, etc., are still basically "magic" to us, since we are still in the position of having no ultimate explanation of causality.

CARLA: One of the concepts most central to the system of study that comes out of research into the contactee messages offered by alleged UFO contact is the concept of the immortality of our individual consciousness. There is a long mystical tradition extending back far beyond biblical times, which posits a type of immortal soul. St. Paul in his Epistles has distinguished between the human body and the spiritual body. Long before St. Paul's century, Egyptian priests had the concept of the ka and posited that this ka, or spiritual personality, existed after death and was the true repository of the essence of consciousness of the person who had lived the life. Egyptians, of course, made very elaborate arrangements for life after death.

If life after death is posited as a probability, one may also posit life before birth. Any mother who has more than one child will testify to the undoubted fact that each child comes into his life or incarnation already equipped with a personality that cannot be explained by environment or heredity. After all the factors of both have been accounted for, there remains a unique personality with which the child seems to have been born. Each child has certain fears that are not explainable in terms of the fears of the parents. A child, for instance, may be terrified of a thunderstorm. The rest of the family may be perfectly comfortable during such a storm. Another child may be extraordinarily gifted at the playing of an instrument when neither parent nor any relative as far back as the parents can remember had musical ability.

This brings us back to the serious consideration of reincarnation. According to the alleged UFO contact messages, reincarnation is one of the most important concepts to be grasped, for through it the universe functions in order to advance the evolution of mankind. This evolution is seen to be not only physical but also metaphysical, not only of the body but also of the spirit, and incarnations are seen in this system of philosophy to be opportunities for an individual to continue his evolution through numerous and varied experiences.

Although perhaps two-thirds of the world's population embraces or is familiar with a religious system that posits reincarnation, those of us of the Judeo-Christian culture are not as familiar with this concept. Nevertheless, Don's early investigations seemed to indicate that reincarnation was a probability and that incarnations contained situations, relationships, and lessons that were far more easily understood in the light of knowledge of previous incarnations.

One succinct example of this relationship, which some are fond of calling karma, is that of a young boy (who requests that his name not be used) who in this life had experienced such intense allergies to all living things that he could not cut the grass, smell the flowers, or, during the blooming season, spend much time at all outside. Under hypnotic regression he experienced in detail a long life in England. He had been a solitary man whose nature was such as to avoid contact with any human being. He had inherited a fairly large estate and he spent his life upon it. His one pleasure was the very extensive garden that he maintained. In it he had his gardeners plant all manner of flowers, fruits, and vegetables.

After the life had been discussed, and while the lad was still in trance, hypnotist Lawrence Allison asked the boy, as he often did, to contact what is loosely referred to as his Higher Self. He had the boy ask his Higher Self if the lesson of putting people first and other things second had been learned. The Higher Self said that indeed the lesson had been learned. The hypnotist then had the boy ask the Higher Self if this allergy could be healed, since the lesson had been learned and the allergy was no longer necessary. The Higher Self agreed. The hypnotist then carefully brought the boy out of the hypnotic state and walked over to his piano on which was placed a magnolia. As magnolia blossoms will do, it had dropped its pollen on the polished surface of the piano, and the hypnotist scraped the pollen onto his hand, took it over to the boy, and deliberately blew the pollen directly at the boy's nose. "How could you do that to me!" exclaimed the boy. "You know how allergic I am." "Oh, really?" asked the hypnotist. "I don't hear you sneezing." The boy remained cured of his allergy.

When we attempt to consider our relationship with the universe, we begin to see that there is a great deal more in heaven and earth than has been dreamt of in most philosophies. It is an unbelievably gigantic universe, and if we have a true relationship to it we must, ourselves, be more than, or other than, our daily lives seem to encompass. In *The Ra*

Material a good deal of information is discussed concerning our true relationship with the universe, but it is good to realize that we do have a long tradition of work upon what may perhaps most simply be called the magical personality.

Magic is, of course, a much misused term and is mostly understood as being the art of prestidigitation, or illusion. When one sees a magician, one accepts the fact that one is seeing very skillfully performed illusions.

However, there is a study of the so-called magical personality that suggests that there is a thread that runs through our daily lives that we can grasp, and, using that thread, remove ourselves from time to time into a framework of reference points in which we see reality as being that of the spiritual body, that of the personality that exists from incarnation to incarnation and indeed "since before the world was." By working upon this magical personality, by interiorizing experience, by accepting responsibility for all that occurs, by carefully analyzing our reactions to all that occurs, and by eventually coming to balance our reactions to all that occurs so that our actions in our environment are generated within the self and are no longer simple reactions to outward stimulus, we strengthen the so-called magical personality until we are able to have some small claim to "the art of causing changes in consciousness at will." This is the classic definition of magic. Each time that a person sustains an unfortunate situation and reacts to it by not giving anger for anger or sadness for sadness but instead offering compassion and comfort where none was expected, we strengthen that thread of inner strength within us and we become more and more associated with a life that is closely related to the organic evolution of the universe.

It is some sense of the wholeness or organic nature of the universe that best informs the student of the UFOs' purposes in being here. They have been here, by many accounts, for thousands of years; at least UFOs have been mentioned, along with many other strange sights, in the annals of all early histories, including the Bible.

Modern-day interest in UFOs can probably be fairly accurately dated from Kenneth Arnold's historic sighting over Mt. Rainier in Washington. Another early and historic sighting, also by an extremely reliable witness, is coincidentally connected with Don Elkins, and so I would choose the Mantell case of January 7, 1948, instead of the Kenneth Arnold case of June 24, 1947, for discussion.

Thomas Mantell had trained as a pilot and had flown missions in Africa, in Europe, and, most notably, on D-day. In 1947 he was out of the Air Corps and had started the Elkins-Mantell Flying School on Bowman Field in Louisville, Kentucky. In 1947 Don Elkins was a youthful student in this school.

At about two o'clock in the afternoon on January 7, 1948, the Kentucky State Police called Fort Knox and reported to the MPs there that they had sighted a circular flying object moving rather quickly in their area. The MPs called the commanding officer at Godman Field at Fort Knox, and through due process the flight service checked with Wright Field in Ohio to see if there were any experimental aircraft that could explain the sighting. Wright Field had none flying.

Meanwhile, the tower at Godman Field, Fort Knox, had already sighted this disc-shaped object, both visually and on radar, and had made a report that was relayed quickly to the commanding officer.

As it happened, four F-51s were in the area en route from Marietta, Georgia, near Atlanta, to Louisville, Kentucky. Since they were already airborne, the commanding officer at Godman Field decided to contact the lead pilot and request that he investigate the UFO. The lead pilot was Captain Thomas Mantell.

Mantell was given a radar vector from Godman tower and moved towards the UFO. He sighted the object and stated that it was traveling slower than he was and that he would close to take a look. Then Mantell informed the tower that the object was now above him, that it appeared to be metallic, and that it was tremendous in size.

None of the F-51s, including Mantell's, were equipped with oxygen. The other pilots leveled off at 15,000 feet. Mantell kept climbing. That was the last transmission from Captain Mantell. Minutes later there was a telephone call stating that a plane had crashed. It was Captain Mantell's. His body lay near the wreckage.

I could spend the length of the book attempting to give you a sketchy introduction to the thousands and thousands of sightings like Captain Mantell's that involve irrefutably puzzling and concrete evidence of something highly strange occurring. There are many radar sightings of UFOs. There is one volume, published by the Center for UFO Studies in Evanston, Illinois, that deals solely with the numerous physical traces that UFOs have left behind, either by irradiating the soil, causing other changes in soil composition, or leaving impressions in the ground. A computer set up by this same organization to carry a program of information regarding UFOs contains well over 80,000 reports, and some things become startlingly clear by the use of "UFOCAT," the computer. For instance, it is now possible, if one measures a landing trace from a UFO sighting, to find out from the computer what the probable description of the UFO itself will be. Thus, in a way, the witness is merely confirming what the computer already knows.

However, this is an introduction to a book that consists of transcripts of messages of a very precise nature having to do with metaphysics, philosophy, and the plan of evolution, both physical and spiritual, of man on Earth. Consequently, what I propose to do is share with you some of the research material that our group has collected through the years. Since all of these examples come from the same group, we never describe who the receiver may be, as we feel that it is the information that is important rather than the person who is transmitting.

According to an entity called Hatonn who has spoken with our group and several others for many years, the purpose in being here of at least some of the UFOs that are seen in our skies at this time is much like the purpose that we might have in sending aid to a disaster-stricken or extremely impoverished country. It is a desire to be of service.

We have been contacting people of planet Earth for many, many of your years. We have been contacting at intervals of thousands of years those who sought our aid. It is time for many of the people of this planet to be contacted, for many now have the understanding and the desire to seek something outside the physical illusion that has for so many years involved the thinking of those of this planet. The process we are stimulating is one which is self-generating. As more and more of those who desire our contact receive it and pass it on to others, then those who receive this passed-on information will then themselves be able to reach a state of thinking and understanding sufficiently in tune, shall I say, with our vibrations in order to receive our contact. For this, my friends, is how contacts work. It is first necessary, if the entity is to be able to receive our contact, for him to become of a certain vibration as a result of his thinking. This is greatly speeded by involvement in groups such as this. And then it is finally done through meditation. In other words, the verbal communications given to the entity by the channels such as this one create a system of thought and a desire for spiritual awareness that raises his vibration.

We of the Confederation of Planets in the Service of the Infinite Creator are very sorry that we cannot step upon your soil and teach those of your people who desire our service. But, my friends, as we have said before, this would be a very great disservice to those who do not desire our service at this time, and we are afraid we would have little effect in bringing understanding even to those who desire it, for understanding, my friends, comes from within. We can only guide. We can only suggest. We are attempting to do this in such a way that the seeking of the individual will be stimulated to turning his thinking inward, inward to that single source of love and understanding, the Creator, that is part of us all, part of everything that exists, for everything that exists, my friends, is the Creator.

We are very privileged to have you join with us in this great service at this time in the history of your planet. For this is a very great time, a great transitional period, in which many of the Earth's people will be raised from their state of confusion to a simple understanding: the love of their Creator.

Hatonn speaks of our desire to seek something outside the physical illusion. What he talks about so persuasively is something that is often referred to by members of what Ra calls the Confederation of Planets in the Service of the Infinite Creator as "the original thought." This is another term for our word "love," but implies a great deal more. It implies a unity that is so great that we do not see each other simply as close friends, or brothers and sisters, but, ideally, as the Creator; and, as we see each other and ourselves as the Creator, we see one being. This concept is at the very heart of telepathy, and Hatonn talks about this concept and the original thought in general:

At this time I am in a craft far above your place of dwelling. I am at this time able to monitor your thoughts. This, my friends, might seem to some of your peoples to be an infringement, but I can assure you that it is not. Our capabilities of knowing the thinking of the peoples of this planet Earth are not designed in any way to infringe upon either their thinking or their activities. We do not consider the knowledge of the thoughts of others to be an infringement for we see these thoughts as our own. We see these thoughts as the thoughts of the Creator.

My friends, it may seem to you that a thought of a nature other than one of love and brotherhood might be a thought generated not of our Creator. This is not possible, my friends. All thought that is generated is generated by the Creator. All things that are generated are generated by the Creator. He is all things and is in all places, and all of the consciousness and all of the thought that exists is the thought of our Creator. His infinite number of parts all have free will, and all may generate in any way they choose. All of His parts communicate with all of the creation, in His entire and infinite sense.

We are not attempting to change the thinking of our Creator. We are only attempting to bring His ideas to some of the more isolated parts for their inspection and appraisal. Isolated parts, I say, my friends, and why should we consider these parts to be isolated? We consider them isolated because from our point of view they have chosen to wander far from the concept that we have found to permeate most of the parts of the creation with which we are familiar. We find, my friends, that man upon planet Earth in his experiences and experiments has become isolated in his thinking and has divorced it from that to which we are accustomed in the vast reaches of creation which we have experienced.

I urge you, my friends, to remember what we have brought to you. The next time that you are, shall we say, backed into a corner by the circumstances which prevail within the illusion of your physical existence, remember what you have learned and do not forget what you have worked so hard to obtain. You will choose at any time to alter your needs and desires from within the physical illusion to your being within the creation of the Father. As long as your objectives lie within this physical illusion it will be necessary for you to be subject to the laws which prevail within this illusion. If your desires can be altered by the application of what you are learning and are lifted in the creation of the Infinite One, then, my friends, you may have a great deal more ability to remove yourself from the corners into which the illusion seems to back you.

To some who may read these words, the concepts may seem to be a less than practical and certainly overly idealistic method of discussing what many have called the new age or the Age of Aquarius. It certainly seems unlikely that an entire planet could go so wrong philosophically and that beings supposedly more advanced than we would care enough about us to attempt to help us.

However, as we look for the heart of the "cosmic" system of philosophy, we find much that is clear and simple without being simplistic in the least, much that is ethical without being dogmatic—in short, much that is informative. Here Hatonn speaks of the nature of reality, which, in the main, seems to have escaped the notice of Earth man:

My friends, man on Earth has become very shortsighted in appreciation of the creation. He does not understand the true meaning of the simple and beautiful life that surrounds him. He does not appreciate its generation and regeneration. He learns that the very atmosphere that he breathes is cycled through the plant life to be regenerated to support him and his fellow beings and creatures, and yet this seems to the vast majority of those who dwell upon this planet to be an exercise in technology rather than one in theology. There is no awareness of the Creator's plan to provide for His children, to provide for their every desire and to provide a state of perfection. Man on Earth has lost the awareness that is rightfully his. And why, my friends, has he lost this awareness? He has lost this because he has focused his attention upon devices and inventions of his own. He has become hypnotized by his playthings and his ideas. He is but a child in his mind.

All of this may be very simply remedied, and man can once more return to an appreciation of reality rather than an appreciation of the illusion created by his mind. All that is necessary, my friends, is that he individually avail himself to this appreciation of reality through the process of meditation, for this process stills his active conscious mind which is continually seeking stimulus within the illusion developed over so many centuries of time upon planet Earth. Very rapidly, then, he can return to an appreciation of the reality in the functioning of the real creation.

This, my friends, is what man of Earth must return to if he is to know reality: this simple thought of absolute love, a thought of total unity with all his brothers regardless of how they might express themselves or whom they might be, for this is the original thought of your Creator.

The creation of the Father, then, as Hatonn calls it, has a very simple nature, a nature in which love is the essence of all things and of all their functions.

Yet this "real" creation obviously is not uppermost in most of our minds because we live in a day-to-day atmosphere to which the Confederation has referred quite often as an illusion.

We of the Confederation of Planets in the Service of the Infinite Creator have been, for many of your years, aware of many principles of reality. We are aware of these principles because we have availed ourselves to them just as the people of your planet may do.

It is possible through meditation to totally reduce the illusion that you now experience that creates the separation—an illusory separation—to what it actually is a total illusion. We have been continuing to speak to you about meditation. We have spoken to you many times about reality and about love and about understanding, and yet you do not seem to be able to overcome the illusion.

The reason for the illusion, my friends, is one that man on Earth has generated. He has generated it out of desire. This illusion is useful.

It is very useful for those who would wish to evolve at a very rapid rate by experiencing it and by using it while within it. Many of us who are now circling your planet would desire to have the opportunity that you have, the opportunity to be within the illusion and then, through the generation of understanding, use the potentials of the illusion. This is a way of gaining progress spiritually and has been sought out by many of our brothers.

I cannot over-emphasize the necessity of becoming able to understand the nature of the potentials within your illusion and then, by self-analysis and meditation, reacting to that in a way that will express the thought that generated us: the thought of our Creator. This was done by the teacher whom you know as Jesus. This man recognized his position. He recognized the illusion. He understood the reason for the potentials within the illusion, and his reaction to these potentials and activities within the illusion was a reaction which was expressing the thought of the Creator, a thought of love.

Keep uppermost in your mind that the illusion that you experience is an illusion, that it is surrounding you for the purpose of teaching you. It can only teach you if you become aware of its teachings. It is said that "He worked His wonders in mysterious ways." This way may seem mysterious; however, it is the way of spiritual evolvement. There are many souls experiencing the illusion in which you find yourself; however, there are few using this illusion to grow. They are not doing this other than at a subliminal level because they have not availed themselves through their seeking to a knowledge of the possibility of doing this.

Once an individual has become aware of the possibility of using the illusion in which he finds himself in your physical world for the progression of spiritual growth, it is necessary that he take the next step and use his knowledge to express, regardless of the potentials that affect him, the love and understanding of his Creator.

As you have by now become aware, meditation is always suggested as the best means of attaining understanding, of progressing spiritually, and of understanding the nature of the illusion and the purpose for which you are experiencing it. Each person is involved in an illusion or game in which we may, if we wish, use our consciousness in meditation in such a way as to create a more rapid growth in personal evolution. But how do we bring ourselves to the point at which this process, which often seems very difficult, is grasped and begun?

Desire, my friends, is the key to what you receive. If you desire it, you shall receive it. This was the Creator's plan, a plan in which all of His parts would receive exactly what they desire. My friends, often in the illusion which you now experience it seems that you do not acquire what you desire. In fact, the opposite seems to be the case in many, many instances. It is a paradox, it seems, that such a statement should be made and that such apparent results of desire are manifested, and yet we state, without exception, that man receives exactly what he desires. Perhaps, my friends, you do not understand desire. Perhaps this understanding is not within the intellectual mind. Perhaps it will be necessary to spend time in meditation to become aware of your real desire. For, my friends, there is much, much more of you and of the creation than you presently appreciate with your intellectual abilities in your present illusion.

It is very difficult for the peoples of this planet to give up their illusion, to give up the preconceived knowledge of what they believe to be cause and effect. However, this is not reality. This is illusion, born of illusion. It is a simple product of the complexity that man upon this planet has generated. Join with us in divorcing your thinking from such complexities and become aware of what has created you, everything that you experience, and everything that is thought. Become aware of your Creator. Become aware of His desire, and when you know this desire you will know your own, for you and your Creator are one, and you are one with all of His parts and, therefore, all of your fellow beings throughout all of the creation. When you know His desire you will feel it. There will be no more confusion. There will be no more questions. You will have found what you have sought. You will have found Love, for this is the desire of your Creator: that all of His parts express and experience the Love that created you. This may be found simply, in meditation. No amount of seeking within the intellectual concepts of your people, no amount of careful planning or careful interpretation of the written or spoken word, will lead you to the simple truth.

The Confederation messages concentrate a great deal upon the concept of seeking and of desire, feeling that the will of each entity is absolutely central to each entity's quest for evolution. In fact, they say, free will is at the foundation of the universe. Each entity is conceived not only as being part of one unity but also as being a totally unique part of that unity. Each person's free will is quite paramount, and the Confederation's concern is always to avoid infringement upon the free will of any person. Their method of contacting man on Earth takes its form from a deep concern for this free will:

> We do not wish to impose our understanding of truth upon your peoples, and this would be something that we would do if we contacted them directly. We could not help it, for our very utterance of truth would be accepted by many of your peoples as being valid. We do not wish to be thought of as the ultimate representatives of the Creator's truth. We wish to give this to your peoples in such a way so that they may accept or reject this at their own will. This, as we understand it, is a necessary provision in the spiritual evolvement of all mankind: that he be, at some state of his evolution, in a position to accept or reject what is necessary for his evolution. In this way, and only in this way, can he *know* the truth, the truth of the Creator, that single truth that is the creation, the truth of the love of the creation.

> It must be realized from within. It cannot be impressed from without. We are attempting to stimulate those of your peoples who would be stimulated to seeking this truth that is within them. We have been required by our understanding of our Creator's principle to remain in hiding, for we cannot serve one individual and at the same time do a disservice to his neighbor by proving within his own mind that we exist, for many of those of planet Earth at this time do not desire to believe in or have proof of our existence. For this reason we find it necessary to speak to those who seek through channels such as this one. We find it necessary to give to those who seek that which they seek in such a way that they, for themselves, may appraise its value and accept or reject, on their own terms, those thoughts that we bring, and understand the reality of the creation in which all of us exist.

Once the desire to receive this message has been developed, the messages are indeed available, not just from our group but from many so-called contactee or channeling groups around the world. Indeed, you will find little new in the "cosmic" system of philosophy. Those concepts are basic, profound, and simple. The Confederation has a name for one of the great goals of this system of meditation and study—understanding:

> Many of your peoples are at this time seeking outside their illusion. To those who seek, we offer our understanding. We do not attempt

to say that we have ultimate wisdom. We only suggest that that which we have to offer may be of value, for we have found, in our experience, as we have passed through the same experiences as those of Earth, that there is a most beneficial direction in seeking to serve. We are acting through instruments such as those here tonight to give, to those who seek, an understanding. Our presence is meant to stimulate seeking. Through this process, we hope to contact as many of the peoples of your planet as would desire our contact. We hope in the very near future to be able to contact many more of the peoples of your planet, the peoples who would desire understanding. It is difficult to contact those people of your planet because of this, shall I say, mixture of types, but it is well worth our effort if we are able to contact but one.

We will continue to act as we do now, speaking through instruments such as this one, until a sufficient number of the peoples of your planet have become aware of truth. We are constantly striving to bring, through many channels of communication, the simple message to the peoples of Earth: the simple message that will leave them with a simple understanding of all that there is, and that is love.

But understanding, that understanding that shows us the love of an Infinite Creator, is again and again described as being possible far more easily through the processes of meditation than by any other method:

There are pieces of information that are of importance and there are pieces of information that are not. Wisdom is a rather lonely matter, my friends. You must accept this truth as you acquire the burden of wisdom. That which you know, you are to be careful of, for what you know in the real creation has power, and that which you desire is all of the direction which that power will be aimed at; but have faith, my friends, in what you know and what you are learning. Feed your faith and your understanding through meditation. The further that you go along this path, my friends, the more meaningful you will find this simple statement: meditate. It begins as a simple process and, little by little, it becomes a way in which you live. Observe it as you progress along your own spiritual path.

It is frequently suggested in contactee messages that the state of mind of the seeker has the opportunity of being continuously in a far more pleasant configuration than is the mind of one who is not actively engaged in pursuing a path of self-knowledge and seeking. However, there are other fruits of the path of meditation and seeking that are predictable and that engage the attention of those who channel these messages.

It is to be remembered, my friends, that service to others is service to one's self. Notice that we do not say that service is like unto service to one's self. There is no similarity between others and ourselves. There is identity. There is completion and unity. Therefore, that which is felt of a negative nature towards a sheep of the flock is felt towards one's self and is felt toward the Creator. This enters the service which you attempt to give to yourself and to the Creator through service to another, and causes a blot or a stain upon the perfect service you would have performed. It must be remembered that each person is a completely free entity whose independence must in no way be shaken and yet whose identity remains one with you.

* * * * * *[1]

There is only one thing of great importance for you to consider at this time. That is your personal preparation for service. You are to serve your fellow man, and, therefore, it is necessary that you prepare yourselves for this service. This of course, my friends, is done in meditation. We cannot overemphasize the importance of meditation. Through this technique you will receive answers to all of your questions. It is difficult to realize this, but this is true. All of your questions can be reduced to an extremely simple concept. This you can become aware of in meditation. Once this has been done you will be ready to serve, just as others have served and are now serving upon your planet. Follow their example; spend time in meditation. Qualify yourself to reach out to your fellow man and lead him from the darkness of confusion that he is experiencing back into the light that he desires.

One service that the Confederation sources greatly appreciate is that provided by vocal channels, which are trained in groups such as the one that we have had in Louisville since 1962. They never suggest in any way that their message is unique or that "salvation" can only be gained by listening to that message. However, they are aware that there are many who seek that message through sources other than orthodox religion and classical philosophy. Consequently, they are here to provide a service of making information available and can perform their service only through vocal channels:

---

1. Asterisks (******) indicate the separation between a quotation from one transcript and a quotation upon the same subject from another transcript.

There are more people upon this planet seeking than there have been in the past. However, many are quite confused in their attempts to seek, and there is a need at this time for many more channels such as this one who can receive directly the thoughts that so many of the people of this planet are seeking. We are attempting at this time to generate greater numbers of proficient vocal channels who can receive our thoughts quite readily. This requires daily meditation. This is all that is required: daily meditation. It is assumed, of course, that as this daily meditation is performed there is a desire for our contact.

As one who has participated in meditation groups for many years, may I suggest that individual meditations not include the attempt to contact Confederation sources. It is best to pursue this attempt only in a group situation, preferably a group that contains at least one experienced receiver. And always, whether meditating alone or in a group, I strongly recommend some means of "tuning" so that the meditation that follows will be at the highest spiritual level possible. This "tuning" can be accomplished in any way preferable to the meditator. The Lord's Prayer, "Aum-ing" or other singing or chanting, the reading of some inspirational writing, or a careful visualization of the "white light" of the Creator, are all useful "tuning" methods.

Reincarnation is very basic to the Confederation message. One of the most highly regarded fruits of the meditation and seeking process is the ability of the seeker to penetrate what Ra calls the "forgetting process," which occurs at the time of our birth into this incarnation so that we might become aware of the lessons that we have to learn during this incarnation. These lessons are always along the lines of how to love better, more fully, more deeply, or with more kindness and understanding. However, each entity has unique lessons:

At the time at which each of you incarnated, my friends, each of you was aware that certain lessons, hitherto unlearned, were to be the goals for achievement in this incarnation. If it seems to you that your entire incarnation within this illusion has been a series of difficulties of one particular type, then you are almost certainly aware in some manner of one of your lessons. As you can see, these lessons are not to be avoided. They are to be learned.

Further, we must point out to you that when a confrontation in such a lesson has been achieved, that which separates you from understanding is most often your own thinking. Your conscious thinking processes are quite capable of being self-destructive in the sense that they may aid you to avoid the lesson that you wish in reality to learn.

Therefore, as you approach a lesson, we suggest that if it is possible to achieve a temporary abeyance of the conscious, analytical processes, then you may return to the problem with a much clearer mentality, ready to learn what you came to this experience to learn, rather than only to avoid what you came to learn.

We know how difficult it is to achieve the meditative state at all times, for we have been where you are and we are aware of that particular type of illusion that you call physical. We urge you, therefore, to depend on meditation of a formal kind, then to attempt a semi-meditative state at all times, and, by this, we mean simply to achieve a state of attention so that your destructive impulses are not free to clog your mind completely and keep you from learning the lessons you came to learn.

Undergirding all of the lessons that we have to learn about love is the basic concept that all things are one:

Meditate upon the complete unity of yourself and all that you see. Do this not once, and not simply in present circumstances, but at all times, and especially in difficult circumstances. For insofar as you love and feel at one with those things which are difficult for you, to that extent will those circumstances be alleviated. This is not due to any laws within our physical illusion but is due to the Law of Love, for that body which is of spirit, which is interpenetrated with the physical body, is higher than your physical body, and those changes which you make by love upon your spiritual body will, of necessity, reflect themselves within the physical illusion.

All is one, my friends. My voice is now the voice of this instrument; my thoughts are her thoughts. Please believe that the vibration we offer to you is not a vibration of personality, but is a vibration of the Creator. We are also channels. There is only one voice. Within this vibration, we are self-consciously aware that this voice is the voice of the Creator. It is simply a matter of lifting vibrations which are not so self-aware of the Creator. All things will eventually come into harmony in relation to your understanding.

Even if the universe for those around you remains disharmonious and difficult, if your mind is stayed upon the unity of the Creator, your own universe will become harmonious, and this is not by your doing but by the simple love of the Creator.

From many sources we have heard that we are in the last days of a particular era of evolution. Popular writers of the Christian faith have taken the writings of the book of Revelation and analyzed them in such a way that it is suggested that the days of Armageddon are near at hand. Scientists have written many books exploring the possibility that unusual planetary configurations such as the Jupiter effect will occur now and in the year 2000, thus enlarging the possibility for Earth changes. Other scientists have examined much evidence indicating that a polar shift by the year 2000 is probable. Prophets such as Edgar Cayce have channeled information having to do with such drastic changes occurring, and in addition, of course, there are our many concerns having strictly to do with the man-made potential for planetary devastation. We also have gathered information in our meetings on the subject of Earth changes:

There is a season upon your planet which shall be highly traumatic within your physical illusion. The physical reasons for this are varied. Your scientists will spend a great deal of time, while they can, in attempting to catalog and describe each of the conditions which will produce disaster on this physical plane of your planet. That which your scientists speak of is quite so, and will be part of the program which has been predicted by all of those holy works which you have upon the face of the Earth.

It is not either permissible or possible for us to tell you precisely what events will occur, or when they will occur, due to the fact that the vibration within the mind and heart of the peoples upon your planet is determining and will determine the precise events. There is within the planet Earth a great deal of karma which must be adjusted as the cycle changes, and these things will manifest. Precisely when, and how, we cannot say, nor would we wish to, my friends. For the rain, and the wind, and fire, will destroy only those things which are in what you call the third density of vibration. You may value those things because you cannot imagine what a fourth-density existence will be like. We suggest to you that you spend no time concerning yourselves with the effort of maintaining your third-density existence after the vibration change to fourth density has been completed.

If, within your spirit, your graduation day has come, those things necessary for your emergence into fourth density will be done for you. All will be accomplished by helpers which you must be aware that you have.

It is extremely possible that damage will occur to those things which you identify with yourself in the third density. If we may speak plainly, you will observe the valley of the shadow of death. These very words, my friends, have been spoken to you before, and yet you cling to that physical body and those physical surroundings as though your spirit were attached quite permanently to them.

May we suggest to you that you can find your spirit neither in your head, nor in your hands, nor in your chest, nor in your legs, nor in your feet, that nowhere can you find your spirit; nowhere can you operate to remove it, nor to aid it. Your spirit resides within a shell. The shell may be removed, but that is no matter. The spirit does not perish.

What is the metaphysical meaning of this suggested physical trauma of our planet? The Confederation suggests that the planet itself is moving into a new vibration, a new portion of space and time, which many have called the New Age, but into which we shall not be able to enter unless we have indeed learned the lessons of love that it has been our choice to learn or not to learn for many incarnations. Therefore, the Confederation suggests that it is very important to choose to follow the positive path or not to follow it:

There is a choice to be made very shortly, and it would be preferable if all of the people of this planet understand the choice that is to be made. It will be difficult for many of the people of this planet to understand what this choice is, because it is a choice that they have not considered. They have been much too involved in their daily activities and their confusion and their desires of a very trivial nature to be concerned with an understanding of the choice that they are very shortly to make. Whether they wish to or not, whether they understand it or not, regardless of any influence, each and every one of the people who dwell upon planet Earth will shortly make a choice. There will be no middle area. There will be those who choose to follow the path of love and light and those who choose otherwise.

This choice will not be made by saying, "I choose the path of love and light," or "I do not choose it." The verbal choice will mean nothing. This choice will be measured by the individual's demonstration of his choice. This demonstration will be very easy for us of the Confederation of Planets in His Service to interpret. This choice is measured by what we term the vibratory rate of the individual. It is necessary, if an individual is to join those who make the choice of love and understanding, for his rate of vibration to be above a certain minimal level. There are many now that are close to this minimum level, but due to continuing conditions of erroneous thought that prevail upon your surface, they are either fluctuating around this point or are even in some cases drifting away from the path of love and understanding. There are many whose vibratory rate at this time is sufficiently high for them to travel with no difficulty into the density of vibration that this planet is shortly to experience.

At some time in the future, then, something that the Confederation has called the harvest will take place. This concept of the Judgment Day differs from the eschatological one in that the one who judges us is not a God apart from us but the God within us. As a result of this harvest some will go on to a new age of love and light and will learn new lessons in a very positive and beautiful density, as the Confederation calls it. Others will have to repeat this particular grade of lessons and relearn the lessons of love. Here the Confederation entity, Hatonn, speaks once again of the harvest and of the Confederation's purpose in speaking through contactee groups:

> There is going to be a Harvest, as you might call it, a harvest of souls that will shortly occur upon your planet. We are attempting to extract the greatest possible harvest from this planet. This is our mission, for we are the Harvesters.

> In order to be most efficient, we are attempting to create first a state of seeking among the people of this planet who desire to seek. This would be those who are close to the acceptable level of vibration. Those above this level are of course not of as great an interest to us since they have, you might say, already made the grade. Those far below this level, unfortunately, cannot be helped by us at this time. We are attempting at this time to increase by a relatively small percentage the number who will be harvested into the path of love and understanding.

> Even a small percentage of those who dwell upon your planet is a vast number, and this is our mission, to act through groups such as this one in order to disseminate information in such a fashion that it may be accepted or rejected, that it may be in a state lacking what the people of your planet choose to call proof.

We offer them no concrete proof, as they have a way of expressing it. We offer them Truth. This is an important function of our mission—to offer Truth without proof. In this way, the motivation will, in each and every case, come from within the individual. In this way, the individual vibratory rate will be increased. An offering of proof or an impressing of this Truth upon an individual in such a way that he would be forced to accept it would have no usable effect upon his vibratory rate.

This, then, my friends, is the mystery of our way of approaching your peoples.

Another concept that has come out of the many communications from alleged UFO entities is that of "Wanderers." They are usually service-oriented people, and, as would be predictable, they often have a great deal of difficulty fitting into the planetary vibrations of Earth. Often they have the feeling that they do not fit in or do not belong, but at the same time, very often, these people are possessed of many gifts, in the arts, in teaching, or in the simple sharing of a cheerful and happy vibration, which certainly does not suggest the normal attitude of a simple malcontent.

This concept is particularly interesting to many people who will be drawn to *The Ra Material* because, according to that material, much of it will be most easily recognized as being useful by Wanderers. There are not just a few Wanderers on Earth today; Ra suggests a figure of approximately sixty-five million. They have left other densities in harmonious environments to take on a kind of job that is most difficult and dangerous, for if a Wanderer cannot at least begin to pierce the forgetting process that occurs at birth into this density during his or her lifetime on planet Earth, and remember the love and the light that the person was intended to share, the Wanderer can conceivably become caught in the third-density illusion, collecting what may loosely be termed as karma, and be delayed in arriving again at the home planet until all that is unbalanced in third density in this lifetime has been balanced.

When Don Elkins and I wrote *Secrets of the UFO* in 1976, we devoted a chapter to the concept of Wanderers and used material gathered in hypnotic regressions of three women who are friends in this lifetime and who, when separately regressed, gave independent and dovetailing stories of their lives on another planet.

After that book went to press, we were able to work with a man whom the women had named as being a part of that experience on another planet. This man, who was then a student working towards his

THE LAW OF ONE

master's degree in chemical engineering, was aware of no detail of our research except that we were involved in doing some hypnosis. On May 10, 1975, Don, along with Lawrence Allison, an accomplished hypnotist with whom we had worked often when he lived in Louisville, sat down with our fourth volunteer and proceeded to explore that other world for a fourth time. The information was especially interesting, since all three previous regressions had been poetic, and beautiful, but scarcely technical. Our fourth subject had a far different background and was able to see things in a far more accurate and explicit manner. This fourth regression fitted perfectly into the story told by the first three subjects.

One of the first things that Don and Larry (the questioning went back and forth) asked about was the clothing.

Q. *How are you dressed?*
A. In white.

Q. *White what?*
A. Loose white clothes.

Q. *OK. What's above the waist now? Above the pants?*
A. Well, it's just like a robe; it's not really a robe but a loose clothing with a sash, like for a belt.

Q. *And what about on the shoulders?*
A. Well, it's just short sleeved. It's warm.

This type of robe suggests a monastic or religious order, and questions were asked to attempt to discover some orthodox religious connection on this planet. No connection was found, so the questioners moved on to the name of this other world since the surroundings were not those of Earth, but the young man, normally incisive in his answers, seemed totally unaware of the concept of naming.

Q. *The name of your planet?*
A. It's just a . . . we live there, and . . . I don't see any mountains, but I see . . . the name?

* * * * *[2]

A. I have a child.
Q. *One child?*

---

2. Asterisks (****) separate two quotations from the same regressive hypnosis session.

A. Yeah. Little boy.
Q. *His name is?*
A. I just don't have a feeling for names. I have, like, you know when you want somebody, and they know when you want them, sort of. I mean, I just don't have a feeling for names.

Not only did their planet seem to lack a proper name, but speech itself seemed to be a far different process, one that we would probably call telepathy.

Q. *All right, if someone calls to you, what do they call you?*
A. I just haven't heard anybody speak. I don't know if you have to speak.

* * * * *

A. It seems, like, kind of a simple life. But there's obviously—well, there was light at my books, so it's obviously mechanized, or perhaps much more than that even. I don't,
    I . . . don't recall people speaking to each other, though. I mean, they seem to, you know, everybody knows each question . . . you know what's going on, but I don't really see. It was singing; there was singing, but there wasn't actually people conversing with each other. You just sort of knew, I guess.

* * * * *

A. I'd be sitting on a stone or a bench and they'd be sitting down, and I'm explaining, but I don't really see myself talking to them.

    The subject, with his engineer's eye, was able to put together the architecture of the place in the way the women had not. All four agreed that the center of the community and its purpose was something that may conveniently be called the temple.

A. . . . think it's a stone . . . I guess limestone, but it's whiter, I guess. That's what it's made of.

Q. *What about the perimeter?*
A. Well, there's, from supports from the side are arches up to the ceiling, but . . . it's not a regular dome, it's . . . well, I haven't seen that kind of dome before.

Q. *Take a good guess. How far across is that dome?*

A. Oh, goodness. It looks like it's 200 feet the long way, and maybe more than that, maybe 250. And, oh, maybe 150 feet wide. It's a huge room, very—

Q. *OK. Now, how is it lighted?*
A. Just, [*laughs a little incredulously*] . . . really, it's just a glow from the ceiling. I mean, you know, like the, well, there's, like the area that's light, and then there's darker, like it's been painted, but the paint, that's light. It seems like it's, well, it just doesn't need any light. The room's bright. Maybe it's coming from the windows, but . . . there doesn't seem to be any shadow in the room.

Q. *What you're saying is that it seems as if the atmosphere in the room is glowing there?*
A. Well, yeah, just like it's bright. I don't see any shadows, like if there was a light source.

Q. *Uh huh. Now I want you to listen inside that big room. What kind of sounds do you hear?*
A. Nothing in that room, but they're singing someplace.

Q. *Very quietly, singing off in the distance?*
A. Um hmm.

Q. *All right. It is, ah, some kind of . . .*
A. It's more like, a kind of choir, a little choir, like.

That music, reported by all four subjects, is not like any music we have ever heard. Two of the subjects actually saw the music sparkling in the air, and none could accurately describe it.

A. I just . . . I can't . . . place the words. It's just, you know, like a sort of praise, a sort of, you know, something like you'd hear in a choir.

Q. *Praise to whom?*
A. Well, uh . . .

Q. *To God?*
A. I'm sure that's who it is, you know, that's . . . it's sort of a happy thing to do, when people get together and sing . . .

The subject spoke of growing up studying in large books.

A. I see myself sitting over . . . over a book and just reading.

Q. History?

A. Well, I don't know.
Q. Practical work? Science? What do you study? Art? The arts?

A. Just great books, big books.
Q. Um hum. Do you have supervised study in classes or . . .
A. Well, in the morning there's a teacher, and in the afternoon or in late evening, I study.

Q. Is there an examination?
A. No exams. You just want to learn; you want to learn. You, uh, it's like you can't learn enough.

Who were these people? Did they represent an entire planetary population or were they a portion only of that population? If they were a portion, how were they chosen to do this work? After looking at this material, Don and I generated a term by which to call this particular group of people: the "clan." Here is one of the questioners on this subject.

Q. Nobody has individual homes?
A. Well, no; this big place is their home. This is, this is home.

＊＊＊＊＊

A. Well, this is one purpose. Like, it's like a school, or a teaching place to teach those that want to learn it in depth, and those that come when they can.

＊＊＊＊＊

A. But this isn't like a ruling-type people, by any means. Like, you know, this isn't . . . like the people have to come here. It's not a class system or anything.

Meditation played a very large part in the lives of the inhabitants of this other world, or at least those in this clan. There were meditations alone and there were daily group meditations with the entire clan.

A. Well, let's see. I don't see myself there, in different states of consciousness. There are prayerful times, in the morning and at night. You have them in your room, and then you have others before meals, before the morning meal, and then, not, well, briefly before the evening meal, but, when, it was like when the food was brought, but then afterwards there's, it's a . . . in a room, like a private sort of devotional, except that you're not—like in meditation. And there are times when the whole group gets together other than meals, just . . . like the whole place is like a family I would guess. Because, like I said, you don't feel that attached, necessarily, to one person. You feel attached to everybody. They're all, like, in your family.

Another function of the clan was to open their great temple from time to time to all of those of the planet who wished to come for spiritual inspiration. The questioners, in attempting to determine just how these large crowds came to fill the temple, happened upon the description of what seemed to be a very large heliport. We discovered later that the vehicle was not a helicopter. However, that is the term that the questioner used here.

Q. OK. Now, the people that leave at that heliport—you have no idea where they go?
A. When I say these ships come, it's not like hordes of people just rushing off and rushing back on or anything, it's just . . . it's, oh, how should I . . . you know, it lands there, and the doors open, and the people come out, and people come in. They're allowed to go on the grounds, you know. In other words, this is their place too. But they come as a visitor, sort of, to it.

Q. How long do they stay there?
A. A day.

The description of the heliport:

A. There's a place, a flat place, a flat place, like, that's stone, out in front, but I don't see roads coming to it, for . . . it . . . I see . . . uh, like, sort of, like, uh, like, well, a huge helicopter pad, for instance, but . . .
The questioners had to find out what was landing on that large stone area, and so the subject was asked to describe the type of transport that used it.

Q. All right. I want you to describe that ship, and what makes it go.
A. I don't . . . um . . . it's . . . well, it's like . . . it seems it's probably a space ship. But I don't see it coming from space. It sort of, suddenly almost being there, I don't see it like zipping off or coming in, you know, across the horizon or anything.

Q. Just describe what it looks like.
A. Yeah, well, it's a, it's longer than it is wide, and it's not real thick compared to the length dimensions and the width dimension. It's a—it's not like, it's not spinning when it comes down, because it's a little sort of, like oblong or . . . it just sort of appears and sets down, you know; I mean, I don't see it actually coming into view from small and getting larger.

It is interesting to note the apparent description of materialization and dematerialization implicit in the subject's answer to that question.

And so the young man grew in wisdom and in years and told a story of teaching, growing somewhat gray haired, beginning to teach fewer and more advanced students, and in time preparing to end the incarnation. As the questioners brought the subject back through the death experience in the previous incarnation and forward in time to the experience in which he was at that moment living, they paused with the subject in between incarnations to ask about the purpose this particular Wanderer came to Earth to fulfill. The answer that he gave is both provocative and all too scanty. Many of us seek to help this planet of ours in one way or another, and the question is always: How shall we accomplish it?

Q. Why are you on Earth? What is the purpose of this life? What do you intend to do here? What were you assigned to do here?
A. It seems like, to help.

Q. Helping with what? Something in particular?
A. Something . . .

Q. Have you already helped in this field? Or is the problem yet to come that you are to help with?
A. It hasn't happened yet.

Q. What do you anticipate?
A. Just . . . just great needs.

Q. What would happen, to require so much help from you that you know about? [pause] Spiritual growth? Spiritual development? Physical needs?
A. Well, not . . . the . . . I get the feeling of some people that are lost, you know?

Q. Can you help them? This is your mission?
A. I feel like that's what I need to do. This . . . Help those people.

Q. Um hum. Which people?
A. The ones that are lost.

Q. Is this a particular group?
A. No.

Q. Just in general.
A. Just people.

The work I did in early 1976 was to be my last. I had had a condition called juvenile rheumatoid arthritis with several complications, one being SLE, commonly known as lupus, since I was thirteen when my kidneys had failed. In 1956, the advanced techniques that are available now to those whose kidneys fail were not available. In fact, it was considered a miracle that I survived, but survive I did with the loss of approximately half of each kidney.

I consider myself very fortunate to have been able to have had a productive and active physical life for so long with the odds going so far against me. Even now, with the help of exercise, diet, friends, and faith, I feel most blessed. But my activities are limited.

The research that Don and I had done up to that point brought us across the knowledge of a highly unusual type of healing, and it was in part my disability that caused us to put ourselves so wholeheartedly into an examination of that type of healing. Psychic surgery bears only a tangential relationship to orthodox surgery and no relationship to orthodox medicine. It is, like all brands of "faith healing," impossible to prove, and the natural and standard response, not only from scientists but from any person who has not done any research into the subject, is an automatic "turn off" and utter disbelief.

This is to be expected. Were it not for many years of research, this would perhaps be our reaction also. However, we, like most who investigate psychic surgery, knew that we had nothing to lose by investigating this possibility. No psychic surgery patient has ever been lost because nothing actually happens to the patient's physical body. It is truly a psychic form of healing. Consequently, we spent some time both in the Philippines and in Mexico taking part in an examination of the possibilities of psychic surgery.

This is an example of what the psychic surgeon creates as a manifestation for the eye: it is a Philippine bedroom; the patient is undressed, retaining those garments that may be needed for personal modesty, and lies down on the bed, which may in some cases be covered with a simple shower curtain, usually that one borrowed from the motel bathroom. The healer, a religious man, and one who has often spent ten or twelve years of his life praying to become a healer "walking in the wilderness" of the volcanic mountains of Luzon in solitude, enters the room. He carries nothing except perhaps a Bible. Often the healer is accompanied by an assistant who functions as interpreter and, to use a term familiar to our culture, surgical assistant; to use a more accurate term, cleanup man.

The healer normally knows very little English. He or she begins by taking the hands and moving them over the body, palms down. We are informed that this is a method of scanning the body just as an x-ray machine would. A site for "surgery" is then selected, and if the healer is right-handed the left hand is pressed firmly against the skin. The skin seems to separate and the interior of the body is seen. This manifestation is very real looking, and anyone who has seen a genuine psychic surgeon at work and has not studied the phenomenon carefully will swear that the body has been opened with the bare hands. The right hand then enters this open site and manipulates within the body.

In the most interesting case in which I took part, the healer was told that I had arthritis. He scanned my body with the help of his assistant. Then he opened the abdominal cavity and with a very liquid-sounding action pulled gently, but firmly, at what seemed to be organs rather than joints. It was not unpleasant but, to me, the patient, it was puzzling, as I had no arthritis in my organs. He then removed what seemed to be three rather small, long pieces of bloody material, at the center of which was a small piece of hard material. This done, he removed his left hand. The "incision" vanished without a scar or trace of any kind. The two men, in this case, mopped up what had become a fairly considerable amount of blood, rinsed their hands, and then took baby oil and worked it over the abdominal skin, massaging in silence.

When I asked what the healer was doing working in the abdominal area, the interpreter relayed my request and relayed back the information that the scanning had produced the knowledge of three cysts upon my right ovary, and the misplacement or dropping of both ovaries, which had occurred through years of very active life. The pulling had been to reposition the ovaries so that I would not be in discomfort during menstruation. The removal of the cysts had had the same purpose.

Although my gynecologist had diagnosed these three small cysts when I was a very young woman, I had never spoken of them to Don Elkins and, indeed, to no one, since such conversation is not fascinating. One other person knew of these cysts, my mother, but she was 12,000 miles away.

Upon returning to the United States I had my gynecologist examine the area, and he confirmed that the three cysts were no longer palpable. They have remained gone, and the comfort level of my menstrual cycle is correspondingly far better.

The massage with baby oil is a very simplified and unostentatious form of magnetic healing in which prayers are offered and a protective light is visualized around the affected area so that healing will be aided.

It is Don's and my belief that the opening of the body for the removal of parts, the closing of the body, and the manifestation of the blood and all other materials are materializations of the same type as the materializations of ghosts and the materialization of UFOs. Therefore, we have never made any attempt to preserve specimens of this psychic surgery. We are aware that this does not fulfill the rigors of the scientific method that exists today, but it is our belief that we would find out nothing by looking at the results of such analysis of manifestation.

It would seem that a person, no matter how great his desire to be healed, would be nervous and apprehensive, since the opening of the body itself, physical or psychic, seems very traumatic. Once the healer's hands are upon you, a distinct emotional and mental attitude change occurs within every individual with whom I have spoken who has experienced this phenomenon. The psychic surgeons call it the presence of the Holy Spirit. It should be considered part of the phenomenon.

In late 1977 and early 1978 we accompanied Dr. Andrija Puharich and his research associates to Mexico City to investigate a Mexican psychic surgeon, a seventy-eight-year-old woman called Pachita, who had been practicing for a great many years. The gift had come to her on the battlefield with Pancho Villa's army, and, as in the Philippines, more of her patients were native than were American. The one difference in her technique was the culture from which she came. In the Philippines, psychic healing came from an extremely literal belief in Christianity as taught by Spanish missionaries for three hundred years. Christianity was the center of almost every Filipino peasant's life. A large percentage went to mass daily, and, as Don and I were there during Holy Week of 1975, we were able to watch evidence of the ruthlessly literal type of Christianity that was practiced there. On Good Friday, for instance, there was a great Catholic parade of the cross through the streets of Manila. What was different about this parade was that there was a human being nailed to that cross. Many had vied for that position. The one who had achieved it, when asked for comment, simply replied that he felt very exalted and hoped that they would choose him again the following year.

In Mexico, if Christianity is present at all, and it often is, it is an overlay to an extremely strong Indian belief that is harsh and brooding. One brings to mind the memories of the Mayan slaughter of innocents on the steep steps of the Mexican pyramids.

Consequently, Pachita used a very dull knife with a 5-inch blade. She passed it around amongst the entire research group watching to see our reactions, especially mine, since I was the guinea pig. Since her "operations" took place with me lying on my stomach, I cannot give a firsthand account of what occurred, but Don informs me that the knife seemed to disappear 4 inches into my back and was then moved rapidly across the spine. This was repeated several times. Pachita was, she said, working on my kidneys. Again we made no attempt to conserve "evidence," as we knew that it would come to nothing. Many have attempted to research psychic surgery by analysis of its products and have found either inconclusive results or null results, indicating that psychic surgery is a fraud.

In the book *Arigo*, by John Fuller, on Dr. Puharich's early work with the South American healer of that nickname, psychic surgery is carefully examined, and for those interested in this unusual subject that book is a good place to begin. I have never had any success in getting any orthodox doctor to test the possible results of this Mexican experience. This is due to the fact that the procedure used to test the kidneys can, if the kidneys are badly enough damaged already, cause the kidneys to go into failure once again, and no orthodox doctor could be expected to take that risk. Dr. Puharich himself was unwilling for me to go through this procedure.

With all of its frustrations, investigation into areas in the very fringe of psychic phenomena are most interesting, informative, and rewarding to the researcher who is patient and whose approach to the subject is simply to gather data rather than attempting to prove, step by step, hypotheses about that which he is doing research. In *The Ra Material*, manifestations of this type of materialization are discussed, and the information is quite interesting.

Back in the United States, although I could no longer work at the typewriter, I was still able to offer the continuing weekly meditations and to take on advanced students for individual work. In 1978 James Allen McCarty heard about our group, first from a number of people who had meditated at our Sunday night meetings and had gone on to form a "light center" and nature preserve in Marion County, Kentucky, and then from a two-hour, call-in radio show that Don and I had done in Lexington, Kentucky. He came up with many people from the Marion County meditation group to experience our meditations. After two meditations the group as a whole stopped coming, but Jim made the 140-mile round trip almost weekly, beginning in the spring of 1980. Jim had, for many years, been searching for some method of aiding humanity. Born in 1947, and equipped with degrees in business and education, he had studied, in addition, alternative methods for teaching consciousness expansion. Some of this time was spent working with inner-city children, but he began to find a very strong desire to discover a clearer idea of what it was he was seeking.

In 1972, he took a course of study in consciousness expansion called "brain self-control" with a gruff old mountain man who lived in a log cabin at 10,000 feet in the Rocky Mountains of Colorado. During this course he learned, for the first time, of the possibility of communication with advanced civilization from outer space, not through any man-made means like radios, telegraphs, or electronic gadgetry but through the use of the frontal lobes of the human brain.

Since this very central experience was in wilderness country, rocks, pine, and juniper, he decided to search for an equally remote piece of land upon which he could then offer these brain self-control experiences to others. On 132 acres in central Kentucky, with a running creek for an access road, he formed the Rock Creek Research and Development Laboratories and began to work on the subject closest to his heart: the evolution of mankind. He gave several workshops on this subject but found little interest in that area and so returned to a life of homesteading and solitude for the next six and one-half years, growing his own food, meditating, and studying. He was still curious as to what it would be like to be in a clear, two-way communication with advanced intelligent beings, and, thus, he very much enjoyed the meditations with the Louisville group, but he also had previously become interested in work being done in a group in Oregon. In the fall of 1980, he traveled from Kentucky to Oregon to work with this group that was supposedly channeling the same source that Edgar Cayce had channeled in deep trance.

However, the learning that he had received from the Sunday night meetings and from the advanced study that he had with me had spoken to his inner seeking, and, seemingly of its own accord, his mind made itself up for him after only two months in Oregon. He found that he needed to return to Louisville and work with Don and me. On December 23, 1980, he arrived in Louisville, having traveled 5,000 miles from the woods of central Kentucky to Oregon and back to Louisville.

Don and I were endlessly grateful for McCarty's aid. His abilities were extraordinary. He had a grasp of the metaphysical material going back to his college days, and he had read extensively through all the intervening years, so he came to this work very informed of our areas of study. He was able to take up the physical part of the research, filing, making notes, transcribing tapes, and carrying on the correspondence that had sorely lapsed since my disability. Jim, always thorough, sold his land. L/L Research merged with the Rock Creek Research and Development Laboratories, keeping our old partnership name for our publishing arm, purchased a new typewriter—Jim's fingers, strengthened by six and one-half years of homesteading, overmatched my old electric typewriter*—and we settled down to do . . . *what?* We didn't know.

We discussed doing a new book, updating what we had learned in *Secrets of the UFO*, and had blank paper ready to be filled. Jim had begun to do back research in our voluminous files. Three weeks after he came, the Ra contact began.

During all the years that I had been channeling, I had always channeled consciously, using my free will to clothe telepathic concepts in my own language. In 1980, a longtime friend and meditation group member, Elaine Flaherty, died a tragically young death. She had had juvenile diabetes and had died in her thirties. I had sat with her for many days in the hospital before she finally left her body, and she had told me several times that she wanted to make sure that her husband, Tom, was made aware that she was all right after her death, for she knew that she was likely to die. She had told Tom, also a longtime meditation group member, as well.

After her funeral, Tom came to me and asked if I would attempt to get in touch with Elaine. Having been through all too many séances and not having a great deal of personal commitment to the type of communication that one was likely to get from one's physically dead relatives, I was at first reluctant to attempt such "mediumship." However, these were my good friends and I could not say no. Tom, Don, and Elaine and Tom's son, Mike, gathered with me for the first attempt. After some moments of consciously offering myself for the contact with Elaine, I became unaware of the passing of time, and when I awakened, Tom had what sounded like Elaine's voice on tape speaking through me. That was my first experience with trance. I did not know, and to this day do not know, how it occurred. Tom asked once more if I would do this, and again I went into what seemed to be a very deep trance, remembering nothing and hearing what sounded like Elaine's voice on tape after the session. Don stated that if he had heard me from the next room without seeing me, he would have been certain it was Elaine.

This work was extremely draining to me, and I asked Tom to accept the fact that I really did not wish to continue being this type of medium. Tom agreed, saying that he had what Elaine had promised, and was satisfied. However, only a few days later, while working with an advanced meditation student, Leonard Cecil, I received a new contact, one that I had never had before. As I do in all cases, I challenged this entity in the name of Christ, demanding that it leave if it did not come as a messenger of Christ-consciousness. It remained, so I opened myself to its channel. Again I went almost immediately into trance, and the entity, which called itself Ra, began its series of contacts with us. This contact is ongoing, fascinating, and, to me, a source of some disquiet.

The person who decides to become a vocal channel in the first place has already taken a step that is, to some people, quite difficult; that is, the willingness to speak the words of one that is not controlled by the self. In free-will channeling, it is possible to choose to stop channeling. However, it is also possible to utter complete nonsense because the channel never knows in advance what the next concept will be. I hasten to add that this nonsense has never occurred in my experience, and that the channelings have always made a reasonable amount of sense and, in many cases, have been quite inspirational. Nevertheless, in a society where you are taught to measure your words with some care, it seems an irresponsible act to simply blurt out that which comes into your mind.

When, in order for the contact to occur, trance has to be obtained, the disquiet grows into something close to a near panic on my part. I do not know how the procedure for a trance works, and I am always afraid that in this session, nothing will happen, I will remain conscious, and I will receive no contact. Again, this has never happened. Since neither I nor either of the others in our group has any real idea of how to aid me beyond a certain point in achieving a state of "trance," there is nothing to be done but simply to move ahead. Don states that although my state of trance is similar to others he has observed, it is what he would call "telepathic reception in the trance state."

Although I studied literature in my undergraduate days and was a librarian for many years, reading the material almost always offers me the opportunity to learn a new word or two and has certainly stretched my mind in the area of science, which in my education was woefully lacking.

What concerns me perhaps more than anything else is that someone who reads this material will consider this human being that I am to have some sort of wisdom that Ra certainly has, but that I certainly do not. If this work impresses you, I can only ask that you please make a sharp differentiation in your mind between the words and the "medium" through which the words come. You would not, for instance, expect the water pipe to be responsible for the quality of the water that runs through it. Certainly all of us in the research group try, through meditation and daily life, to prepare ourselves as best we can for these sessions. Nevertheless, what comes through our group stands on its own and cannot be said to reflect on the wisdom or so-called spiritual advancement of any of its members. As our popular philosophy has it, "We are all bozos on this bus."

If you have any questions as you read, please feel free to write the Rock Creek group. Its correspondent, Jim, will never ignore a letter, and since he has his own experiences of the sessions themselves to share, he will finish this introduction.

JIM McCARTY: We are beginners when it comes to knowing how the Ra contact occurs, and it has only been through a process of trial and error, session by session, that we have learned more about how to support our instrument, Carla, in the mental, physical, and spiritual senses. We were so excited about the Ra contact when it first began that we had two sessions per day for days at a time, but we have since learned that this procedure was much too wearing on Carla. We average about one session every week to ten days now, which allows us to prepare for each session with the greater degree of care that seems to be required as sessions accumulate.

A great deal of thought goes into the questions that Don asks during each session. Each of us contributes ideas, but the great bulk of the line of questioning is accomplished by Don, since he has the years of experience in investigating the UFO contactee phenomenon necessary to develop the intellectual foundation required in any attempt to fit the diverse pieces of this puzzle together. He also has the intuitive sense that is vital in following the unexpected and profoundly revealing answers that Ra so often gives with further questions, developed on the spur of the moment, to take advantage of the new insights.

With the decision made to hold a session the night before the session is to occur, we arise the morning of the session, have a light breakfast, and begin the series of steps that will best aid us in successfully completing the session. I give Carla a half-hour back massage to loosen her muscles and joints before each session because she will have to remain absolutely motionless for between an hour and an hour and forty-five minutes. Then we meditate so that the harmony we try to produce in our daily lives is intensified, and so that our desires are unified into the single desire to see contact with Ra. We then perform our ritual of protection and cleansing of the room in which the contact will be made, and situate Carla in a prone position on the bed, covering her body with a white blanket, her eyes with a white cloth, and hook up the three tape recorder microphones just below her chin so that we don't miss any of the session if one or two tape recorders malfunction.

By this time, all that is visible of Carla is her hair flowing down both of her shoulders and her nose poking out of the sea of cloth white surrounding it. As she mentally recites the Prayer of St. Francis, Don is aligning the table, which holds the Bible, candle, incense, and chalice of water in a straight line with her head, as recommended by Ra. After Don lights the candle and incense, he and I walk the Circle of One around Carla and repeat the words that begin each contact.

At some point after that, Carla departs her physical body, and Ra then uses it to make the words that form the responses to Don's questions. I meditate and send light to Carla for the duration of the session, only taking time out to flip the tapes over as they finish each side. When the session is over, Don waits a few moments for Carla to return to her usually quite stiff body, calls her name a few times until she responds, helps her to sit up, rubs her neck a bit, and gives her the chalice full of water to drink after he and I have filled it as full of our love vibrations as we can.

Since Carla has no idea of what has occurred during the session, she is always most curious to know how it went. She has to settle for secondhand bits and pieces of information until I can get the session transcribed from the tapes, which is usually very easy since Ra speaks quite slowly and forms each syllable with precise enunciation.

Participating in this communication with Ra has been most inspiring for each of us because of the blend of eloquence and simplicity that characterizes Ra's responses. The information contained in *The Ra Material* has been most helpful to us in increasing our knowledge of the mystery of the creation and our evolution through it. We hope that it might also be useful to you.

L/L Research

Don Elkins
Carla L. Rueckert
Jim McCarty

Louisville, Kentucky
July 7, 1983

From the Ra material, Session no. 88, May 29, 1982:

Firstly, if pictures be taken of a working, the visual image must needs be that which is; that is, it is well for you to photograph only an actual working and no sham nor substitution of any material. There shall be no distortions which this group can avoid any more than we would wish distortions in our words.

Secondly, it is inadvisable to photograph the instrument or any portion of the working room while the instrument is in trance. This is a narrow band contact, and we wish to keep electrical and electromagnetic energies constant when their presence is necessary and not present at all otherwise.

Thirdly, once the instrument is aware of the picture taking, whether before or after the working, the instrument shall be required to continuously respond to speech, thus assuring that no trance is imminent.

* * * * *

We ask that any photographs tell the truth, that they be dated and shine with a clarity so that there is no shadow of any but genuine expression which may be offered to those who seek truth.

We come as humble messengers of the Law of One, desiring to decrease distortions. We ask that you, who have been our friends, work with any considerations such as above discussed, not with the thought of quickly removing an unimportant detail, but, as in all ways, regard such as another opportunity to, as the adept must, be yourselves and offer that which is in and with you without pretense of any kind.

RA, Session no. 2, January 20, 1981: "Place at the entity's head a virgin chalice of water. Place to the center the book most closely aligned with the instrument's mental distortions, which are allied most closely with the Law of One—that being the Bible that she touches most frequently. To the other side of the Bible, place a small amount of cense, or incense, in a virgin censer. To the rear of the book symbolizing One, opened to the Gospel of John, Chapter One, place a white candle." June 9, 1982

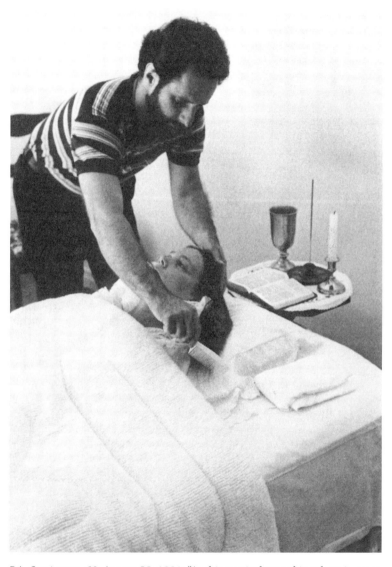

RA, Session no. 69, August 29, 1981: "At this particular working there is some slight interference with the contact due to the hair of the instrument. We may suggest the combing of this antenna-like material into a more orderly configuration prior to the working." June 9, 1982

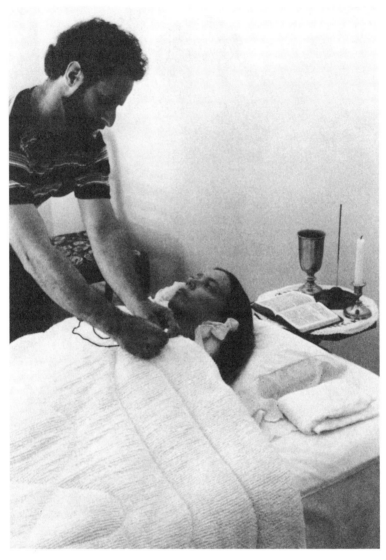

"We hook up three tape recorder microphones just below her chin so that we don't miss any of the session if tape recorder one or two malfunctions, which has happened." From the introduction to *The Ra Material*. June 9, 1982

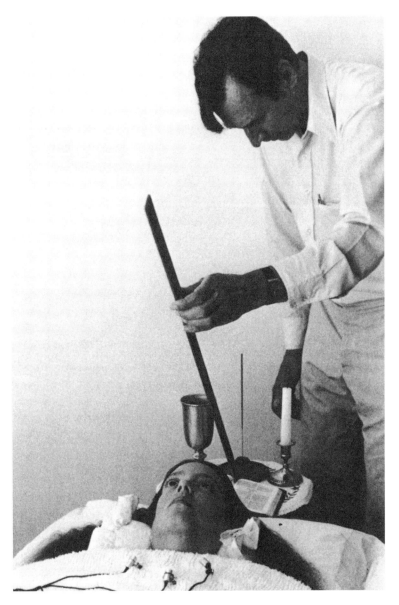

RA, Session no. 2, January 20, 1981: "The proper alignment is with the head pointed 20 degrees north by northeast. This is the direction from which the newer or New Age distortions of love/light, which are less distorted, are emanating, and this instrument will find comfort therein." June 9, 1982

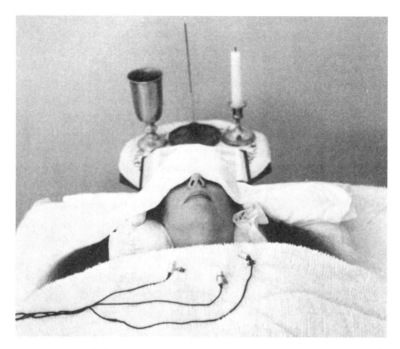

RA, Session no. 2, January 20, 1981: "The instrument would be strengthened by the wearing of a white robe. The instrument shall be covered and prone, the eyes covered." June 9, 1982

From the introduction to *The Ra Material*: "Each of us contributes ideas, but the great bulk of the line of questioning is accomplished by Don, who is the questioner, since he has years of experience in investigating the UFO contactee phenomenon necessary to develop the intellectual foundation which is required in any attempt to fit the diverse pieces of this puzzle together." June 9, 1982

From the introduction to *The Ra Material*: "We average about one session every week or ten days now, which allows us to prepare for each session with the greater degree of care that seems to be required as sessions accumulate. A great deal of thought goes into the questions that Don asks during each session." June 9, 1982

From the introduction to *The Ra Material*: "After Don lights the candle and incense, he and I walk the Circle of One around Carla and repeat the words that begin each contact. At some point after that, Carla departs her physical body, and Ra then uses it to make the words that form the responses to Don's questions. I meditate and send light to Carla for the duration of the session, only taking time out to flip the tapes over as they finish each side."

In this picture, Carla is not channeling Ra but is singing "Amazing Grace" as per Ra's instructions for the instrument to be constantly speaking if her eyes are covered during the picture-taking session. June 9, 1982

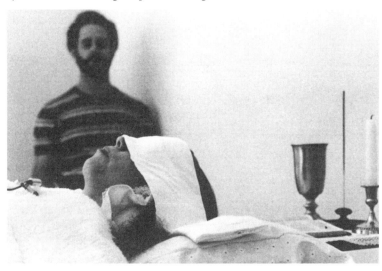

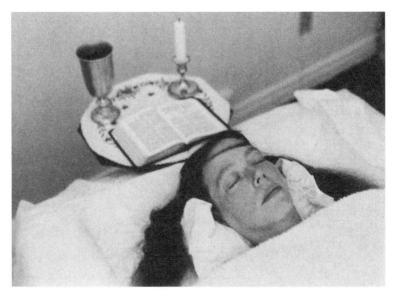

This picture was taken immediately after Carla responded to her name and the eye covering was removed from her face, somewhat mussing her hair. June 9, 1982

From the introduction to *The Ra Material*: "When the session is over, Don waits a few moments for Carla to return to her usually quite stiff body; he calls her name a few times until she responds, helps her to sit up, rubs her neck a bit, and gives her the chalice full of water to drink after he and I have filled it as full of our love vibrations as we can." June 9, 1982

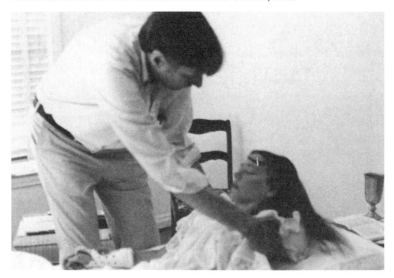

Jim is transcribing Session no. 89 on the afternoon of June 9, 1982, while Chocolate Bar, one of our four cats, observes. June 9, 1982

The exterior of the Ra room: the door and corner windows are part of the outside of the room in which the Ra sessions have taken place since January 1981. June 9, 1982

Carla holding our longtime friend, thirteen-year-old Gandalf. June 26, 1982

Don, in the office, talking to the picture taker, Jim, and attracting a feline audience as well. June 26, 1982

Jim and Carla prepare for the meditation that always precedes a Ra session.
June 26, 1982

Carla, after Ra session no. 92, July 8, 1982

On January 15, 1981, our research group began receiving a communication from the social memory complex, Ra. From this communication precipitated the Law of One and some of the distortions of the Law of One.

The pages of this book contain an exact transcript, edited only to remove some personal material, of the communications received in the first twenty-six sessions with Ra.

Session 1,
January 15, 1981

RA: I am Ra. I have not spoken through this instrument before. We had to wait until she was precisely tuned, as we send a narrow band vibration. We greet you in the love and in the light of our Infinite Creator.

We have watched your group. We have been called to your group, for you have a need for the diversity of experiences in channeling which go with a more intensive, or as you might call it, advanced approach to the system of studying the pattern of the illusions of your body, your mind, and your spirit, which you call seeking the truth. We hope to offer you a somewhat different slant upon the information which is always and ever the same.

At this time we would be glad to attempt to speak to any subject or question which those entities in the room may have potential use in the requesting.

QUESTIONER: Do you have a specific purpose, and if so, could you tell us something of what your purpose is?

RA: I am Ra. We communicate now. We are those who are of the Law of One. In our vibration the polarities are harmonized; the complexities are simplified; the paradoxes have a solution. We are one. That is our nature and our purpose.

We are old upon your planet and have served with varying degrees of success in transmitting the Law of One, of Unity, of Singleness to your peoples. We have walked your planet. We have seen the faces of your peoples. However, we now feel the great responsibility of staying in the capacity of removing the distortions and powers that have been given to the Law of One. We will continue in this, until, shall we say, your cycle is appropriately ended. If not this one, then the next. We are not a part of time and, thus, are able to be with you in any of your times.

Does this give you enough information from which to extract our purpose, my brother?

QUESTIONER: Yes. Thank you.

RA: I am Ra. We appreciate your vibrations. Is there another query?

QUESTIONER: I've heard of the name "Ra" in connection with the Egyptians. Are you connected with that Ra in any way?

RA: I am Ra. Yes, the connection is congruency. May we elucidate? What do you not understand?

QUESTIONER: Could you give me a little more detail about your role with the Egyptians?

RA: I am Ra. The identity of the vibration Ra is our identity. We as a group, or what you would call a social memory complex, made contact with a race of your planetary kind which you call Egyptians. Others from our density made contact at the same time in South America, and the so-called "lost cities" were their attempts to contribute to the Law of One.

We spoke to one who heard and understood and was in a position to decree the Law of One. However, the priests and peoples of that era quickly distorted our message, robbing it of the, shall we say, compassion with which unity is informed by its very nature. Since it contains all, it cannot abhor any.

When we were no longer able to have appropriate channels through which to enunciate the Law of One, we removed ourselves from the now-hypocritical position which we had allowed ourselves to be placed in. Other myths, shall we say, having more to do with polarity and the things of your vibration that are complex, again took over in that particular society/complex.

Does this form a sufficient amount of information, or could we speak further?

Is there another query?

QUESTIONER: [The question was lost because the questioner was sitting too far from the tape recorder to be recorded.]

RA: I am Ra. Consider, if you will, that the universe is infinite. This has yet to be proven or disproven, but we can assure you that there is no end to your selves, your understanding, what you would call your journey of seeking, or your perceptions of the creation.

That which is infinite cannot be many, for manyness is a finite concept. To have infinity you must identify or define the infinity as unity; otherwise, the term does not have any referent or meaning. In an Infinite Creator there is only unity. You have seen simple examples of unity. You have seen the prism which shows all colors stemming from the sunlight. This is a simplistic example of unity.

In truth there is no right or wrong. There is no polarity, for all will be, as you would say, reconciled at some point in your dance through the mind/body/spirit complex which you amuse yourself by distorting in various ways at this time. This distortion is not in any case necessary. It is chosen by each of you as an alternative to understanding the complete unity of thought which binds all things. You are not speaking of similar or somewhat like entities or things. You are every thing, every being, every emotion, every event, every situation. You are unity. You are infinity. You are love/light, light/love. You are. This is the Law of One.

May we enunciate in more detail?

QUESTIONER: No.

RA: I am Ra. Is there another query at this time?

QUESTIONER: Can you comment on the coming planetary changes in our physical reality?

RA: I am Ra. I preferred to wait till this instrument had again reached a proper state of depth of singleness or one-pointedness before we spoke.

The changes are very, very trivial. We do not concern ourselves with the conditions which bring about harvest.

QUESTIONER: If an individual makes efforts to act as a catalyst in general to increase the awareness of planetary consciousness, is he of any aid in that direction, or is he doing nothing but acting upon himself?

RA: I am Ra. We shall answer your question in two parts, both of which are important equally.

Firstly, you must understand that the distinction between yourself and others is not visible to us. We do not consider that a separation exists between the consciousness-raising efforts of the distortion which you project as a personality and the distortion that you project as another personality. Thus, to learn is the same as to teach unless you are not teaching what you are learning, in which case you have done you/them little good. This understanding should be pondered by your mind/body/spirit complex as it is a distortion which plays a part in your experiences at this nexus.

To turn to the second part of our response, may we state our understanding, limited though it is.

Group-individuated consciousness is that state of sharing understanding with the other distortions of mind/body/spirit complexes, which are within the evident reach of the mind/body/spirit complex individual or group. Thus, we are speaking to you and accepting both our distortions and your own in order to enunciate the laws of creation, more especially the Law of One. We are not available to many of your peoples, for this is not an easily understood way of communication or type of philosophy. However, our very being is hopefully a poignant example of both the necessity and the near hopelessness of attempting to teach.

Each of those in this group is striving to use, digest, and diversify the information which we are sending this instrument into the channels of the mind/body/spirit complex without distortion. The few whom you will illuminate by sharing your light are far more than enough reason for the greatest possible effort. To serve one is to serve all. Therefore, we offer the question back to you to state that indeed it is the only activity worth doing: to learn/teach or teach/learn. There is nothing else which is of aid in demonstrating the original thought except your very being, and the distortions that come from the unexplained, inarticulate, or mystery-clad being are many. Thus, to attempt to discern and weave your way through as many group mind/body/spirit distortions as possible among your peoples in the course of your teaching is a very good effort to make. We can speak no more valiantly of your desire to serve.

May we speak in any other capacity upon this subject?

QUESTIONER: Will you be available for communication? Can we call on you in the future?

RA: I am Ra. We have good contact with this instrument because of her recent experiences with trance. She is to be able to communicate our thoughts in your future. However, we advise care in disturbing the channel for a few moments and then the proper procedure for aiding an instrument who has, to some extent, the need of reentering the mind/body/spirit complex which the instrument has chosen for the life experience of this time/space. Do you understand how to nurture this instrument?

QUESTIONER: No. Could you explain it?

RA: We suggest first a brief period of silence. Then the repetition of the instrument's vibratory complex of sound in your density which you call name. Repeat until an answer is obtained. Then the laying on of the hands at the neck region for a brief period so that the instrument may recharge batteries, which are not, shall we say, full of the essence of this particular field at this time. And finally, a gift of water into which the love of all present has been given. This will restore this entity, for her distortions contain great sensitivity towards the vibrations of love and the charged water will effect comfort. Do you now understand?

QUESTIONER: Not completely.

RA: I am Ra. We search your mind to find the vibration (nickname). It is this vibration from you which contains the largest amount of what you would call love. Others would call this entity (first name). The charging of the water is done by those present placing their hands over the glass and visualizing the power of love entering the water. This will charge that very effective medium with those vibrations.

This instrument is, at this time, quite fatigued. However, her heart is such that she continues to remain open to us and useful as a channel. This is why we have spent the time/space explaining how the distortions of what you may call fatigue may be ameliorated.

Under no circumstances should this instrument be touched until she has responded to her name. I do not wish to take this instrument beyond her capacity for physical energy. It grows low. Therefore, I must leave this instrument. I leave you in the glory and peace of unity. Go forth in peace, rejoicing in the power of the One Creator. I am Ra.

Session 2,
January 20, 1981

RA: I am Ra. I greet you in the love and the light of our Infinite Creator. I am with this mind/body/spirit complex which has offered itself for a channel. I communicate with you.

Queries are in order in your projections of mind distortion at this time/space. Thusly would I assure this group that my own social memory complex has one particular method of communicating with those few who may be able to harmonize their distortions with ours, and that is to respond to queries for information. We are comfortable with this format. May the queries now begin.

QUESTIONER: I'm guessing that there are enough people who would understand what you are saying, who would be interested enough in it, for us to make a book of your communications, and I wondered if you would agree to this?

If so, I was thinking that possibly a bit of historical background of yourself might be in order.

RA: I am Ra. The possibility of communication, as you would call it, from the One to the One, through distortion, acceptable for meaning is the reason we contacted this group. There are few who will grasp, without significant distortion, that which we communicate through this connection with this mind/body/spirit complex. However, if it be your desire to share our communications with others, we have the distortion towards a perception that this would be most helpful in regularizing and crystallizing your own patterns of vibration upon the levels of experience which you call the life. If one is illuminated, are not all illuminated? Therefore, we are oriented towards speaking for you in whatever supply of speakingness you may desire. To teach/learn is the Law of One in one of its most elementary distortions.

QUESTIONER: Could you tell us something of your historical background and your contact with earlier races on this planet? Then we would have something to start with.

RA: I am Ra. We are aware that your mind/body is calculating the proper method of performing the task of creating a teach/learning instrument. We are aware that you find our incarnate, as you call it, state of interest. We waited for a second query so as to emphasize that the time/space of several thousand of your years creates a spurious type of interest. Thus in giving this information, we ask the proper lack of stress be placed upon our experiences in your local space/time. The teach/learning which is our responsibility is philosophical rather than historical. We shall proceed with your request which is harmless if properly evaluated.

We are those of the Confederation who eleven thousand of your years ago came to two of your planetary cultures which were at that time closely in touch with the creation of the One Creator. It was our naive belief that we could teach/learn by direct contact and that the free-will distortions of individual feeling or personality were in no danger. We had no thought of their being disturbed, as these cultures were already closely aligned with an all-embracing belief in the live-ness or consciousness of all. We came and were welcomed by the peoples whom we wished to serve. We attempted to aid them in technical ways having to do with the healing of mind/body/spirit complex distortions through the use of the crystal, appropriate to the distortion, placed within a certain appropriate series of ratios of time/space material. Thus were the pyramids created.

We found that the technology was reserved largely for those with the effectual mind/body distortion of power. This was not intended by the Law of One. We left your peoples. The group that was to work with those in the area of South America, as you call that portion of your sphere, gave up not so easily. They returned. We did not. However, we have never left your vibration due to our responsibility for the changes in consciousness we had first caused and then found distorted in ways not relegated to the Law of One. We attempted to contact the rulers of the land to which we had come, that land which you call Egypt, or in some areas, the Holy Land.

In the Eighteenth Dynasty, as it is known in your records of space/ time distortions, we were able to contact a pharaoh, as you would call him. The man was small in life experience on your plane and was a . . . what this instrument would call Wanderer. Thus, this mind/body/spirit complex received our communication distortions and was able to blend his distortions with our own. This young entity had been given a vibratory complex of sound which vibrated in honor of a prosperous god, as this mind/body complex, which we call instrument for convenience, would call "Ammon." The entity decided that this name, being in honor of one among many gods, was not acceptable for inclusion in his vibratory sound complex. Thus, he changed his name to one which honored the sun disc. This distortion, called "Aten," was a close distortion to our reality as we understand our own nature of mind/body/spirit complex distortion. However, it does not come totally into alignment with the intended teach/learning which was sent. This entity, Ikhnaton, became convinced that the vibration of One was the true spiritual vibration and thus decreed the Law of One.

However, this entity's beliefs were accepted by very few. His priests gave lip service only, without the spiritual distortion towards seeking. The peoples continued in their beliefs. When this entity was no longer in this density, again the polarized beliefs in the many gods came into their own and continued so until the one known as Mohammed delivered the peoples into a more intelligible distortion of mind/body/spirit relationships.

Do you have a more detailed interest at this time?

QUESTIONER: We are very interested in the entire story that you have to tell and getting in to the Law of One in quite some detail. There will be several questions that I'll ask as we go along that may or may not be related directly to understanding the Law of One. However, I believe that the proper way of presenting this as a teach/learning vehicle is to investigate different facets of what you tell us. You spoke of crystal healing. (One other thing I want to mention is that when the instrument becomes fatigued, we want to cut off communication and continue questions at a later time when the instrument is recharged.) If the instrument is suitable at this time, we would like a little information about the crystal healing that you mentioned.

RA: I am Ra. The principle of crystal healing is based upon an understanding of the hierarchical nature of the structure of the illusion which is the physical body, as you would call it. There are crystals which work upon the energies coming into the spiritual body; there are crystals which work upon the distortions from spirit to mind; there are crystals which balance the distortions between the mind and the body. All of these crystal healings are charged through purified channels. Without the relative crystallization of the healer working with the crystal, the crystal will not be properly charged. The other ingredient is the proper alignment with the energy fields of the planet upon which you dwell and the holistic or cosmic distortions or streamings which enter the planetary aura in such a manner that an appropriate ratio of shapes and placement within these shapes is of indicated aid in the untangling or balancing process.

To go through the various crystals to be used would be exhaustive to this instrument, although you may ask us if you wish in another session. The delicacy, shall we say, of the choosing of the crystal is very critical and, in truth, a crystalline structure such as a diamond or ruby can be used by a purified channel who is filled with the Love/Light of One, in almost any application.

This, of course, takes initiation, and there never have been many to persevere to the extent of progressing through the various distortion leavings which initiation causes.

May we further inform you in any fairly brief way upon this or another subject?

QUESTIONER: Yes. You mentioned that the pyramids were an outgrowth of this. Could you expand a little on that? Were you responsible for the building of the pyramid, and what was the purpose of the pyramid?

RA: I am Ra. The larger pyramids were built by our ability using the forces of One. The stones are alive. It has not been so understood by the mind/body/spirit distortions of your culture. The purposes of the pyramids were two:

Firstly, to have a properly oriented place of initiation for those who wished to become purified or initiated channels for the Law of One.

Two, we wished then to carefully guide the initiates in developing a healing of the people whom they sought to aid, and of the planet itself. Pyramid after pyramid charged by the crystal and Initiate were designed to balance the incoming energy of the One Creation with the many and multiple distortions of the planetary mind/body/spirit. In this effort we were able to continue work that brothers within the Confederation had effected through building of other crystal-bearing structures and thus complete a ring, if you will, of these about the Earth's, as this instrument would have us vibrate it, surface.

This instrument begins to lose energy. We ask for one more query or subject and then we shall take our leave for this time/space.

QUESTIONER: You might mention that originally there was a capstone on the pyramid at the top: what was it made of and how you moved the heavy blocks to build the pyramid. What technique was used for that?

RA: I am Ra. I request that we be asked this question in our next work-time, as you would term the distortion/sharing that our energies produce.

If you have any questions about the proper use of this mind/body/spirit, we would appreciate your asking them now.

QUESTIONER: Consider them asked. I don't have anything to go on. What is the proper use of this instrument? What should we do? What should we do to maximize her ability and her comfort?

RA: I am Ra. We are pleased that you have asked this question, for it is not our understanding that we have the right/duty to share our perceptions on any subject but philosophy without direct question. However, this mind/body/spirit is not being correctly used and therefore is experiencing unnecessary distortions of body in the area of fatigue.

The vibrations may well be purified by a simple turning to the circle of One and the verbal vibration while doing so of the following dialogue:

Question: "What is the Law?"

Answer: "The Law is One."

Question: "Why are we here?"

Answer: "We seek the Law of One."

Question: "Why do we seek Ra?"

Answer: "Ra is an humble messenger of the Law of One." Both Together: "Rejoice then and purify this place in the Law of One. Let no thought-form enter the circle we have walked about this instrument, for the Law is One."

The instrument at this time should be in trance. The proper alignment is the head pointed 20 degrees north by northeast. This is the direction from which the newer or New Age distortions of love/light, which are less distorted, are emanating, and this instrument will find comfort therein. This is a sensitive instrument, by which we mean the distortions which enter her mind/body/spirit complex come from any of her senses. Thus, it is well to do the following:

Place at the entity's head a virgin chalice of water.

To the center, the book most closely aligned with the instrument's mental distortions which are allied most closely with the Law of One, that being the Bible that she touches most frequently.

To the other side of the Bible, a small amount of cense, or incense, in a virgin censer.

To the rear of the book symbolizing One, opened to the Gospel of John, Chapter One, a white candle.

The instrument would be strengthened by the wearing of a white robe. The instrument shall be covered and prone, the eyes covered.

We feel that, though this is a complex of activity/circumstance and may seem very distorted from a purposeful teach/learning experience, these elaborations on the technique of trance will ease the mind distortions of those about the instrument as they perceive improvement in the instrument's distortions with regard to fatigue. We add only that if these teach/learning sessions are held during time/space during which your sun body does not light your room that it is best to call the instrument before the lighting of the illuminatory mechanism.

I am Ra. I leave you in the glory and the peace of the One Creator. Rejoice in the love/light, and go forth in the power of the One Creator. In joy, we leave you. Adonai.

Session 3,
January 21, 1981

RA: I am Ra. I greet you in love and the light of the One Infinite Creator. I communicate with you now.

QUESTIONER: My first question is, did we correctly perform the ritual for starting the communication?

RA: I am Ra. The placement of the artifacts designated to balance the instrument should be placed at the instrument's head for the least distortion of effect. The remainder of the beginning account of purpose is quite acceptable, for those speaking desire to serve. Otherwise, the attendant emphasis in mind complexities would not have been affected properly. We caution you to guard against those who are not wishing to serve others above all else, from taking part in the beginning or in lending their distortions of mind/body/spirit complex to any session as we should then be unable to properly blend our distortions with those of this instrument.

QUESTIONER: Should I move the Bible, candle, and incense at this time?

RA: I am Ra. This would be appropriate.

QUESTIONER: [*After moving the items*] Is this the proper position?

RA: I am Ra. Please correct the angle of the incense so that it is perpendicular to the plane of 20 degrees north by northeast.

QUESTIONER: [*After making the correction*] Is this satisfactory?

RA: I am Ra. Please check by eye to make fine correction. We will explain the process by which this becomes a significant distortion balancer. The incense acts as energizer to the physical body of this instrument, signifying its humanity. This is, therefore, a necessity that the wafted smoke is perceived from the same relative angle as the instrument perceives the opened Bible balanced by the lighted candle signifying love/light and light/love and, therefore, give the mental and emotional, shall we call it, distortion complex of this instrument the sight of paradise and peace which it seeks. Thus energized from the lower to the higher, the instrument becomes balanced and does not grow fatigued.

We appreciate your concern, for this will enable our teach/learning to proceed more easily.

QUESTIONER: Does everything appear correctly aligned now?

RA: I am Ra. I judge it within limits of acceptability.

QUESTIONER: At the last session we had two questions that we were saving for this session: one having to do with the possible capstone on top of the Great Pyramid at Giza; the other having to do with how you moved the heavy blocks that make up the pyramid. I know these questions are of no importance with respect to the Law of One, but it was my judgment—and please correct me if I am wrong, and make the necessary suggestions—that this would provide an easy entry for those who would read the material that will eventually become a book. We are very grateful for your contact and will certainly take any suggestions as to how we should receive this information.

RA: I am Ra. I will not suggest the proper series of questions. This is your prerogative as free agent of the Law of One having learned/understood that our social memory complex cannot effectually discern the distortions of the societal mind/body/spirit complex of your peoples. We wish now to fulfill our teach/learning honor/responsibility by answering what is asked. This only will suffice for we cannot plumb the depths of the distortion complexes which infect your peoples.

The first question, therefore, is the capstone. We iterate the unimportance of this type of data.

The so-called Great Pyramid had two capstones. One was of our design and was of smaller and carefully contrived pieces of the material upon your planet which you call "granite." This was contrived for crystalline properties and for the proper flow of your atmosphere via a type of what you would call "chimney."

At a time when we as a people had left your density, the original was taken away and a more precious one substituted. It consisted, in part, of a golden material. This did not change the properties of the pyramid, as you call it, at all and was a distortion due to the desire of a few to mandate the use of the structure as a royal place only.

Do you wish to query further upon this first question?

QUESTIONER: What did you mean by chimney? What was its specific purpose?

RA: I am Ra. There is a proper flow of your atmosphere which, though small, freshens the whole of the structure. This was designed by having air-flow ducts, as this instrument might call them, situated so that there was a freshness of atmosphere without any disturbance or draft.

QUESTIONER: How were the blocks moved?

RA: I am Ra. You must picture the activity within all that is created. The energy is, though finite, quite large compared to the understanding/distortion by your peoples. This is an obvious point well known to your people, but little considered.

This energy is intelligent. It is hierarchical. Much as your mind/body/spirit complex dwells within a hierarchy of vehicles and retains, therefore, the shell or shape or field, and the intelligence of each ascendingly intelligent or balanced body, so does each atom of such a material as rock. When one can speak to that intelligence, the finite energy of the physical or chemical rock/body is put into contact with that infinite power which is resident in the more well-tuned bodies, be they human or rock.

With this connection made, a request may be given. The intelligence of infinite rockness communicates to its physical vehicle, and that splitting and moving which is desired is then carried out through the displacement of the energy field of rockness from finity to a dimension which we may conveniently call, simply, infinity.

In this way, that which is required is accomplished due to a cooperation of the infinite understanding of the Creator indwelling in the living rock. This is, of course, the mechanism by which many things are accomplished, which are not subject to your present means of physical analysis of action at a distance.

QUESTIONER: I am reminded of the statement—approximately— that if you had faith to move a mountain, the mountain would move. This seems to be approximately what you were saying. That if you are fully aware of the Law of One, you would be able to do these things. Is that correct?

RA: I am Ra. The vibratory distortion of sound, faith, is perhaps one of the stumbling blocks between those of what we may call the infinite path and those of the finite proving/understanding.

You are precisely correct in your understanding of the congruency of faith and intelligent infinity; however, one is a spiritual term, the other more acceptable perhaps to the conceptual framework distortions of those who seek with measure and pen.

QUESTIONER: Then if an individual is totally informed with respect to the Law of One and lives the Law of One, then such things as the building of the pyramids by direct mental effort would be commonplace. Is that what I am to understand?

RA: I am Ra. You are incorrect in that there is a distinction between the individual power through the Law of One and the combined or societal memory complex mind/body/spirit understanding of the Law of One.

In the first case only the one individual, purified of all flaws, could move a mountain. In the case of mass understanding of unity, each individual may contain an acceptable amount of distortion and yet the mass mind could move mountains. The progress is normally from the understanding which you now seek to a dimension of understanding which is governed by the laws of love, and which seeks the laws of light. Those who are vibrating with the Law of Light seek the Law of One. Those who vibrate with the Law of One seek the Law of Foreverness.

We cannot say what is beyond this dissolution of the unified self with all that there is, for we still seek to become all that there is, and still are we Ra. Thus our paths go onward.

QUESTIONER: Was the pyramid then built by the mutual action of many?

RA: I am Ra. The pyramids which we thought/built were constructed thought-forms created by our social memory complex.

QUESTIONER: Then the rock was created in place rather than moved from someplace else? Is that correct?

RA: I am Ra. We built with everlasting rock the Great Pyramid, as you call it. Other of the pyramids were built with stone moved from one place to another.

QUESTIONER: What is everlasting rock?

RA: I am Ra. If you can understand the concept of thought-forms you will realize that the thought-form is more regular in its distortion than the energy fields created by the materials in the rock which has been created through thought-form from thought to finite energy and being-ness in your, shall we say, distorted reflection of the level of the thought-form.
May we answer you in any more helpful way?

QUESTIONER: This is rather trivial, but I was wondering why the pyramid was built with many blocks rather than creating the whole thing as one form created at once?

RA: I am Ra. There is a law which we believe to be one of the more significant primal distortions of the Law of One. That is the Law of Confusion. You have called this the Law of Free Will. We wished to make an healing machine, or time/space ratio complex which was as efficacious as possible. However, we did not desire to allow the mystery to be penetrated by the peoples in such a way that we became worshipped as builders of a miraculous pyramid. Thus it appears to be made, not thought.

QUESTIONER: Well, then you speak of the pyramid, the Great Pyramid, I assume, as primarily a healing machine, and also you spoke of it as a device for initiation. Are these one and the same concept?

RA: I am Ra. They are part of one complex of love/light intent/sharing. To use the healing properly it was important to have a purified and dedicated channel, or energizer, for the love/light of the Infinite Creator to flow through; thus the initiatory method was necessary to prepare the mind, the body, and the spirit for service in the Creator's work. The two are integral.

QUESTIONER: Does the shape of the pyramid have a function in the initiation process?

RA: I am Ra. This is a large question. We feel that we shall begin and ask you to reevaluate and ask further at a later session, this somewhat, shall we say, informative point.

To begin. There are two main functions of the pyramid in relation to the initiatory procedures. One has to do with the body. Before the body can be initiated, the mind must be initiated. This is the point at which most adepts of your present cycle find their mind/body/spirit complexes distorted from. When the character and personality that is the true identity of the mind has been discovered, the body then must be known in each and every way. Thus, the various functions of the body need understanding and control with detachment. The first use of the pyramid, then, is the going down into the pyramid for purposes of deprivation of sensory input so that the body may, in a sense, be dead and another life begin.

We advise, at this time, any necessary questions and a fairly rapid ending of this session. Have you any query at this time/space?

QUESTIONER: The only question is, is there anything that we have done wrong, or that we could do to make the instrument more comfortable?

RA: I am Ra. We scan this instrument.

This instrument has been much aided by these precautions. We suggest only some attention to the neck, which seems in this body/distortion to be distorted in the area of strength/weakness. More support, therefore, to the neck area may be an aid.

QUESTIONER: Should we have the instrument drink the water from the chalice behind her head, or should we have her drink from another glass after we charge it with love?

RA: I am Ra. That and only that chalice shall be the most beneficial as the virgin material living in the chalice accepts, retains, and responds to the love vibration activated by your beingness.

I am Ra. I will now leave this group rejoicing in the power and peace of the One Creator. Adonai.

Session 4,
January 22, 1981

RA: I am Ra. I greet you in the love and the light of the Infinite Creator. I communicate with you now.

QUESTIONER: When we finished the last session, I had asked a question that was too long to answer. It had to do with the shape of the pyramid, its relationship to the initiation. Is this the appropriate time to ask this question?

RA: I am Ra. Yes, this is an appropriate time/space to ask that question.

QUESTIONER: Does the shape of the pyramid have an effect upon the initiation?

RA: I am Ra. As we began the last session question, you have already recorded in your individual memory complex the first use of the shape having to do with the body complex initiation. The initiation of spirit was a more carefully designed type of initiation as regards the time/space ratios about which the entity to be initiated found itself.

If you will picture with me the side of the so-called pyramid shape and mentally imagine this triangle cut into four equal triangles, you will find the intersection of the triangle, which is at the first level on each of the four sides, forms a diamond in a plane which is horizontal. The middle of this plane is the appropriate place for the intersection of the energies streaming from the infinite dimensions and the mind/body/ spirit complexes of various interwoven energy fields. Thus it was designed that the one to be initiated would, by mind, be able to perceive and then channel this, shall we say, gateway to intelligent infinity. This, then, was the second point of designing this specific shape.

May we provide a further description of any kind to your query?

QUESTIONER: Yes. As I understand it then, the initiate was to be on the centerline of that pyramid, but at an altitude above the base as defined by the intersection of the four triangles made by dividing each side. Is that correct?

RA: I am Ra. This is correct.

QUESTIONER: Then at this point there is a focusing of energy that is extra-dimensional in respect to our dimensions. Am I right?

RA: I am Ra. You may use that vibratory sound complex. However, it is not totally and specifically correct. There are no "extra" dimensions. We would prefer the use of the term "multidimensional."

QUESTIONER: Is the size of the pyramid a function of the effectiveness of the initiation?

RA: I am Ra. Each size pyramid has its own point of streaming in of intelligent infinity. Thus, a tiny pyramid that can be placed below a body or above a body will have specific and various effects depending upon the placement of the body in relationship to the entrance point of intelligent infinity.

For the purposes of initiation, the size needed to be large enough to create the impression of towering size so that the entrance point of multidimensional intelligent infinity would completely pervade and fill the channel, the entire body being able to rest in this focused area. Furthermore, it was necessary for healing purposes that both channel and the one to be healed be able to rest within that focused point.

QUESTIONER: Is the large pyramid at Giza still usable for this purpose, or is it no longer functional?

RA: I am Ra. That, like many other pyramid structures, is like the piano out of tune. It, as this instrument would express it, plays the tune but, oh, so poorly. The disharmony jangles the sensitivity. Only the ghost of the streaming still remains due to the shifting of the streaming points which is in turn due to the shifting electromagnetic field of your planet; due also to the discordant vibratory complexes of those who have used the initiatory and healing place for less compassionate purposes.

QUESTIONER: Would it be possible to build a pyramid and properly align it and use it today from the materials that we have available?

RA: I am Ra. It is quite possible for you to build a pyramid structure. The material used is not critical, merely the ratios of time/space complexes. However, the use of the structure for initiation and healing depends completely upon the inner disciplines of the channels attempting such work.

QUESTIONER: My question then would be, are there individuals incarnate upon the planet today who would have the inner disciplines to, using your instructions, construct and initiate in a pyramid they built? Is this within the limits of what anyone on the planet today can do? Or is there no one available for this?

RA: I am Ra. There are people, as you call them, who are able to take this calling at this nexus. However, we wish to point out once again that the time of the pyramids, as you would call it, is past. It is indeed a timeless structure. However, the streamings from the universe were, at the time we attempted to aid this planet, those which required a certain understanding of purity. This understanding has, as the streamings revolved and all things evolve, changed to a more enlightened view of purity. Thus, there are those among your people at this time whose purity is already one with intelligent infinity. Without the use of structures, healer/patient can gain healing.

May we further speak to some specific point?

QUESTIONER: Is it possible for you to instruct in these healing techniques if we could make available an individual who had the native ability?

RA: I am Ra. It is possible. We must add that many systems of teach/learning the healing/patient nexus are proper given the various mind/body/spirit complexes. We ask your imagination to consider the relative simplicity of the mind in the earlier cycle and the less distorted, but often overly complex, views and thought/spirit processes of the same mind/body/spirit complexes after many incarnations. We also ask your imagination to conceive of those who have chosen the distortion of service and have removed their mind/body/spirit complexes from one dimension to another, thus bringing with them in totally latent form many skills and understandings which more closely match the distortions of the healing/patient processes.

QUESTIONER: I would very much like to continue investigation into the possibility of this healing process, but I'm a little lost as to where to begin. Can you tell me where my first step would be?

RA: I am Ra. I cannot tell you what to ask. I may suggest that you consider the somewhat complex information just given and thus discover several avenues of inquiry. There is one "health," as you call it, in your polarized environment, but there are several significantly various distortions of types of mind/body/spirit complexes. Each type must pursue its own learn/teaching in this area.

QUESTIONER: Would you say, then, that the first step would be to find an individual with ability brought with him into this incarnation? Is this correct?

RA: I am Ra. This is correct.

QUESTIONER: Once I have selected an individual to perform the healing, it would be helpful to receive instruction from you. Is this possible?

RA: I am Ra. This is possible given the distortions of vibratory sound complexes.

QUESTIONER: I'm assuming, then, that the selected individual would be one who was very much in harmony with the Law of One. Even though he may not have any intellectual understanding of it, he should be living the Law of One?

RA: I am Ra. This is both correct and incorrect. The first case, that being correctness, would apply to one such as the questioner himself who has the distortions towards healing, as you call it.

The incorrectness which shall be observed is the healing of those whose activities in your space/time illusion do not reflect the Law of One, but whose ability has found its pathway to intelligent infinity regardless of the plane of existence from which this distortion is found.

QUESTIONER: I'm a little confused. I partially understand you, but I'm not sure that I fully understand you. Could you restate that in another way?

RA: I am Ra. I can restate that in many ways, given this instrument's knowledge of your vibratory sound complexes. I will strive for a shorter distortion at this time.

Two kinds there are who can heal: those such as yourself who, having the innate distortion towards knowledge-giving of the Law of One, can heal but do not; and those who, having the same knowledge, but showing no significant distortions toward the Law of One in mind, body, or spirit, yet, and nevertheless have opened a channel to the same ability.

The point being that there are those who, without proper training, shall we say, nevertheless heal. It is a further item of interest that those whose life does not equal their work may find some difficulty in absorbing the energy of intelligent infinity and thus become quite distorted in such a way as to cause disharmony in themselves and others and perhaps even find it necessary to cease the healing activity. Therefore, those of the first type, those who seek to serve and are willing to be trained in thought, word, and action are those who will be able to comfortably maintain the distortion toward service in the area of healing.

QUESTIONER: Then would it be possible for you to train us in healing awareness?

RA: I am Ra. It is possible.

QUESTIONER: Will you train us?

RA: I am Ra. We will.

QUESTIONER: I have no idea how long this would take. Is it possible for you to give a synopsis of the program of training required? I have no knowledge of what questions to ask at this point.

RA: I am Ra. We consider your request for information, for as you noted, there are a significant number of vibratory sound complexes which can be used in sequence to train the healer.

The synopsis is a very appropriate entry that you might understand what is involved.

Firstly, the mind must be known to itself. This is perhaps the most demanding part of healing work. If the mind knows itself then the most important aspect of healing has occurred. Consciousness is the microcosm of the Law of One.

The second part has to do with the disciplines of the body complexes. In the streamings reaching your planet at this time, these understandings and disciplines have to do with the balance between love and wisdom in the use of the body in its natural functions.

The third area is the spiritual, and in this area the first two disciplines are connected through the attainment of contact with intelligent infinity.

QUESTIONER: I believe I have a little idea of the accomplishment of the first step. Can you elaborate a little bit on the other two steps which I am not at all familiar with.

RA: I am Ra. Imagine the body. Imagine the more dense aspects of the body. Proceed therefrom to the very finest knowledge of energy pathways which revolve and cause the body to be energized. Understand that all natural functions of the body have all aspects from dense to fine and can be transmuted to what you may call sacramental. This is a brief investigation of the second area.

To speak to the third, if you will, imagine the function of the magnet. The magnet has two poles. One reaches up. The other goes down. The function of the spirit is to integrate the up-reaching yearning of the mind/body energy with the downpouring and streaming of infinite intelligence. This is a brief explication of the third area.

QUESTIONER: Then would this training program involve specific things to do, specific instructions and exercises?

RA: I am Ra. We are not at this time incarnate among your peoples; thus, we can guide and attempt to specify, but we cannot, by example, show. This is an handicap. However, there should indeed be fairly specific exercises of mind, body, and spirit during the teach/learning process we offer. It is to be once more iterated that healing is but one distortion of the Law of One. To reach an undistorted understanding of that law, it is not necessary to heal or to show any manifestation but only to exercise the discipline of understanding.

We would ask that one or two more questions be the ending of this session.

QUESTIONER: My objective is primarily to discover more of the Law of One, and it would be very helpful to discover the techniques of healing. I am aware of your problem with respect to free will. Can you state the Law of One and the laws of healing to me?

RA: I am Ra. The Law of One, though beyond the limitation of name, as you call vibratory sound complexes, may be approximated by stating that all things are one, that there is no polarity, no right or wrong, no disharmony, but only identity. All is one, and that one is love/light, light/love, the Infinite Creator.

One of the primal distortions of the Law of One is that of healing. Healing occurs when a mind/body/spirit complex realizes, deep within itself, the Law of One; that is, that there is no disharmony, no imperfection; that all is complete and whole and perfect. Thus, the intelligent infinity within this mind/body/spirit complex reforms the illusion of body, mind, or spirit to a form congruent with the Law of One. The healer acts as energizer or catalyst for this completely individual process.

One item which may be of interest is that a healer asking to learn must take the distortion understood as responsibility for that ask/receiving. This is an honor/duty which must be carefully considered in free will before the asking.

QUESTIONER: I assume that we should continue tomorrow.

RA: I am Ra. Your assumption is correct unless you feel a certain question is necessary. This instrument is nurtured by approximately this length of work.

QUESTIONER: I have one more short question. Is this instrument capable of two of these sessions per day, or should we remain with one?

RA: I am Ra. This instrument is capable of two sessions a day. However, she must be encouraged to keep her bodily complex strong by the ingestion of your foodstuffs to an extent which exceeds this instrument's normal intake of your foodstuffs, this due to the physical material which we use to speak.

Further, this instrument's activities must be monitored to prevent overactivity, for this activity is equivalent to a strenuous working day on the physical level.

If these admonishments are considered, the two sessions would be possible. We do not wish to deplete this instrument.

QUESTIONER: Thank you, Ra.

RA: I am Ra. I leave you in the love and the light of the one Infinite Intelligence which is the Creator. Go forth rejoicing in the power and the peace of the One. Adonai.

Session 5,
January 23, 1981

RA: I am Ra. I greet you in the love and the light of the Infinite Creator. I communicate now.

QUESTIONER: The last time that we communicated we were speaking of the learning of healing. It is my impression from what you gave to us in the earlier session that it is necessary to first purify the self by certain disciplines and exercises. Then in order to heal a patient, it is necessary, by example, and possibly certain exercises, to create the mental configuration in the patient that allows him to heal himself. Am I correct?

RA: I am Ra. Although your learn/understanding distortion is essentially correct, your choice of vibratory/sound complex is not entirely as accurate as this language allows.

It is not by example that the healer does the working. The working exists in and of itself. The healer is only the catalyst, much as this instrument has the catalysis necessary to provide the channel for our words, yet by example or exercise of any kind can take no thought for this working.

The healing/working is congruent in that it is a form of channeling some distortion of the intelligent infinity.

QUESTIONER: We have decided to accept, if offered, the honor/duty of learning/teaching the healing process. I would ask as to the first step which we should accomplish in becoming effective healers.

RA: I am Ra. We shall begin with the first of the three teachings/learnings.

We begin with the mental learn/teaching necessary for contact with intelligent infinity. The prerequisite of mental work is the ability to retain silence of self at a steady state when required by the self. The mind must be opened like a door. The key is silence.

Within the door lies an hierarchical construction you may liken unto geography and in some ways geometry, for the hierarchy is quite regular, bearing inner relationships.

To begin to master the concept of mental disciplines it is necessary to examine the self. The polarity of your dimension must be internalized. Where you find patience within your mind you must consciously find the corresponding impatience and vice versa. Each thought a being has, has in its turn an antithesis. The disciplines of the mind involve, first of all, identifying both those things of which you approve and those things of which you disapprove within yourself, and then balancing each and every positive and negative charge with its equal. The mind contains all things. Therefore, you must discover this completeness within yourself.

The second mental discipline is acceptance of the completeness within your consciousness. It is not for a being of polarity in the physical consciousness to pick and choose among attributes, thus building the roles that cause blockages and confusions in the already distorted mind complex. Each acceptance smooths part of the many distortions that the faculty you call judgment engenders.

The third discipline of the mind is a repetition of the first but with the gaze outward toward the fellow entities that it meets. In each entity there exists completeness. Thus, the ability to understand each balance is necessary. When you view patience, you are responsible for mirroring in your mental understandings, patience/impatience. When you view impatience, it is necessary for your mental configuration of understanding to be impatience/patience. We use this as a simple example. Most configurations of mind have many facets, and understanding of either self polarities, or what you would call other-self polarities, can and must be understood as subtle work.

The next step is the acceptance of the other-self polarities, which mirrors the second step. These are the first four steps of learning mental disciplines. The fifth step involves observing the geographical and geometrical relationships and ratios of the mind, the other mind, the mass mind, and the infinite mind.

The second area of learn/teaching is the study/understanding of the body complexes. It is necessary to know your body well. This is a matter of using the mind to examine how the feelings, the biases, what you would call the emotions, affect various portions of the body complex. It shall be necessary to both understand the bodily polarity and to accept them, repeating in a chemical/physical manifestation the work you have done upon the mind bethinking the consciousness.

The body is a creature of the mind's creation. It has its biases. The biological bias must be first completely understood and then the opposite bias allowed to find full expression in understanding. Again, the process of acceptance of the body as a balanced, as well as polarized, individual may then be accomplished. It is then the task to extend this understanding to the bodies of the other-selves whom you will meet.

The simplest example of this is the understanding that each biological male is female; each biological female is male. This is a simple example. However, in almost every case wherein you are attempting the understanding of the body of self or other-self, you will again find that the most subtle discernment is necessary in order to fully grasp the polarity complexes involved.

At this time we would suggest closing the description until the next time of work so that we may devote time to the third area commensurate with its importance.

We can answer a query if it is a short one before we leave this instrument.

QUESTIONER: Is the instrument comfortable? Is there anything that we can do to increase the comfort of the instrument?

RA: I am Ra. The candle could be rotated clockwise approximately 10 degrees each session to improve the flow of spiraled energy through the being's receiving mechanisms. This particular configuration is well otherwise. But we ask that the objects described and used be centered with geometric care and checked from time to time. Also that they not be exposed to that space/time in which work is not of importance.

I am Ra. I leave this instrument in the love and in the light of the One Infinite Creator. Go forth rejoicing in the power and the peace of the One Creator. Adonai.

Session 6,
January 24, 1981

RA: I am Ra. I greet you in the love and the light of the Infinite Creator. I communicate now.

QUESTIONER: We would like to continue the material from yesterday.

RA: I am Ra. This is well with us.

We proceed now with the third part of the teach/learning concerning the development of the energy powers of healing.

The third area is the spiritual complex which embodies the fields of force and consciousness which are the least distorted of your mind/body/spirit complex. The exploration and balancing of the spirit complex is indeed the longest and most subtle part of your learn/teaching. We have considered the mind as a tree. The mind controls the body. With the mind single-pointed, balanced, and aware, the body comfortable in whatever biases and distortions make it appropriately balanced for that instrument, the instrument is then ready to proceed with the greater work.

That is the work of wind and fire. The spiritual body energy field is a pathway, or channel. When body and mind are receptive and open, then the spirit can become a functioning shuttle or communicator from the entity's individual energy/will upwards, and from the streamings of the creative fire and wind downwards.

The healing ability, like all other, what this instrument would call, paranormal abilities, is affected by the opening of a pathway or shuttle into intelligent infinity. There are many upon your plane who have a random hole or gateway in their spirit energy field, sometimes created by the ingestion of chemicals such as what this instrument would call LSD, who are able, randomly and without control, to tap into energy sources. They may or may not be entities who wish to serve. The purpose of carefully and consciously opening this channel is to serve in a more dependable way, in a more commonplace or usual way, as seen by the distortion complex of the healer. To others there may appear to be miracles. To the one who has carefully opened the door to intelligent infinity, this is ordinary; this is commonplace; this is as it should be. The life experience becomes somewhat transformed. The great work goes on.

At this time we feel these exercises suffice for your beginning. We will, at a future time, when you feel you have accomplished that which is set before you, begin to guide you into a more precise understanding of the functions and uses of this gateway in the experience of healing.

QUESTIONER: I think this might be an appropriate time to include a little more background on yourself, possibly information having to do with where you came from prior to your involvement with planet Earth, if this is possible.

RA: I am Ra. I am, with the social memory complex of which I am a part, one of those who voyaged outward from another planet within your own solar system, as this entity would call it. The planetary influence was that you call Venus. We are a race old in your measures. When we were at the sixth dimension our physical beings were what you would call golden. We were tall and somewhat delicate. Our physical body complex covering, which you call the integument, had a golden luster.

In this form we decided to come among your peoples. Your peoples at that time were much unlike us in physical appearance, as you might call it. We, thus, did not mix well with the population and were obviously other than they. Thus, our visit was relatively short, for we found ourselves in the hypocritical position of being acclaimed as other than your other-selves. This was the time during which we built the structures in which you show interest.

QUESTIONER: How did you journey from Venus to this planet?

RA: I am Ra. We used thought.

QUESTIONER: Would it have been possible to have taken one of the people of this planet at that time and placed him on Venus? Would he have survived? Were conditions on Venus hospitable?

RA: I am Ra. The third-density conditions are not hospitable to the life forms of your peoples. The fifth and sixth dimensions of that planetary sphere are quite conducive to growing/learning/teaching.

QUESTIONER: How were you able to make the transition from Venus? Did you have to change your dimension to walk upon the Earth?

RA: I am Ra. You will remember the exercise of the wind. The dissolution into nothingness is the dissolution into unity, for there is no nothingness. From the sixth dimension, we are capable of manipulating, by thought, the intelligent infinity present in each particle of light or distorted light so that we were able to clothe ourselves in a replica visible in the third density of our mind/body/spirit complexes in the sixth density. We were allowed this experiment by the Council which guards this planet.

QUESTIONER: Where is this Council located?

RA: I am Ra. This Council is located in the octave, or eighth dimension, of the planet Saturn, taking its place in an area which you understand in third-dimension terms as the rings.

QUESTIONER: Are there any people such as you find on Earth on any of the other planets in our solar system?

RA: I am Ra. Do you request space/time present information or space/time continuum information?

QUESTIONER: Both.

RA: I am Ra. At one time/space, in what is your past, there was a population of third-density beings upon a planet which dwelt within your solar system. There are various names by which this planet has been named. The vibratory sound complex most usually used by your peoples is Maldek. These entities, destroying their planetary sphere, thus were forced to find room for themselves upon this third density, which is the only one in your solar system at their time/space present which was hospitable and capable of offering the lessons necessary to decrease their mind/body/spirit distortions with respect to the Law of One.

QUESTIONER: How did they come here?

RA: I am Ra. They came through the process of harvest and were incarnated through the processes of incarnation from your higher spheres within this density.

QUESTIONER: How long ago did this happen?

RA: I am Ra. I am having difficulty communicating with this instrument. We must deepen her state.
This occurred approximately 500,000 of your years ago.

QUESTIONER: Is all of the Earth's human population then originally from Maldek?

RA: I am Ra. This is a new line of questioning and deserves a place of its own. The ones who were harvested to your sphere from the sphere known before its dissolution as other names, but to your peoples as

Maldek, incarnated, many within your Earth's surface rather than upon it. The population of your planet contains many various groups harvested from other second-dimension and cycled third-dimension spheres. You are not all one race or background of beginning. The experience you share is unique to this time/space continuum.

QUESTIONER: I think that it would be appropriate to discover how the Law of One acts in this transfer of beings to our planet and the action of harvest?

RA: I am Ra. The Law of One states simply that all things are one, that all beings are one. There are certain behaviors and thought-forms consonant with the understanding and practice of this law. Those who, finishing a cycle of experience, demonstrate grades of distortion of that understanding of thought and action will be separated by their own choice into the vibratory distortion most comfortable to their mind/body/spirit complexes. This process is guarded or watched by those nurturing beings who, being very close to the Law of One in their distortions, nevertheless move towards active service.

Thus, the illusion is created of light, or more properly but less understandably, light/love. This is in varying degrees of intensity. The spirit complex of each harvested entity moves along the line of light until the light grows too glaring, at which time the entity stops. This entity may have barely reached third density or may be very, very close to the ending of the third-density light/love distortion vibratory complex. Nevertheless, those who fall within this octave of intensifying light/love then experience a major cycle during which there are opportunities for the discovery of the distortions which are inherent in each entity and, therefore, the lessening of these distortions.

QUESTIONER: What is the length, in our years, of one of these cycles?

RA: I am Ra. One major cycle is approximately 25,000 of your years. There are three cycles of this nature during which those who have progressed may be harvested at the end of three major cycles. That is, approximately between 75 and 76,000 of your years. All are harvested regardless of their progress, for during that time the planet itself has moved through the useful part of that dimension and begins to cease being useful for the lower levels of vibration within that density.

QUESTIONER: What is the position of this planet with respect to the progression of cycles at this time?

RA: I am Ra. This sphere is at this time in fourth-dimension vibration. Its material is quite confused due to the society memory complexes embedded in its consciousness. It has not made an easy transition to the vibrations which beckon. Therefore, it will be fetched with some inconvenience.

QUESTIONER: Is this inconvenience imminent within a few years?

RA: I am Ra. This inconvenience, or disharmonious vibratory complex, has begun several of your years in your past. It shall continue unabated for a period of approximately thirty of your years.

QUESTIONER: After this period of thirty years I am assuming that this will be a fourth-density planet. Is this correct?

RA: I am Ra. This is so.

QUESTIONER: Is it possible to estimate what percent of the present population will inhabit the fourth-density planet?

RA: I am Ra. The harvesting is not yet; thus, estimation is meaningless.

QUESTIONER: Does the fact that we are in this transition period now have anything to do with the reason that you have made your information available to the population?

RA: I am Ra. We have walked among your people. We remember. We remember sorrow: have seen much. We have searched for an instrument of the proper parameters of distortion in mind/body/spirit complex and supporting and understanding of mind/body/spirit complexes to accept this information with minimal distortion and maximal desire to serve for some of your years. The answer, in short, is yes. However, we wished you to know that in our memory we thank you.

QUESTIONER: The disc-shaped craft that we call UFOs—some have been said to have come from the planet Venus. Would any of these be your craft?

RA: I am Ra. We have used crystals for many purposes. The craft of which you speak have not been used by us in your space/time present memory complex. However, we have used crystals and the bell shape in the past of your illusion.

QUESTIONER: How many years in the past did you use the bell-shaped craft to come to Earth?

RA: I am Ra. We visited your peoples 18,000 of your years ago and did not land; again, 11,000 years ago.

QUESTIONER: Photographs of bell-shaped craft and reports of contact of such from Venus exist from less than thirty years ago. Do you have any knowledge of these reports?

RA: I am Ra. We have knowledge of Oneness with these forays of your time/space present. We are no longer of Venus. However, there are thought-forms created among your peoples from our time of walking among you. The memory and thought-forms created, therefore, are a part of your society-memory complex. This mass consciousness, as you may call it, creates the experience once more for those who request such experience. The present Venus population is no longer sixth density.

QUESTIONER: Do any of the UFOs presently reported at this time come from other planets, or do you have this knowledge?

RA: I am Ra. I am one of the members of the Confederation of Planets in the Service of the Infinite Creator. There are approximately fifty-three civilizations, comprising approximately five hundred planetary consciousness complexes in this Confederation. This Confederation contains those from your own planet who have attained dimensions beyond your third. It contains planetary entities within your solar system, and it contains planetary entities from other galaxies.* It is a true Confederation in that its members are not alike, but allied in service according to the Law of One.

* Ra often uses the word "galaxy" where we would say planetary system. This meaning is listed in the unabridged dictionary but is not in common use.

QUESTIONER: Do any of them come here at this time in spacecraft? In the past, say, thirty years?

RA: I am Ra. We must state that this information is unimportant. If you will understand this, we feel that the information may be acceptably offered. The Law of One is what we are here to express. However, we will speak upon this subject.

Each planetary entity which wishes to appear within your third dimension of space/time distortion requests permission to break quarantine, as you may call it, and appear to your peoples. The reason and purpose for this appearance is understood and either accepted or rejected. There have been as many as fifteen of the Confederation entities in your skies at any one time. The others are available to you through thought.

At present there are seven which are operating with craft in your density. Their purposes are very simple: to allow those entities of your planet to become aware of infinity, which is often best expressed to the uninformed as the mysterious or unknown.

QUESTIONER: I am fully aware that you are primarily interested in disseminating information concerning the Law of One. However, it is my judgment, and I could be wrong, that in order to disseminate this material it will be necessary to include questions such as the one I have just asked. If this is not the objective, then I could limit my questions to the application of the Law of One. But I understand that at this time it is the objective to widely disseminate this material. Is this correct?

RA: I am Ra. This perception is only slightly distorted in your understand/learning. We wish you to proceed as you deem proper. That is your place. We, in giving this information, find our distortion of understanding of our purpose to be that not only of the offering of information, but the weighting of it according to our distorted perceptions of its relative importance. Thus, you will find our statements, at times, to be those which imply that a question is unimportant. This is due to our perception that the given question is unimportant. Nevertheless, unless the question contains the potential for answer giving which may infringe upon free will, we offer our answers.

QUESTIONER: Thank you very much. We do not want to overtire the instrument. We have gone considerably over our normal working time. Could you tell me what condition the instrument is in?

RA: I am Ra. The instrument is balanced due to your care. However, her physical vehicle is growing stiff.

QUESTIONER: In that case perhaps we should continue at a later time.

RA: I am Ra. I leave you in the love and the light of the One Infinite Creator. Go forth rejoicing in the power and the peace of the One Creator. Adonai.

Session 7,
January 25, 1981

RA: I am Ra. I greet you in the love and the light of our Infinite Creator. I communicate now.

QUESTIONER: You mentioned that there were a number of members of the Confederation of Planets. What avenues of service, or types of service, are available to the members of the Confederation?

RA: I am Ra. I am assuming that you intend the service which we of the Confederation can offer, rather than the service which is available to our use.

The service available for our offering to those who call us is equivalent to the square of the distortion/need of that calling divided by, or integrated with, the basic Law of One in its distortion indicating the free will of those who are not aware of the unity of creation.

QUESTIONER: From this, I am assuming that the difficulty that you have in contacting this planet at this time is the mixture of people here, some being aware of the unity, and some not, and for this reason you cannot come openly or give proof of your contact. Is this correct?

RA: I am Ra. As we just repeated through this instrument, we must integrate all of the portions of your social memory complex in its illusory disintegration form. Then the product of this can be seen as the limit of our ability to serve. We are fortunate that the Law of Service squares the desires of those who call. Otherwise, we would have no beingness in this time/space at this present continuum of the illusion. In short, you are basically correct. The thought of not being able is not a part of our basic thought-form complex towards your peoples, but rather it is a maximal consideration of what is possible.

QUESTIONER: By squared, do you mean that if ten people call, you can count that, when comparing it to the planetary ratio, as 100 people, squaring ten and getting 100?

RA: I am Ra. This is incorrect. The square is sequential—one, two, three, four, each squared by the next number.

QUESTIONER: If only ten entities on Earth required your services, how would you compute their calling by using this square method?

RA: I am Ra. We would square one ten sequential times, raising the number to the tenth square.

QUESTIONER: What would be the result of this calculation?

RA: I am Ra. The result is difficult to transmit. It is 1,012, approximately. The entities who call are sometimes not totally unified in their calling and, thus, the squaring slightly less. Thus, there is a statistical loss over a period of call. However, perhaps you may see by this statistically corrected information the squaring mechanism.

QUESTIONER: About how many entities at present on planet Earth are calling for your services?

RA: I am Ra. I am called personally by 352,000. The Confederation, in its entire spectrum of entity complexes, is called by 632,000,000 of your mind/body/spirit complexes. These numbers have been simplified.

QUESTIONER: Can you tell me what the result of the application of the Law of Squares is to those figures?

RA: I am Ra. The number is approximately meaningless in the finite sense as there are many, many digits. It, however, constitutes a great calling which we of all creation feel and hear as if our own entities were distorted towards a great and overwhelming sorrow. It demands our service.

QUESTIONER: At what point would this calling be great enough for you to come openly among the people on Earth? How many entities on Earth would have to call the Confederation?

RA: I am Ra. We do not calculate the possibility of coming among your peoples by the numbers of calling, but by a consensus among an entire societal-memory complex which has become aware of the infinite consciousness of all things. This has been possible among your peoples only in isolated instances.

In the case wherein a social memory complex which is a servant of the Creator sees this situation and has an idea for the appropriate aid which can only be done among your peoples, the social memory complex desiring this project lays it before the Council of Saturn. If it is approved, quarantine is lifted.

QUESTIONER: I have a question about that Council. Who are the members, and how does the Council function?

RA: I am Ra. The members of the Council are representatives from the Confederation and from those vibratory levels of your inner planes bearing responsibility for your third density. The names are not important because there are no names. Your mind/body/spirit complexes request names, and so, in many cases, the vibratory sound complexes which are consonant with the vibratory distortions of each entity are used. However, the name concept is not part of the Council. If names are requested, we will attempt them. However, not all have chosen names.

In number, the Council that sits in constant session, though varying in its members by means of balancing, which takes place what you would call irregularly, is nine. That is the Session Council. To back up this Council, there are twenty-four entities which offer their services as requested. These entities faithfully watch and have been called Guardians.

The Council operates by means of what you would call telepathic contact with the oneness or unity of the nine, the distortions blending harmoniously so that the Law of One prevails with ease. When a need for thought is present, the Council retains the distortion complex of this need, balancing it as described, and then recommends what it considers as appropriate action. This includes: One, the duty of admitting social memory complexes to the Confederation; Two, offering aid to those who are unsure how to aid the social memory complex requesting aid in a way consonant with both the call, the Law, and the number of those calling (that is to say, sometimes the resistance of the call); Three, internal questions in the Council are determined.

These are the prominent duties of the Council. They are, if in any doubt, able to contact the twenty-four, who then offer consensus/judgment/thinking to the Council. The Council then may reconsider any question.

QUESTIONER: You mentioned the nine who sit on the Council. Is this "nine" the same nine as those mentioned in this book? [Questioner gestures to *Uri*]

RA: I am Ra. The Council of Nine has been retained in semi-undistorted form by two main sources, that known in your naming as Mark and that known in your naming as Henry. In one case, the channel became the scribe. In the other, the channel was not the scribe. However, without the aid of the scribe, the energy would not have come to the channel.

QUESTIONER: The names that you spoke of. Were they Mark Probert and Henry Puharich?

RA: I am Ra. This is correct.

QUESTIONER: I am interested in the application of the Law of One as it pertains to free will with respect to what I would call the advertising done by UFO contacts with the planet Earth. The Council seems to have allowed the quarantine to be lifted many times over the past thirty years. This seems to me to be a form of advertising for what we are doing right now, so that more people will be awakened. Am I correct?

RA: I am Ra. It will take a certain amount of untangling of conceptualization of your mental complex to reform your query into an appropriate response. Please bear with us.

The Council of Saturn has not allowed the breaking of quarantine in the time/space continuum you mentioned. There is a certain amount of landing taking place. Some are of the entities known to you as the group of Orion.

Secondly, there is permission granted, not to break quarantine by dwelling among you, but to appear in thought-form capacity for those who have eyes to see.

Thirdly, you are correct in assuming that permission was granted at the time/space in which your first nuclear device was developed and used for Confederation members to minister to your peoples in such a way as to cause mystery to occur. This is what you mean by advertising and is correct. The mystery and unknown quality of the occurrences we are allowed to offer have the hoped-for intention of making your peoples aware of infinite possibility. When your peoples grasp infinity, then and only then can the gateway be opened to the Law of One.

QUESTIONER: You said that Orion was the source of some of these contacts with UFOs. Can you tell me something of that contact, its purpose?

RA: I am Ra. Consider, if you will, a simple example of intentions which are bad/good. This example is Adolf. This is your vibratory sound complex. The intention is to presumably unify by choosing the distortion complex called elite from a social memory complex and then enslaving, by various effects, those who are seen by the distortion as not elite. There is then the concept of taking the social memory complex thus weeded and adding it to a distortion thought of by the so-called Orion group as an empire. The problem facing them is that they face a great deal of random energy released by the concept of separation. This causes them to be vulnerable, as the distortions amongst their own members are not harmonized.

QUESTIONER: What is the density of the Orion group?

RA: I am Ra. Like the Confederation, the densities of the mass consciousnesses which comprise that group are varied. There are a very few third density, a larger number of fourth density, a similarly large number of fifth density, and very few sixth-density entities comprising this organization. Their numbers are perhaps one-tenth ours at any point in the space/time continuum, as the problem of spiritual entropy causes them to experience constant disintegration of their social memory complexes. Their power is the same as ours. The Law of One blinks neither at the light nor the darkness, but is available for service to others and service to self. However, service to others results in service to self, thus preserving and further harmonizing the distortions of those entities seeking intelligent infinity through these disciplines.

Those seeking intelligent infinity through the use of service to self create the same amount of power but, as we said, have constant difficulty because of the concept of separation, which is implicit in the manifestations of the service to self which involve power over others. This weakens and eventually disintegrates the energy collected by such mind/body/spirit complexes who call the Orion group and the social memory complexes which comprise the Orion group.

It should be noted, carefully pondered, and accepted that the Law of One is available to any social memory complex which has decided to strive together for any seeking of purpose, be it service to others or service to self. The laws, which are the primal distortions of the Law of One, then are placed into operation, and the illusion of space/time is used as a medium for the development of the results of those choices freely made. Thus all entities learn, no matter what they seek. All learn the same; some rapidly, some slowly.

QUESTIONER: Using as an example the fifth density concerning the social memory complex of the Orion group, what was their previous density before they became fifth density?

RA: I am Ra. The progress through densities is sequential. A fifth-density social memory complex would be comprised of mind/body/spirit complexes harvested from fourth density. Then the conglomerate or mass mind/body/spirit complex does its melding, and the results are due to the infinitely various possibilities of combinations of distortions.

QUESTIONER: I'm trying to understand how a group such as the Orion group would progress. How it would be possible, if you were in the Orion group and pointed toward self-service, to progress from our third density to the fourth. What learning would be necessary for that?

RA: I am Ra. This is the last question of length for this instrument at this time.

You will recall that we went into some detail as to how those not oriented towards seeking service for others yet, nevertheless, found and could use the gateway to intelligent infinity. This is true at all densities in our octave. We cannot speak for those above us, as you would say, in the next quantum or octave of beingness. This is, however, true of this octave of density. The beings are harvested because they can see and enjoy the light/love of the appropriate density. Those who have found this light/love, love/light without benefit of a desire for service to others nevertheless, by the Law of Free Will, have the right to the use of that light/love for whatever purpose. Also, it may be inserted that there are systems of study which enable the seeker of separation to gain these gateways.

This study is as difficult as the one which we have described to you, but there are those with the perseverance to pursue the study just as you desire to pursue the difficult path of seeking to know in order to serve. The distortion lies in the effect that those who seek to serve the self are seen by the Law of One as precisely the same as those who seek to serve others, for are all not one? To serve yourself and to serve others is a dual method of saying the same thing, if you can understand the essence of the Law of One.

At this time we would answer any brief questions you may have.

QUESTIONER: Is there anything that we can do to make the instrument more comfortable?

RA: I am Ra. There are small adjustments you may make. However, we are now able to use this instrument with minimal distortion and without depleting the instrument to any significant extent.

Do you wish to ask further?

QUESTIONER: We do not wish to tire the instrument. Thank you very much. That was very helpful, and we would like to continue in the next session from this point.

RA: I am Ra. I leave you in the love and the light of the One Infinite Creator. Go forth then rejoicing in the power and the peace of the One Creator. Adonai.

Session 8,
January 26, 1981

RA: I am Ra. I greet you in the love and the light of the Infinite Creator. I communicate now.

QUESTIONER: I have a question regarding what I call the advertising of the Confederation. It has to do with free will. There have been certain contacts allowed, as I understand, by the Confederation, but this is limited because of free will of those who are not oriented in such a way as to want contact. Many people on our planet want this material, but even though we disseminate it, many will not be aware that it is available. Is there any possibility of creating some effect which I would call advertising, or is this against the principle of free will?

RA: I am Ra. Consider, if you will, the path your life-experience complex has taken. Consider the coincidences and odd circumstances by which one thing flowed to the next. Consider this well.

Each entity will receive the opportunity that each needs. This information source beingness does not have uses in the life-experience complex of each of those among your peoples who seek. Thus the advertisement is general and not designed to indicate the searching out of any particular material, but only to suggest the noumenal aspect of the illusion.

QUESTIONER: You said that some of the landings at this time were of the Orion group. Why did the Orion group land here? What is their purpose?

RA: I am Ra. Their purpose is conquest, unlike those of the Confederation who wait for the calling. The so-called Orion group calls itself to conquest. As we have said previously, their objective is to locate certain mind/body/spirit complexes which vibrate in resonance with their own vibrational complex, then to enslave the unelite, as you may call those who are not of the Orion vibration.

QUESTIONER: Was the landing at Pascagoula in 1973 when Charlie Hixson was taken aboard this type of landing?

RA: I am Ra. The landing of which you speak was what you would call an anomaly. It was neither the Orion influence nor our peoples in thought-form, but rather a planetary entity of your own vibration which came through quarantine in all innocence in a random landing.

QUESTIONER: What did they do to Charlie Hixson when they took him onboard?

RA: I am Ra. They used his mind/body/spirit complex's life experience, concentrating upon the experience of the complexes of what you call war.

QUESTIONER: How did they use them?

RA: I am Ra. The use of experience is to learn. Consider a race who watches a movie. It experiences a story and identifies with the feelings, perceptions, and experiences of the hero.

QUESTIONER: Was Charlie Hixson originally of the same social memory complex of the ones who picked him up?

RA: I am Ra. This entity of vibratory sound complex did not have a connection with those who used him.

QUESTIONER: Did those who used him use his war experiences to learn more of the Law of One?

RA: I am Ra. This is correct.

QUESTIONER: Did the entities who picked him up have the normal configuration? His description of them was rather unusual.

RA: I am Ra. The configuration of their beings is their normal configuration. The unusualness is not remarkable. We ourselves, when we chose a mission among your peoples, needed to study your peoples, for had we arrived in no other form than our own, we would have been perceived as light.

QUESTIONER: What density were the entities who picked up Charlie Hixson from?

RA: I am Ra. The entities in whom you show such interest are third-density beings of a fairly advanced order. We should express the understanding to you that these entities would not have used the mind/body/spirit complex, Charlie, except for the resolve of this entity before incarnation to be of service.

QUESTIONER: What was the home or origin of the entities who picked up Charlie?

RA: I am Ra. These entities are of the Sirius galaxy.

QUESTIONER: Would it be possible for any of us to have contact with the Confederation in a more direct way?

RA: I am Ra. In observing the distortions of those who underwent this experiential sequence, we decided to gradually back off, shall I say, from direct contact in thought-form. The least distortion seems to be available in mind-to-mind communication. Therefore, the request to be taken aboard is not one we care to comply with. You are most valuable in your present orientation.

May we ask at this time if you have a needed short query before we end this session?

QUESTIONER: Is there anything that we can do to make the instrument more comfortable?

RA: I am Ra. The instrument is well balanced. It is possible to make small corrections in the configuration of the spine of the instrument that it be straighter. Continue also to continually monitor the placement and orientation of the symbols used. This particular session, the censer is slightly off and, therefore, this instrument will experience a slight discomfort.

QUESTIONER: Is the censer off in respect to angle or in respect to lateral displacement?

RA: I am Ra. There is an approximate 3 degrees' displacement from proper perpendicularity.

I am Ra. I leave you in the love and the light of the One Infinite Creator. Go forth, therefore, rejoicing in the power and the peace of the One Creator. Adonai.

Session 9,
January 27, 1981

RA: I am Ra. I greet you in the love and the light of our Infinite Creator. We communicate now.

QUESTIONER: The healing exercises that you gave us are of such a nature that it is best to concentrate on a particular exercise at a certain time. I would like to ask what exercise that I should concentrate on tonight?

RA: I am Ra. Again, to direct your judgment is an intrusion upon your space/time continuum distortion called future. To speak of past or present within our distortion/judgment limits is acceptable. To guide rather than teach/learn is not acceptable to our distortion in regards to teach/learning. We, instead, can suggest a process whereby each chooses the first of the exercises given in the order in which we gave them, which you, in your discernment, feel is not fully appreciated by your mind/body/spirit complex.

This is the proper choice, building from the foundation, making sure the ground is good for the building. We have assessed for you the intensity of this effort in terms of energy expended. You will take this in mind and be patient for we have not given a short or easy program of consciousness learn/teaching.

QUESTIONER: The way that I understand the process of evolution is that our planetary population has a certain amount of time to progress. This is generally divided into three 25,000-year cycles. At the end of 75,000 years the planet progresses itself. What caused this situation to come about with the preciseness of the years in each cycle?

RA: I am Ra. Visualize, if you will, the particular energy which, outward flowing and inward coagulating, formed the tiny realm of the creation governed by your Council of Saturn. Continue seeing the rhythm of this process. The living flow creates a rhythm which is as inevitable as one of your timepieces. Each of your planetary entities began the first cycle when the energy nexus was able in that environment to support such mind/body experiences. Thus, each of your planetary entities is on a different cyclical schedule, as you might call it. The timing of these cycles is a measurement equal to a portion of intelligent energy.

This intelligent energy offers a type of clock. The cycles move as precisely as a clock strikes your hour. Thus, the gateway from intelligent energy to intelligent infinity opens regardless of circumstance on the striking of the hour.

QUESTIONER: The original, first entities on this planet—what was their origin? Where were they before they were on this planet?

RA: I am Ra. The first entities upon this planet were water, fire, air, and earth.

QUESTIONER: Where did the people who are like us who were the first ones here, where did they come from? From where did they evolve?

RA: I am Ra. You speak of third-density experience. The first of those to come here were brought from another planet in your solar system called by you the Red Planet, Mars. This planet's environment became inhospitable to third-density beings. The first entities, therefore, were of this race, as you may call it, manipulated somewhat by those who were guardians at that time.

QUESTIONER: What race is that, and how did they get from Mars to here?

RA: I am Ra. The race is a combination of the mind/body/spirit complexes of those of your so-called Red Planet and a careful series of genetical adjustments made by the guardians of that time. These entities arrived, or were preserved, for the experience upon your sphere by a type of birthing which is nonreproductive but consists of preparing genetic material for the incarnation of the mind/body/spirit complexes of those entities from the Red Planet.

QUESTIONER: I assume from what you are saying that the guardians transferred the race here after the race had died from the physical as we know it on Mars. Is that correct?

RA: I am Ra. This is correct.

QUESTIONER: The guardians were obviously acting within an understanding of the Law of One in doing this. Can you explain the application of the Law of One in this process?

RA: I am Ra. The Law of One was named by these guardians as the bringing of the wisdom of the guardians in contact with the entities from the Red Planet, thus melding the social memory complex of the guardian race and the Red Planet race. It, however, took an increasing amount of distortion into the application of the Law of One from the viewpoint of other guardians, and it is from this beginning action that the quarantine of this planet was instituted, for it was felt that the free will of those of the Red Planet had been abridged.

QUESTIONER: Were the entities of the Red Planet following the Law of One prior to leaving the Red Planet?

RA: I am Ra. The entities of the Red Planet were attempting to learn the Laws of Love which form one of the primal distortions of the Law of One. However, the tendencies of these people towards bellicose actions caused such difficulties in the atmospheric environment of their planet that it became inhospitable for third-density experience before the end of its cycle. Thus, the Red Planet entities were unharvested and continued in your illusion to attempt to learn the Law of Love.

QUESTIONER: How long ago did this transfer occur from the Red Planet to Earth?

RA: I am Ra. In your time this transfer occurred approximately 75,000 years ago.

QUESTIONER: 75,000 years ago?

RA: I am Ra. This is approximately correct.

QUESTIONER: Were there any entities of the form that I am now—two arms, two legs—on this planet before this transfer occurred?

RA: I am Ra. There have been visitors to your sphere at various times for the last four million of your years, speaking approximately. These visitors do not affect the cycling of the planetary sphere. It was not third density in its environment until the time previously mentioned.

QUESTIONER: Then there were second-density entities here prior to approximately 75,000 years ago. What type of entities were these?

RA: I am Ra. The second density is the density of the higher plant life and animal life which exists without the upward drive towards the infinite. These second-density beings are of an octave of consciousness just as you find various orientations of consciousness among the conscious entities of your vibration.

QUESTIONER: Did any of these second-density entities have shapes like ours—two arms, two legs, head, and walk upright on two feet?

RA: I am Ra. The two higher of the sub-vibrational levels of second-density beings had the configuration of the biped, as you mentioned. However, the erectile movement which you experience was not totally effected in these beings who were tending towards the leaning forward, barely leaving the quadrupedal position.

QUESTIONER: Where did these beings come from? Were they a product of evolution as understood by our scientists? Were they evolved from the original material of the earth that you spoke of?

RA: I am Ra. This is correct.

QUESTIONER: Do these beings then evolve from second density to third density?

RA: I am Ra. This is correct, although no guarantee can be made of the number of cycles it will take an entity to learn the lessons of consciousness of self which are the prerequisite for transition to third density.

QUESTIONER: Is there any particular race of people on our planet now who were incarnated here from second density?

RA: I am Ra. There are no second-density consciousness complexes here on your sphere at this time. However, there are two races which use the second-density form. One is the entities from the planetary sphere you call Maldek. These entities are working their understanding complexes through a series of what you would call karmic restitutions. They dwell within your deeper underground passageways and are known to you as "Bigfoot." The other race is that being offered a dwelling in this density by guardians who wish to give the mind/body/spirit complexes of those who are of this density at this time appropriately engineered physical vehicles, as you would call these chemical complexes, in the event that there is what you call nuclear war.

QUESTIONER: I didn't understand what these vehicles or beings were for that were appropriate in the event of nuclear war.

RA: I am Ra. These are beings which exist as instinctual second-density beings which are being held in reserve to form what you would call a gene pool in case these body complexes are needed. These body complexes are greatly able to withstand the rigors of radiation, which the body complexes you now inhabit could not do.

QUESTIONER: Where are these body complexes located?

RA: I am Ra. These body complexes of the second race dwell in uninhabited deep forest. There are many in various places over the surface of your planet.

QUESTIONER: Are they Bigfoot-type creatures?

RA: I am Ra. This is correct although we would not call these Bigfoot, as they are scarce and are very able to escape detection. The first race is less able to be aware of proximity of other mind/body/spirit complexes, but these beings are very able to escape due to their technological understandings before their incarnations here. These entities of the glowing eyes are those most familiar to your peoples.

QUESTIONER: Then there are two different types of Bigfoot. Correct?

RA: I am Ra. This will be the final question.

There are three types of Bigfoot, if you will accept that vibratory sound complex used for three such different races of mind/body/spirit complexes. The first two we have described. The third is a thought-form.

QUESTIONER: I would like to ask if there is anything that we can do to aid the instrument's comfort.

RA: I am Ra. This instrument will require some adjustment of the tender portions of her body complex. The distortions are due to the energy center blockage you would call pineal.

I leave you in the love and the light of the One Infinite Creator. Go forth, therefore, rejoicing in the power and the peace of the One Creator. Adonai.

Session 10,
January 27, 1981

RA: I am Ra. I greet you in the love and light of the Infinite Creator. I communicate now.

QUESTIONER: I think that it would clarify things for us if we went back to the time just before the transfer of souls from Maldek to see how the Law of One operated with respect to this transfer and why this transfer was necessary. What happened to the people of Maldek that caused them to lose their planet? How long ago did this event occur?

RA: I am Ra. The peoples of Maldek had a civilization somewhat similar to that of the societal complex known to you as Atlantis, in that it gained much technological information and used it without care for the preservation of their sphere following to a majority extent the complex of thought, ideas, and actions which you may associate with your so-called negative polarity or the service to self. This was, however, for the most part, couched in a sincere belief/thought structure which seemed to the perception of the mind/body complexes of this sphere to be positive and of service to others. The devastation that wracked their biosphere and caused its disintegration resulted from what you call war.

The escalation went to the furthest extent of the technology this social complex had at its disposal in the space/time present of the then time. This time was approximately 705,000 of your years ago. The cycles had begun much, much earlier upon this sphere due to its relative ability to support the first-dimensional life forms at an earlier point in the space/time continuum of your solar system. These entities were so traumatized by this occurrence that they were in what you may call a social complex knot or tangle of fear. Some of your time passed. No one could reach them. No beings could aid them.

Approximately 600,000 of your years ago the then-existing members of the Confederation were able to deploy a social memory complex and untie the knot of fear. The entities were then able to recall that they were conscious. This awareness brought them to the point upon what you would call the lower astral planes, where they could be nurtured until each mind/body/spirit complex was able to finally be healed of this trauma to the extent that each entity was able to examine the distortions it had experienced in the previous life/illusion complex.

After this experience of learn/teaching, the group decision was to place upon itself a type of what you may call karma alleviation. For this purpose they came into incarnation within your planetary sphere in what were not acceptable human forms. This then they have been experiencing until the distortions of destruction are replaced by distortions towards the desire for a less distorted vision of service to others. Since this was the conscious decision of the great majority of those beings in the Maldek experience, the transition to this planet began approximately 500,000 of your years ago, and the type of body complex available at that time was used.

QUESTIONER: Was the body complex available at that time what we refer to as the ape body?

RA: I am Ra. That is correct.

QUESTIONER: Have any of the Maldek entities transformed since then? Are they still second density now or are some of them third density?

RA: I am Ra. The consciousness of these entities has always been third density. The alleviation mechanism was designed by the placement of this consciousness in second-dimensional physical chemical complexes which are not able to be dexterous or manipulative to the extent which is appropriate to the working of the third-density distortions of the mind complex.

QUESTIONER: Have any of the entities moved on now, made a graduation at the end of a cycle and made the transition from second-density bodies to third-density bodies?

RA: I am Ra. Many of these entities were able to remove the accumulation of what you call karma, thus being able to accept a third-density cycle within a third-density body. Most of those beings so succeeding have incarnated elsewhere in the creation for the succeeding cycle in third density. As this planet reached third density, some few of these entities became able to join the vibration of this sphere in third-density form. There remain a few who have not yet alleviated through the mind/body/spirit coordination of distortions the previous action taken by them. Therefore, they remain.

QUESTIONER: Are these the Bigfoot that you spoke of?

RA: I am Ra. These are one type of Bigfoot.

QUESTIONER: Then our human race is formed of a few who originally came from Maldek and quite a few who came from Mars. Are there entities here from other places?

RA: I am Ra. There are entities experiencing your time/space continuum who have originated from many, many places, as you would call them, in the creation, for when there is a cycle change, those who must repeat then find a planetary sphere appropriate for this repetition. It is somewhat unusual for a planetary mind/body/spirit complex to contain those from many, many various loci, but this explains much, for, you see, you are experiencing the third-dimension occurrence with a large number of those who must repeat the cycle. The orientation, thus, has been difficult to unify even with the aid of many of your teach/learners.

QUESTIONER: When Maldek was destroyed, did all the people of Maldek have the fear problem or were some advanced enough to transfer to other planets?

RA: I am Ra. In the occurrence of planetary dissolution none escaped, for this is an action which redounds to the social complex of the planetary complex itself. None escaped the knot or tangle.

QUESTIONER: Is there any danger of this happening to Earth at this time?

RA: I am Ra. We feel this evaluation of your planetary mind/body/spirit complexes' so-called future may be less than harmless. We say only the conditions of mind exist for such development of technology and such deployment. It is the distortion of our vision/understanding that the mind and spirit complexes of those of your people need orientation rather than the "toys" needing dismantlement, for are not all things that exist part of the Creator? Therefore, freely to choose is your own duty.

QUESTIONER: When graduation occurs at the end of a cycle, and entities are moved from one planet to another, by what means do they go to a new planet?

RA: I am Ra. In the scheme of the Creator, the first step of the mind/body/spirit/totality/beingness is to place its mind/body/spirit complex distortion in the proper place of love/light. This is done to ensure proper healing of the complex and eventual attunement with the totality/beingness complex. This takes a very variable length of your time/space. After this is accomplished, the experience of the cycle is dissolved and filtered until only the distillation of distortions in its pure form remains. At this time, the harvested mind/body/spirit/totality/beingness evaluates the density needs of its beingness and chooses the more appropriate new environment for either a repetition of the cycle or a moving forward into the next cycle. This is the manner of the harvesting, guarded and watched over by many.

QUESTIONER: When the entity is moved from one planet to the next, is he moved in thought or by a vehicle?

RA: I am Ra. The mind/body/spirit/totality/beingness is one with the Creator. There is no time/space distortion. Therefore, it is a matter of thinking the proper locus in the infinite array of time/spaces.

QUESTIONER: While an entity is incarnate in this third density at this time, he may either learn unconsciously without knowing what he is learning, or he may learn after he is consciously aware that he is learning in the ways of the Law of One. By the second way of learning consciously, it is possible for the entity to greatly accelerate his growth. Is this correct?

RA: I am Ra. This is correct.

QUESTIONER: Then although many entities are not consciously aware of it, what they really desire is to accelerate their growth, and it is their job to discover this while they are incarnate. Is it correct that they can accelerate their growth much more while in the third density than in between incarnations of this density?

RA: I am Ra. This is correct. We shall attempt to speak upon this concept.

The Law of One has as one of its primal distortions the free-will distortion; thus each entity is free to accept, reject, or ignore the mind/body/spirit complexes about it and ignore the creation itself. There are many among your social memory complex distortion who, at this time/space, engage daily, as you would put it, in the working upon the Law of One in one of its primal distortions; that is, the ways of love. However, if this same entity, being biased from the depths of its mind/body/spirit complex towards love/light, were then to accept the responsibility for each moment of the time/space accumulation of present moments available to it, such an entity can empower its progress in much the same way as we described the empowering of the call of your social complex distortion to the Confederation.

QUESTIONER: Could you state this in a little different way . . . how you empower this call?

RA: I am Ra. We understand you to speak now of our previous information. The call begins with one. This call is equal to infinity and is not, as you would say, counted. It is the cornerstone. The second call is added. The third call empowers or doubles the second, and so forth, each additional calling doubling or granting power to all the preceding calls. Thus, the call of many of your peoples is many, many powered and overwhelmingly heard to the infinite reaches of the One Creation.

QUESTIONER: For the general development of the reader of this book, could you state some of the practices or exercises to perform to produce an acceleration toward the Law of One?

RA: I am Ra.

Exercise One. This is the most nearly centered and usable within your illusion complex. The moment contains love. That is the lesson/goal of this illusion or density. The exercise is to consciously see that love in awareness and understanding distortions. The first attempt is the cornerstone. Upon this choosing rests the remainder of the life experience of an entity. The second seeking of love within the moment begins the addition. The third seeking empowers the second, the fourth powering or doubling the third. As with the previous type of empowerment, there will be some loss of power due to flaws within the seeking in the distortion of insincerity. However, the conscious statement of self to self of the desire to seek love is so central an act of will that, as before, the loss of power due to this friction is inconsequential.

Exercise Two. The universe is one being. When a mind/body/spirit complex views another mind/body/spirit complex, see the Creator. This is an helpful exercise.

Exercise Three. Gaze within a mirror. See the Creator.

Exercise Four. Gaze at the creation which lies about the mind/body/spirit complex of each entity. See the Creator.

The foundation or prerequisite of these exercises is a predilection towards what may be called meditation, contemplation, or prayer. With this attitude, these exercises can be processed. Without it, the data will not sink down into the roots of the tree of mind, thus enabling and ennobling the body and touching the spirit.

QUESTIONER: I was wondering about the advent of the civilizations of Atlantis and Lemuria, when these civilizations occurred, and where did they come from?

RA: I am Ra. This is the last question of this working. The civilizations of Atlantis and Lemuria were not one but two. Let us look first at the Mu entities.

They were beings of a somewhat primitive nature, but those who had very advanced spiritual distortions. The civilization was part of this cycle, experienced early within the cycle at a time of approximately 53,000 of your years ago. It was an helpful and harmless place which was washed beneath the ocean during a readjustment of your sphere's tectonic plates through no action of their own. They sent out those who survived and reached many places in what you call Russia, North America, and South America. The Indians of whom you come to feel some sympathy in your social complex distortions are the descendants of these entities. Like the other incarnates of this cycle, they came from elsewhere. However, these particular entities were largely from a second-density planet which had some difficulty, due to the age of its sun, in achieving third-density life conditions. This planet was from the galaxy Deneb.

The Atlantean race was a very conglomerate social complex which began to form approximately 31,000 years in the past of your space/time continuum illusion. It was a slow-growing and very agrarian one until approximately 15,000 of your years ago. It reached quickly a high technological understanding which caused it to be able to use intelligent infinity in an informative manner. We may add that they used intelligent energy as well, manipulating greatly the natural influxes of the indigo or pineal ray from divine or infinite energy. Thus, they were able to create life forms. This they began to do instead of healing and perfecting their own mind/body/spirit complexes, turning their distortions towards what you may call negative.

Approximately 11,000 of your years ago, the first of the, what you call, wars, caused approximately 40 percent of this population to leave the density by means of disintegration of the body. The second and most devastating of the conflicts occurred approximately 10,821 years in the past according to your illusion. This created an Earth-changing configuration, and the large part of Atlantis was no more, having been inundated. Three of the positively oriented of the Atlantean groups left this geographical locus before that devastation, placing themselves in the mountain areas of what you call Tibet, what you call Peru, and what you call Turkey.

Do you have any brief questions before we close this meeting?

QUESTIONER: Only one, other than what we can do to make the instrument more comfortable. I would like to have your definition of galaxy, the word "galaxy" as you have used it.

RA: I am Ra. We use the term known to your people by the sound vibration "galaxy." We accept that some galaxies contain one system of planetary and solar groups. Others contain several. However, the importance of the locus in infinite time/space dimensionality is so little that we accept the distortion implicit in such an ambiguous term.

QUESTIONER: Then the nine planets and sun which we have here in our system, would you refer to that as a galaxy?

RA: I am Ra. We would not.

QUESTIONER: How many stars would be—approximately—in a galaxy?

RA: I am Ra. It depends upon the galactic system. Your own, as you know, contains many, many, millions of planetary entities and star bodies.

QUESTIONER: I was just trying to get to the definition that you were using for galaxy. You mentioned a couple of times the term "galaxy" in reference to what we call a planetary system and it was causing some confusion. Is there any way that we can make the instrument more comfortable?

RA: I am Ra. This instrument could be made somewhat more comfortable if more support were given the body complex. Other than this, we can only repeat the request to carefully align the symbols used to facilitate this instrument's balance. Our contact is narrow banded, and thus the influx brought in with us must be precise.

I am Ra. I leave you in the love and the light of the One Infinite Creator. Go forth, therefore, rejoicing in the power and peace of the One Creator. Adonai.

Session 11,
January 28, 1981

RA: I am Ra. I greet you in the love and the light of the Infinite Creator. I communicate now.

QUESTIONER: Should we include the ritual that you have suggested that we use to call you in the book that will result from these sessions?

RA: I am Ra. This matter is of small importance, for our suggestion was made for the purpose of establishing contact through this instrument with this group.

QUESTIONER: Is it of any assistance to the instrument to have [name] and [name] present during these sessions? Does the number in the group make any difference in these sessions?

RA: I am Ra. The most important of the entities are the questioner and the vibratory sound complex [name]. The two entities additional aid the instrument's comfort by energizing the instrument with their abilities to share the physical energy complex which is a portion of your love vibration.

QUESTIONER: You said yesterday that Maldek was destroyed due to warfare. If Maldek hadn't destroyed itself due to warfare, would it have become a planet that evolved in self-service, and would the entities involved have increased in density and gone on to, say, the fourth density in the negative sense or the sense of self-service?

RA: I am Ra. The planetary social memory complex, Maldek, had in common with your own sphere the situation of a mixture of energy direction. Thus it, though unknown, would most probably have been a mixed harvest—a few moving to fourth density, a few moving towards fourth density in service to self, the great majority repeating third density. This is approximate due to the fact that parallel possibility/ probability vortices cease when action occurs and new probability/possibility vortices are begun.

QUESTIONER: Is there a planet opposite our sun, in relation to us, that we do not know about?

RA: I am Ra. There is a sphere in the area opposite your sun of a very, very cold nature, but large enough to skew certain statistical figures. This sphere should not properly be called a planet as it is locked in first density.

QUESTIONER: You say that entities from Maldek might go to fourth density negative. Are there people who go out of our present third density to places in the universe and serve, which are fourth-density self-service negative type of planets?

RA: I am Ra. Your question is unclear. Please restate.

QUESTIONER: As our cycle ends and graduation occurs, is it possible for anyone to go from our third density to a fourth-density planet that is of a self-service or negative type?

RA: I am Ra. We grasp now the specificity of your query. In this harvest the probability/possibility vortex is an harvest, though small, of this type. That is correct.

QUESTIONER: Can you tell us what happened to Adolf [Hitler]?

RA: I am Ra. The mind/body/spirit complex known as Adolf is at this time in an healing process in the middle astral planes of your spherical force field. This entity was greatly confused and, although aware of the circumstance of change in vibratory level associated with the cessation of the chemical body complex, nevertheless needed a great deal of care.

QUESTIONER: Is there anyone in our history who is commonly known who went to a fourth-density self-service or negative type of planet or any who will go there?

RA: I am Ra. The number of entities thus harvested is small. However, a few have penetrated the eighth level, which is only available from the opening up of the seventh through the sixth. Penetration into the eighth or intelligent infinity level allows a mind/body/spirit complex to be harvested if it wishes at any time/space during the cycle.

QUESTIONER: Are any of these people known in the history of our planet by name?

RA: I am Ra. We will mention a few. The one known as Taras Bulba, the one known as Genghis Khan, the one known as Rasputin.

QUESTIONER: How did they accomplish this? What was necessary for them to accomplish this?

RA: I am Ra. All of the aforementioned entities were aware, through memory, of Atlantean understandings having to do with the use of the various centers of mind/body/spirit complex energy influx in attaining the gateway to intelligent infinity.

QUESTIONER: Did this enable them to do what we refer to as magic? Could they do paranormal things while they were incarnate?

RA: I am Ra. This is correct. The first two entities mentioned made little use of these abilities consciously. However, they were bent single-mindedly upon service to self, sparing no efforts in personal discipline to double, redouble, and so empower this gateway. The third was a conscious adept and also spared no effort in the pursuit of service to self.

QUESTIONER: Where are these three entities now?

RA: I am Ra. These entities are in the dimension known to you as fourth. Therefore the space/time continua are not compatible. An approximation of the space/time locus of each would net no actual understanding. Each chose a fourth-density planet which was dedicated to the pursuit of the understanding of the Law of One through service to self, one in what you know as the Orion group, one in what you know as Cassiopeia, one in what you know as Southern Cross; however, these loci are not satisfactory. We do not have vocabulary for the geometric calculations necessary for transfer of this understanding to you.

QUESTIONER: Who went to the Orion group?

RA: I am Ra. The one known as Genghis Khan.

QUESTIONER: What does he presently do there? What is his job or occupation?

RA: I am Ra. This entity serves the Creator in its own way.

QUESTIONER: Is it impossible for you to tell us precisely how he does this service?

RA: I am Ra. It is possible for us to speak to this query. However, we use any chance we may have to reiterate the basic understanding/learning that all beings serve the Creator.

The one you speak of as Genghis Khan, at present, is incarnate in a physical light body which has the work of disseminating material of thought control to those who are what you may call crusaders. He is, as you would term this entity, a shipping clerk.

QUESTIONER: What do the crusaders do?

RA: I am Ra. The crusaders move in their chariots to conquer planetary mind/body/spirit social complexes before they reach the stage of achieving social memory.

QUESTIONER: At what stage does a planet achieve social memory?

RA: I am Ra. A mind/body/spirit social complex becomes a social memory complex when its entire group of entities are of one orientation or seeking. The group memory lost to the individuals in the roots of the tree of mind then becomes known to the social complex, thus creating a social memory complex. The advantages of this complex are the relative lack of distortion in understanding the social beingness and the relative lack of distortion in pursuing the direction of seeking, for all understanding/distortions are available to the entities of the society.

QUESTIONER: Then we have crusaders from Orion coming to this planet for mind control purposes. How do they do this?

RA: I am Ra. As all, they follow the Law of One observing free will. Contact is made with those who call. Those then upon the planetary sphere act much as do you to disseminate the attitudes and philosophy of their particular understanding of the Law of One which is service to self. These become the elite. Through these, the attempt begins to create a condition whereby the remainder of the planetary entities are enslaved by their free will.

QUESTIONER: Can you name any names that may be known on the planet that are recipients of the crusaders' efforts?

RA: I am Ra. I am desirous of being in nonviolation of the free-will distortion. To name those involved in the future of your space/time is to infringe; thus, we withhold this information. We request your contemplation of the fruits of the actions of those entities whom you may observe enjoying the distortion towards power. In this way you may discern for yourself this information. We shall not interfere with the, shall we say, planetary game. It is not central to the harvest.

QUESTIONER: How do the crusaders pass on their concepts to the individuals on Earth?

RA: I am Ra. There are two main ways, just as there are two main ways of, shall we say, polarizing towards service to others. There are those mind/body/spirit complexes upon your plane who do exercises and perform disciplines in order to seek contact with sources of information and power leading to the opening of the gate to intelligent infinity. There are others whose vibratory complex is such that this gateway is opened, and contact with total service to self with its primal distortion of manipulation of others is then afforded with little or no difficulty, no training, and no control.

QUESTIONER: What type of information is passed on from the crusaders to these people?

RA: I am Ra. The Orion group passes on information concerning the Law of One with the orientation of service to self. The information can become technical just as some in the Confederation, in attempts to aid this planet in service to others, have provided what you would call technical information. The technology provided by this group is in the form of various means of control or manipulation of others to serve the self.

QUESTIONER: Do you mean to say then that some scientists receive technical information, shall we say, telepathically that comes out then as usable gadgetry?

RA: I am Ra. That is correct. However, very positively, as you would call this distortion, oriented scientists have received information intended to unlock peaceful means of progress which redounded unto the last echoes of potential destruction due to further reception of other scientists of a negative orientation/distortion.

QUESTIONER: Is this how we learned of nuclear energy? Was it mixed with both positive and negative orientation?

RA: I am Ra. That is correct. The entities responsible for the gathering of the scientists were of a mixed orientation. The scientists were overwhelmingly positive in their orientation. The scientists who followed their work were of mixed orientation, including one extremely negative entity, as you would term it.

QUESTIONER: Is this extremely negative entity still incarnate on Earth?

RA: I am Ra. This is correct.

QUESTIONER: Then I would assume that you can't name him. So I will ask you where Nikola Tesla got his information?

RA: I am Ra. The one known as Nikola received information from Confederation sources desirous of aiding this extremely, shall we say, angelically positive entity in bettering the existence of its fellow mind/body/spirit complexes. It is unfortunate, shall we say, that like many Wanderers, the vibratory distortions of third-density illusion caused this entity to become extremely distorted in its perceptions of its fellow mind/body/spirit complexes so that its mission was hindered and, in the result, perverted from its purposes.

QUESTIONER: How was Tesla's work supposed to benefit man on Earth, and what were its purposes?

RA: I am Ra. The most desired purpose of the mind/body/spirit complex, Nikola, was the freeing of all planetary entities from the darkness. Thus, it attempted to give to the planet the infinite energy of the planetary sphere for use in lighting and power.

QUESTIONER: By freeing the planetary entities from darkness, precisely what do you mean?

RA: I am Ra. [Most of the following answer was lost due to tape recorder malfunction. The core of the response was as follows.] We spoke of freeing people from darkness in a literal sense.

QUESTIONER: Would this freeing from darkness be commensurate with the Law of One, or does this have any real product?

RA: I am Ra. The product of such a freeing would create two experiences.
Firstly, the experience of no need to find the necessary emolument for payment, in your money, for energy.

Secondly, the leisure afforded, thereby exemplifying the possibility and enhancing the probability of the freedom to then search the self, the beginning of seeking the Law of One.

Few there are working physically from daybreak to darkness, as you name them, upon your plane who can contemplate the Law of One in a conscious fashion.

QUESTIONER: What about the Industrial Revolution in general. Was this planned in any way?

RA: I am Ra. This will be the final question of this session.

That is correct. Wanderers incarnated in several waves, as you may call them, in order to bring into existence the gradual freeing from the demands of the diurnal cycles and lack of freedom of leisure.

QUESTIONER: That was the last question, so I will do as usual and ask if there is anything that we can do to make the instrument more comfortable?

RA: I am Ra. You are doing well. The most important thing is to carefully align the symbols. The adjustment made this particular time/space present will aid this instrument's physical complex in the distortion towards comfort.

May we ask if you have any short questions which we may resolve before closing the session?

QUESTIONER: I don't know if this is a short question or not, so we can save it till next time, but my question is, why do the crusaders from Orion do this? What is their ultimate objective? This is probably too long to answer.

RA: I am Ra. This is not too long to answer. To serve the self is to serve all. The service of the self, when seen in this perspective, requires an ever-expanding use of the energies of others for manipulation to the benefit of the self with distortion towards power.

If there are further queries to further explicate this subject, we shall be with you again.

QUESTIONER: There was one thing that I forgot. Is it possible to have another session later on today?

RA: I am Ra. It is well.

QUESTIONER: Thank you.

RA: I am Ra. I leave you in the love and the light of the One Infinite Creator. Go forth, then, rejoicing in the power and the peace of the One Creator. Adonai.

Session 12,
January 28, 1981

RA: I am Ra. I greet you in the love and the light of the Infinite Creator. I communicate now.

QUESTIONER: In the last session you mentioned that the Orion crusaders came here in chariots. Could you describe the chariots?

RA: I am Ra. The term "chariot" is a term used in warfare among your peoples. That is its significance. The shape of the Orion craft is one of the following: firstly, the elongated, ovoid shape which is of a darker nature than silver but which has a metallic appearance if seen in the light. In the absence of light, it appears to be red or fiery in some manner.

Other craft include disc-shaped objects of a small nature approximately 12 feet in your measurement in diameter, the boxlike shape approximately 40 feet to a side in your measurement. Other craft can take on a desired shape through the use of thought control mechanisms. There are various civilization complexes which work within this group. Some are more able to use intelligent infinity than others. The information is very seldom shared; therefore, the chariots vary greatly in shape and appearance.

QUESTIONER: Is there any effort on the part of the Confederation to stop the Orion chariots from arriving here?

RA: I am Ra. Every effort is made to quarantine this planet. However, the network of guardians, much like any other pattern of patrols on whatever level, does not hinder each and every entity from penetrating quarantine, for if request is made in light/love, the Law of One will be met with acquiescence. If the request is not made, due to the slipping through the net, then there is penetration of this net.

QUESTIONER: Who makes this request?

RA: I am Ra. Your query is unclear. Please restate.

QUESTIONER: I don't understand how the Confederation stops the Orion chariots from coming through the quarantine?

RA: I am Ra. There is contact at the level of light-form or light-body-being depending upon the vibratory level of the guardian. These guardians sweep reaches of your Earth's energy fields to be aware of any entities approaching. An entity which is approaching is hailed in the name of the One Creator. Any entity thus hailed is bathed in love/light and will of free will obey the quarantine due to the power of the Law of One.

QUESTIONER: What would happen to the entity if he did not obey the quarantine after being hailed?

RA: I am Ra. To not obey quarantine after being hailed on the level of which we speak would be equivalent to your not stopping upon walking into a solid brick wall.

QUESTIONER: What would happen to the entity if he did this? What would happen to his chariot?

RA: I am Ra. The Creator is one being. The vibratory level of those able to breach the quarantine boundaries is such that upon seeing the love/light net, it is impossible to break this Law. Therefore, nothing happens. No attempt is made. There is no confrontation. The only beings who are able to penetrate the quarantine are those who discover windows or distortions in the space/time continua surrounding your planet's energy fields. Through these windows they come. These windows are rare and unpredictable.

QUESTIONER: Does this account for what we call "UFO flaps" where a large number of UFOs show up like in 1973?

RA: I am Ra. This is correct.

QUESTIONER: Are most of the UFOs which are seen in our skies from the Orion group?

RA: I am Ra. Many of those seen in your skies are of the Orion group. They send out messages. Some are received by those who are oriented toward service to others. These messages then are altered to be acceptable to those entities while warning of difficulties ahead. This is the most that self-serving entities can do when faced with those whose wish is to serve others. The contacts which the group finds most helpful to their cause are those contacts made with entities whose orientation is towards service to self. There are many thought-form entities in your skies which are of a positive nature and are the projections of the Confederation.

QUESTIONER: You mentioned that the Orion crusaders, when they get through the net, give both technical and nontechnical information. I think I know what you mean by technical information, but what type of nontechnical information do they give? And am I right in assuming that this is done by telepathic contact?

RA: I am Ra. This is correct. Through telepathy the philosophy of the Law of One with the distortion of service to self is promulgated. In advanced groups there are rituals and exercises given, and these have been written down just as the service to others oriented entities have written down the promulgated philosophy of their teachers. The philosophy concerns the service of manipulating others that they may experience service towards the other self, thus through this experience becoming able to appreciate service to self. These entities would become oriented towards service to self and in turn manipulate yet others so that they in turn might experience the service towards the other self.

QUESTIONER: Would this be the origin of what we call black magic?

RA: I am Ra. This is correct in one sense, incorrect in another. The Orion group has aided the so-called negatively oriented among your mind/body/spirit complexes. These same entities would be concerning themselves with service to self in any case, and there are many upon your so-called inner planes which are negatively oriented and thus available as inner teachers or guides and so-called possessors of certain souls who seek this distortion of service to self.

QUESTIONER: Is it possible for an entity here on Earth to be so confused as to call both the Confederation and the Orion group in an alternating way, first one, then the other, and then back to the first again?

RA: I am Ra. It is entirely possible for the untuned channel, as you call that service, to receive both positive and negative communications. If the entity at the base of its confusion is oriented toward service to others, the entity will begin to receive messages of doom. If the entity at the base of the complex of beingness is oriented towards service to self, the crusaders, who in this case do not find it necessary to lie, will simply begin to give the philosophy they are here to give. Many of your so-called contacts among your people have been confused and self-destructive because the channels were oriented towards service to others but, in the desire for proof, were open to the lying information of the crusaders, who then were able to neutralize the effectiveness of the channel.

QUESTIONER: Are most of these crusaders fourth density?

RA: I am Ra. There is a majority of fourth density. That is correct.

QUESTIONER: Is an entity in the fourth density normally invisible to us?

RA: I am Ra. The use of the word "normal" is one which befuddles the meaning of the question. Let us rephrase for clarity. The fourth density is, by choice, not visible to third density. It is possible for fourth density to be visible. However, it is not the choice of the fourth-density entity to be visible due to the necessity for concentration upon a rather difficult vibrational complex which is the third density you experience.

QUESTIONER: Are there any Confederation or Orion entities living upon the Earth and operating visibly among us in our society at this time?

RA: I am Ra. There are no entities of either group walking among you at this time. However, the crusaders of Orion use two types of entities to do their bidding, shall we say. The first type is the thought-form; the second, a kind of robot.

QUESTIONER: Could you describe the robot?

RA: I am Ra. The robot may look like any other being. It is a construct.

QUESTIONER: Is the robot what is normally called the "Men in Black?"

RA: I am Ra. This is incorrect.

QUESTIONER: Who are the Men in Black?

RA: I am Ra. The Men in Black are a thought-form type of entity which have some beingness to their makeup. They have certain physical characteristics given them. However, their true vibrational nature is without third-density vibrational characteristics, and, therefore, they are able to materialize and dematerialize when necessary.

QUESTIONER: Are all of these Men in Black then used by the Orion crusaders?

RA: I am Ra. This is correct.

QUESTIONER: You spoke of Wanderers. Who are Wanderers? Where do they come from?

RA: I am Ra. Imagine, if you will, the sands of your shores. As countless as the grains of sand are the sources of intelligent infinity. When a social memory complex has achieved its complete understanding of its desire, it may conclude that its desire is service to others with the distortion towards reaching their hand, figuratively, to any entities who call for aid. These entities whom you may call the Brothers and Sisters of Sorrow move toward this calling of sorrow. These entities are from all reaches of the infinite creation and are bound together by the desire to serve in this distortion.

QUESTIONER: How many of them are incarnate on Earth now?

RA: I am Ra. The number is approximate due to an heavy influx of those birthed at this time due to an intensive need to lighten the planetary vibration and thus aid in harvest. The number approaches sixty-five million.

QUESTIONER: Are most of these from the fourth density? Or what density do they come from?

RA: I am Ra. Few there are of fourth density. The largest number of Wanderers, as you call them, are of the sixth density. The desire to serve must be distorted towards a great deal of purity of mind and what you may call foolhardiness or bravery, depending upon your distortion complex judgment. The challenge/danger of the Wanderer is that it will forget its mission, become karmically involved, and thus be swept into the maelstrom of which it had incarnated to avert the destruction.

QUESTIONER: What could one of these entities do to become karmically involved? Could you give an example of that?

RA: I am Ra. An entity which acts in a consciously unloving manner in action with other beings can become karmically involved.

QUESTIONER: Do many of these Wanderers have physical ailments in this third-density situation?

RA: I am Ra. Due to the extreme variance between the vibratory distortions of third density and those of the more dense densities, if you will, Wanderers have, as a general rule, some form of handicap, difficulty, or feeling of alienation which is severe. The most common of these difficulties are alienation, the reaction against the planetary vibration by personality disorders, as you would call them, and body complex ailments indicating difficulty in adjustment to the planetary vibrations such as allergies, as you would call them.

QUESTIONER: Thank you. Is there anything that we can do to make the instrument more comfortable?

RA: I am Ra. We ask you to realign the object upon which the symbols sit. It is not a significant distortion for only one session, but you will find upon measuring the entire assemblage that the resting place is 1.4 degrees from the correct alignment, the resting place an additional 0.5 degrees away from proper orientation. Do not concern yourselves with this in the space/time nexus present, but do not allow these distortions to remain over a long period or the contact will be gradually impaired.

I am Ra. I leave you in the love and in the light of the One Infinite Creator. Go forth rejoicing in the power and the peace of the One Creator. Adonai.

Session 13,
January 29, 1981

RA: I am Ra. I greet you in the love and the light of the Infinite Creator. I communicate now.

QUESTIONER: First of all I would like to apologize for asking so many stupid questions while searching for what we should do. I consider what we are doing to be a great honor and privilege to also be humble messengers of the Law of One. I now believe that the way to prepare this book is to start at the beginning of creation and follow through the evolution of man on Earth, investigating at all times how the Law of One was used. I would also like to make as the title of the book *The Law of One*, and I would like to state as the author, Ra. Would you agree to this?

RA: I am Ra. Your query is unclear. Would you please state as separate queries each area of agreement?

QUESTIONER: First, I would like to start at the beginning of creation, as far back as we can go, and follow the development of man to the present time. Is this agreeable?

RA: I am Ra. This is completely your discernment/understanding/decision.

QUESTIONER: Secondly, I would like to title the book *The Law of One*, by Ra. Is this agreeable?

RA: I am Ra. The title of the book is acceptable. The authorship by vibratory sound complex Ra is, in our distortion of understanding, incomplete. We are messengers.

QUESTIONER: Can you state who then should author the book?

RA: I am Ra. I can only request that if your discernment/understanding suggests the use of this vibratory sound complex, Ra, the phrase "An humble messenger of the Law of One" be appended.

QUESTIONER: Thank you. Can you tell me of the first known thing in the creation?

RA: I am Ra. The first known thing in the creation is infinity. The infinity is creation.

QUESTIONER: From this infinity then must come what we experience as creation. What was the next step or the next evolvement?

RA: I am Ra. Infinity became aware. This was the next step.

QUESTIONER: After this, what came next?

RA: I am Ra. Awareness led to the focus of infinity into infinite energy. You have called this by various vibrational sound complexes, the most common to your ears being "Logos" or "Love." The Creator is the focusing of infinity as an aware or conscious principle called by us, as closely as we can create understanding/learning in your language, intelligent infinity.

QUESTIONER: Can you state the next step?

RA: I am Ra. The next step is still at this space/time nexus in your illusion achieving its progression as you may see it in your illusion. The next step is an infinite reaction to the creative principle following the Law of One in one of its primal distortions, freedom of will. Thus many, many dimensions, infinite in number, are possible. The energy moves from the intelligent infinity due first to the outpouring of randomized creative force, this then creating patterns which in holographic style appear as the entire creation no matter which direction or energy is explored. These patterns of energy begin then to regularize their own local, shall we say, rhythms and fields of energy, thus creating dimensions and universes.

QUESTIONER: Then can you tell me how the galaxy and planetary systems were formed?

RA: I am Ra. You must imagine a great leap of thought in this query, for at the last query, the physical, as you call it, universes were not yet born.

The energies moved in increasingly intelligent patterns until the individualization of various energies emanating from the creative principle of intelligent infinity became such as to be co-Creators. Thus the so-called physical matter began. The concept of light is instrumental in grasping this great leap of thought, as this vibrational distortion of infinity is the building block of that which is known as matter, the light being intelligent and full of energy, thus being the first distortion of intelligent infinity which was called by the creative principle.

This light of love was made to have in its occurrences of being certain characteristics, among them the infinite whole paradoxically described by the straight line, as you would call it. This paradox is responsible for the shape of the various physical illusion entities you call solar systems, galaxies, and planets of revolving and tending towards the lenticular.

QUESTIONER: I think I made an error in getting ahead of the process you were describing. Would it be helpful to fill in that great leap due to the mistake I made?

RA: I am Ra. I attempted to bridge the gap. However, you may question me in any manner you deem appropriate.

QUESTIONER: Taking the question just before the one I asked about the galaxies and planets and tell me what the next step was from there?

RA: I am Ra. The steps, as you call them, are, at the point of question, simultaneous and infinite.

QUESTIONER: Can you tell me how intelligent infinity became, shall we say (I'm having difficulty with the language), how intelligent infinity became individualized from itself?

RA: I am Ra. This is an appropriate question.

The intelligent infinity discerned a concept. This concept was discerned to be freedom of will of awareness. This concept was finity. This was the first and primal paradox or distortion of the Law of One. Thus the one intelligent infinity invested itself in an exploration of manyness. Due to the infinite possibilities of intelligent infinity, there is no ending to manyness. The exploration, thus, is free to continue infinitely in an eternal present.

QUESTIONER: Was the galaxy that we are in created by the infinite intelligence, or was it created by a portion of the infinite intelligence?

RA: I am Ra. The galaxy and all other things of material of which you are aware are products of individualized portions of intelligent infinity. As each exploration began, it, in turn, found its focus and became co-Creator. Using intelligent infinity, each portion created an universe, and allowing the rhythms of free choice to flow, playing with the infinite spectrum of possibilities, each individualized portion channeled the love/light into what you might call intelligent energy, thus creating the so-called Natural Laws of any particular universe.

Each universe, in turn, individualized to a focus becoming, in turn, co-Creator and allowing further diversity, thus creating further intelligent energies regularizing or causing Natural Laws to appear in the vibrational patterns of what you would call a solar system. Thus, each solar system has its own, shall we say, local coordinate system of illusory Natural Laws. It shall be understood that any portion, no matter how small, of any density or illusory pattern contains, as in an holographic picture, the One Creator which is infinity. Thus all begins and ends in mystery.

QUESTIONER: Can you tell me how the individualized infinity created our galaxy and if the same portion created our planetary system, and, if so, how this came about?

RA: I am Ra. We may have misperceived your query. We were under the distortion/impression that we had responded to this particular query. Would you restate the query?

QUESTIONER: I am wondering if the planetary system that we are in now was all created at once, or if our sun was created first and the planets later?

RA: I am Ra. The process is from the larger, in your illusion, to the smaller. Thus the co-Creator, individualizing the galaxy, created energy patterns which then focused in multitudinous focuses of further conscious awareness of intelligent infinity. Thus, the solar system of which you experience inhabitation is of its own patterns, rhythms, and so-called natural laws which are unique to itself. However, the progression is from the galaxy spiraling energy to the solar spiraling energy, to the planetary spiraling energy, to the experiential circumstances of spiraling energy which begin the first density of awareness of consciousness of planetary entities.

QUESTIONER: Could you tell me about this first density of planetary entities?

RA: I am Ra. Each step recapitulates intelligent infinity in its discovery of awareness. In a planetary environment, all begins in what you would call chaos, energy undirected and random in its infinity. Slowly, in your terms of understanding, there forms a focus of self-awareness. Thus the Logos moves. Light comes to form the darkness, according to the co-Creator's patterns and vibratory rhythms, so constructing a certain type of experience. This begins with first density, which is the density of consciousness, the mineral and water life upon the planet learning from fire and wind the awareness of being. This is the first density.

QUESTIONER: How does this first density then progress to greater awareness?

RA: I am Ra. The spiraling energy, which is the characteristic of what you call "light," moves in a straight line spiral, thus giving spirals an inevitable vector upwards to a more comprehensive beingness with regards to intelligent infinity. Thus, first-dimensional beingness strives towards the second-density lessons of a type of awareness which includes growth rather than dissolution or random change.

QUESTIONER: Could you define what you mean by growth?

RA: I am Ra. Picture, if you will, the difference between first-vibrational mineral or water life and the lower second-density beings which begin to move about within and upon its being. This movement is the characteristic of second density, the striving towards light and growth.

QUESTIONER: By striving towards light, what do you mean?

RA: I am Ra. A very simplistic example of second-density growth striving towards light is that of the leaf striving towards the source of light.

QUESTIONER: Is there any physical difference between first and second density? For instance, if I could see both a first- and second-density planet side by side, in my present condition, could I see both of them? Would they both be physical to me?

RA: I am Ra. This is correct. All of the octave of your densities would be clearly visible were not the fourth through the seventh freely choosing not to be visible.

QUESTIONER: Then how does the second density progress to the third?

RA: I am Ra. The second density strives towards the third density, which is the density of self-consciousness or self-awareness. The striving takes place through the higher second density forms who are invested by third-density beings with an identity to the extent that they become self-aware mind/body complexes, thus becoming mind/body/spirit complexes and entering third density, the first density of consciousness of spirit.

QUESTIONER: What is the density level of our planet Earth at this time?

RA: I am Ra. The sphere upon which you dwell is third density in its beingness of mind/body/spirit complexes. It is now in a space/time continuum, fourth density. This is causing a somewhat difficult harvest.

QUESTIONER: How does a third-density planet become a fourth-density planet?

RA: I am Ra. This will be the last full question.

The fourth density is, as we have said, as regularized in its approach as the striking of a clock upon the hour. The space/time of your solar system has enabled this planetary sphere to spiral into space/time of a different vibrational configuration. This causes the planetary sphere to be able to be molded by these new distortions. However, the thought-forms of your people during this transition period are such that the mind/body/spirit complexes of both individual and societies are scattered throughout the spectrum instead of becoming able to grasp the needle, shall we say, and point the compass in one direction.

Thus, the entry into the vibration of love, sometimes called by your people the vibration of understanding, is not effective with your present societal complex. Thus, the harvest shall be such that many will repeat the third-density cycle. The energies of your Wanderers, your teachers, and your adepts at this time are all bent upon increasing the harvest. However, there are few to harvest.

QUESTIONER: I would like to apologize for sometimes asking inappropriate questions. It's difficult sometimes to ask precisely the right question. I don't wish to go over any ground that we've already covered. I notice that this period is slightly shorter than previous work sessions. Is there a reason for this?

RA: I am Ra. This instrument's vital energy is somewhat low.

QUESTIONER: I am assuming from this that it would be a good idea not to have another session today. Is that correct?

RA: I am Ra. It is well to have a session later if it is acceptable that we monitor this instrument and cease using it when it becomes low in the material which we take from it. We do not wish to deplete this instrument.

QUESTIONER: This is always acceptable in any session. I will ask my final question. Is there anything that we can do to make the instrument more comfortable or aid in this communication?

RA: I am Ra. It is well. Each is most conscientious. Continue in the same.
    I am Ra. I leave you in the love and the light of the One Infinite Creator. Go forth, therefore, rejoicing in the power and the peace of the One Creator. Adonai.

Session 14,
January 29, 1981

RA: I am Ra. I greet you in the love and the light of the Infinite Creator. We communicate now.

QUESTIONER: After going over this morning's work, I thought it might be helpful to fill in a few things. You said that the second density strives towards the third density, which is the density of self-consciousness, or self-awareness. The striving takes place through higher second-density forms being invested by third-density beings. Could you explain what you mean by this?

RA: I am Ra. Much as you would put on a vestment, so do your third-density beings invest or clothe some second-density beings with self-awareness. This is often done through the opportunity of what you call pets. It has also been done by various other means of investiture. These include many so-called religious practice complexes which personify and send love to various natural second-density beings in their group form.

QUESTIONER: When this Earth was second density, how did the second-density beings on it become so invested?

RA: I am Ra. There was not this type of investment as spoken, but the simple third-density investment which is the line of spiraling light calling distortion upward from density to density. The process takes longer when there is no investment made by incarnate third-density beings.

QUESTIONER: Then what was the second-density form—what did it look like—that became Earthman in the third density? What did he look like in the second density?

RA: I am Ra. The difference between second- and third-density bodily forms would in many cases have been more like one to the other. In the case of your planetary sphere, the process was interrupted by those who incarnated here from the planetary sphere you call Mars. They were adjusted by genetic changing, and, therefore, there was some difference which was of a very noticeable variety rather than the gradual raising of the bipedal forms upon your second-density level to third-density level. This has nothing to do with the so-called placement of the soul. This has only to do with the circumstances of the influx of those from that culture.

QUESTIONER: I understand from previous material that this occurred 75,000 years ago. It was then that our third-density process of evolution began. Can you tell me the history, hitting only the points of development, shall I say, that occurred within this 75,000 years, any point when contact was made to aid this development?

RA: I am Ra. The first attempt to aid your peoples was at the time 75,000. This attempt 75,000 of your years ago has been previously described by us. The next attempt was approximately 58,000 of your years ago, continuing for a long period in your measurement, with those of Mu as you call this race or mind/body/spirit social complex. The next attempt was long in coming and occurred approximately 13,000 of your years ago when some intelligent information was offered to those of Atlantis, this being of the same type of healing and crystal working of which we have spoken previously. The next attempt was 11,000 of your years ago. These are approximations, as we are not totally able to process your space/time continuum measurement system. This was in what you call Egypt, and of this we have also spoken. The same beings who came with us returned approximately 3,500 years later in order to attempt to aid the South American mind/body/spirit social complex once again. However, the pyramids of those so-called cities were not to be used in the appropriate fashion.

Therefore, this was not pursued further. There was a landing approximately 3,000 of your years ago also in your South America, as you call it. There were a few attempts to aid your peoples approximately 2,300 years ago, this in the area of Egypt. The remaining part of the cycle, we have never been gone from your fifth dimension and have been working in this last minor cycle to prepare for harvest.

QUESTIONER: Was the Egyptian visit of 11,000 years ago the only one where you actually walked the Earth?

RA: I am Ra. I understand your question distorted in the direction of selves rather than other-selves. We of the vibratory sound complex, Ra, have walked among you only at that time.

QUESTIONER: I understood you to say in an earlier session that pyramids were built to ring the Earth. How many pyramids were built?

RA: I am Ra. There are six balancing pyramids and fifty-two others built for additional healing and initiatory work among your mind/body/spirit social complexes.

QUESTIONER: What is a balancing pyramid?

RA: I am Ra. Imagine, if you will, the many force fields of the Earth in their geometrically precise web. Energies stream into the Earth planes, as you would call them, from magnetically determined points. Due to growing thought-form distortions in understanding of the Law of One, the planet itself was seen to have the potential for imbalance. The balancing pyramidal structures were charged with crystals which drew the appropriate balance from the energy forces streaming into the various geometrical centers of electromagnetic energy which surround and shape the planetary sphere.

QUESTIONER: Let me make a synopsis and you tell me if I am correct. All of these visits for the last 75,000 years were for the purpose of giving to the people of Earth an understanding of the Law of One, and in this way allowing them to progress upward through the fourth, fifth, and sixth densities. This was to be a service to Earth. The pyramids were used also in giving the Law of One in their own way. The balancing pyramids, I'm not quite sure of. Am I right so far?

RA: I am Ra. You are correct to the limits of the precision allowed by language.

QUESTIONER: Did the balancing pyramid prevent the Earth from changing its axis?

RA: I am Ra. This query is not clear. Please restate.

QUESTIONER: Does the balancing refer to the individual who is initiated in the pyramid, or does it refer to the physical balancing of the Earth on its axis in space?

RA: I am Ra. The balancing pyramidal structures could be and were used for individual initiation. However, the use of these pyramids was also designed for the balancing of the planetary energy web. The other pyramids are not placed correctly for Earth healing but for healing of mind/body/spirit complexes. It came to our attention that your density was distorted towards what is called, by our distortion/understanding of third density on your planetary sphere, more of a time/space continuum in one incarnation pattern in order to have a fuller opportunity to learn/teach the Laws or Ways of the primal distortion of the Law of One which is Love.

QUESTIONER: I want to make this statement and you tell me if I am correct. The balancing pyramids were to do what we call increase the life span of entities here so that they would gain more wisdom of the Law of One while they were in the physical at one time. Is this correct?

RA: I am Ra. This is correct. However, the pyramids not called by us by the vibrational sound complex, balancing pyramids, were more numerous and were used exclusively for the above purpose and the teach/learning of healers to charge and enable these processes.

QUESTIONER: George Van Tassel built a machine in our western desert called an integratron. Will this machine work for that purpose, of increasing the life span?

RA: I am Ra. The machine is incomplete and will not function for the above-mentioned purpose.

QUESTIONER: Who gave George the information on how to build it?

RA: I am Ra. There were two contacts which gave the entity with the vibratory sound complex, George, this information. One was of the Confederation. The second was of the Orion group. The Confederation was caused to find the distortion towards noncontact due to the alteration of the vibrational mind complex patterns of the one called George. Thus, the Orion group used this instrument; however, this instrument, though confused, was a mind/body/spirit complex devoted at the heart to service to others, so the, shall we say, worst that could be done was to discredit this source.

QUESTIONER: Would there be any value to the people of this planet now to complete this machine?

RA: I am Ra. The harvest is now. There is not at this time any reason to include efforts along these distortions toward longevity, but rather to encourage distortions toward seeking the heart of self, for this which resides clearly in the violet-ray energy field will determine the harvesting of each mind/body/spirit complex.

QUESTIONER: Going back to when we started this 75,000-year period, there was a harvest 25,000 years after the start, which would make it 50,000 years ago. Can you tell me how many were harvested at that time?

RA: I am Ra. The harvest was none.

QUESTIONER: There was no harvest? What about 25,000 years ago?

RA: I am Ra. A harvesting began taking place in the latter portion, as you measure time/space, of the second cycle, with individuals finding the gateway to intelligent infinity. The harvest of that time, though extremely small, was those entities of extreme distortion towards service to the entities who were now to repeat the major cycle. These entities, therefore, remained in third density, although they could, at any moment/present nexus, leave this density through use of intelligent infinity.

QUESTIONER: Then in the harvest 25,000 years ago, the entities who could have been harvested into the fourth density chose to remain here in service to this planetary population. Is this correct?

RA: I am Ra. This is correct. Thus, there was no harvest, but there were harvestable entities who shall choose the manner of their entrance into fourth dimension.

QUESTIONER: Then for the last 2,300 years you have been working to create as large a harvest as possible at the end of the total 75,000-year cycle. Can you state with respect to the Law of One why you do this?

RA: I am Ra. I speak for the social memory complex termed Ra. We came among you to aid you. Our efforts in service were perverted. Our desire then is to eliminate as far as possible the distortions caused by those misreading our information and guidance. The general cause of service such as the Confederation offers is that of the primal distortion of the Law of One, which is service. The One Being of the creation is like unto a body, if you will accept this third-density analogy. Would we ignore a pain in the leg? A bruise upon the skin? A cut which is festering? No. There is no ignoring a call. We, the entities of sorrow, chose as our service the attempt to heal the sorrow which we are calling analogous to the pains of a physical body complex/distortion.

QUESTIONER: Of what density level is Ra?

RA: I am Ra. I am sixth density with a strong seeking towards seventh density. The harvest for us will be in only approximately two and one-half million of your years, and it is our desire to be ready for harvest as it approaches in our space/time continuum.

QUESTIONER: And you ready yourselves for this harvest through the service you can provide. Is this correct?

RA: I am Ra. This is correct. We offer the Law of One, the solving of paradoxes, the balancing of love/light and light/love.

QUESTIONER: How long is one of your cycles?

RA: I am Ra. One of our cycles computes to 75 million of your years.

QUESTIONER: 75 million years?

RA: I am Ra. That is correct.

QUESTIONER: In your service in giving the Law of One, do you work with any other planets than Earth at this time, or just Earth?

RA: I am Ra. We work only with this planetary sphere at this time.

QUESTIONER: You stated that you were called by 352,000 Earth entities. Does this mean that it is this number that will understand and accept the Law of One?

RA: I am Ra. We cannot estimate the correctness of your statement, for those who call are not in every case able to understand the answer to their calling. Moreover, those who were not calling previously may, with great trauma, discover the answers to the call nearly simultaneously with their late call. There is no time/space in call. Therefore, we cannot estimate the number of your mind/body/spirit complexes which will, in your space/time continuum/distortion, hear and understand.

QUESTIONER: How do you normally perform your service of giving the Law of One? How have you done this over the last 2,300 years? How have you normally given this to Earth people?

RA: I am Ra. We have used channels such as this one, but in most cases the channels feel inspired by dreams and visions without being aware, consciously, of our identity or existence. This particular group has been accentuatedly trained to recognize such contact. This makes this group able to be aware of a focal or vibrational source of information.

QUESTIONER: When you contact the entities in their dreams and otherwise, these entities first have to be seeking in the direction of the Law of One. Is this correct?

RA: I am Ra. This is correct. For example, the entities of the nation Egypt were in a state of pantheism, as you may call the distortion toward separate worship of various portions of the Creator. We were able to contact one whose orientation was toward the One.

QUESTIONER: I assume that as the cycle ends and inconveniences occur, there will be some entities who start seeking or be catalyzed into seeking because of the trauma and will then hear your words telepathically or in written form such as this book. Is this correct?

RA: I am Ra. You are correct except in understanding that the inconveniences have begun.

QUESTIONER: Can you tell me who was responsible for transmitting the book *Oahspe*?

RA: I am Ra. This was transmitted by one of Confederation social memory complex status whose idea, as offered to the Council, was to use some of the known physical history of the so-called religions or religious distortions of your cycle in order to veil and partially unveil aspects or primal distortions of the Law of One. All names can be taken to be created for their vibrational characteristics. The information buried within has to do with a deeper understanding of love and light, and the attempts of infinite intelligence through many messengers to teach/learn those entities of your sphere.

QUESTIONER: Have there been any other books that you can name that are available for this purpose that have been given by the Confederation?

RA: I am Ra. We cannot share this information, for it would distort your discernment patterns in your future. You may ask about a particular volume.

QUESTIONER: Who transmitted *The Urantia Book*?

RA: I am Ra. This was given by a series of discarnate entities of your own Earth planes, the so-called inner planes. This material is not passed by the Council.

QUESTIONER: Who spoke through Edgar Cayce?

RA: I am Ra. No entity spoke through Edgar Cayce.

QUESTIONER: Where did the information come from that Edgar Cayce channeled?

RA: I am Ra. We have explained before that the intelligent infinity is brought into intelligent energy from eighth density or octave. The one sound vibratory complex called Edgar used this gateway to view the present, which is not the continuum you experience but the potential social memory complex of this planetary sphere. The term your peoples have used for this is the "Akashic Record" or the "Hall of Records." This is the last question which you may now ask.

QUESTIONER: Is there anything that we can do to make the instrument more comfortable or to help during the transmission?

RA: I am Ra. We only reiterate the importance of alignment. This instrument is placed 0.2 degrees away from the direction of the resting place, which is correct. This may be "eyed," shall we say, by sight and the instrument reminded. You are being conscientious. Is there any brief question we may answer before this session is closed?

QUESTIONER: Can you tell me if we are accomplishing our effort reasonably well?

RA: I am Ra. The Law is One. There are no mistakes.

I am Ra. I leave this instrument in the love and the light of the One Infinite Creator. Go forth, therefore, rejoicing in the power and the peace of the One Creator. Adonai.

Session 15,
January 30, 1981

RA: I am Ra. I greet you in the love and the light of the Infinite Creator. I communicate now.

QUESTIONER: I would like to apologize for any past and future stupid questions. They are due to the fact that I am searching for the proper entry into the investigation of the Law of One.

I would like to ask about the use of the instrument, if it is a function of the time we use the instrument or the amount of words or information the instrument gives? In other words, do I have to hurry and ask questions, or can I take my time to ask questions?

RA: I am Ra. There are two portions to your query. Firstly, this instrument's reserve of vital energy, which is a product of body, mind, and spirit distortions in the various complexes, is the key to the length of time which we may expend using this instrument. We searched your group and we contacted you, for each in your group possesses significantly more vital energy of the body complex. However, this instrument was tuned most appropriately by the mind/body/spirit complex distortions of its beingness in this illusion. Therefore, we remained with this instrument.

Secondly, we communicate at a set rate which is dependent upon our careful manipulation of this instrument. We cannot be more, as you would say, quick. Therefore, you may ask questions speedily, but the answers we have to offer are at a set pace given.

QUESTIONER: This isn't exactly what I meant. If it takes me, say, forty-five minutes to ask my questions, does that give the instrument only fifteen minutes to answer, or could the instrument go over an hour, all totaled, with her answers?

RA: I am Ra. The energy required for this contact is entered into this instrument by a function of time. Therefore, the time is the factor, as we understand your query.

QUESTIONER: Then I should ask my questions rapidly so that I do not reduce the time. Is this correct?

RA: I am Ra. You shall do as you deem fit. However, we may suggest that to obtain the answers you require may mean that you invest some of what you experience as time. Although you lose the answer time, you gain thereby in the specificity of the answer. At many times in the past, we have needed clarification of hastily phrased questions.

QUESTIONER: Thank you. The first question is this: Why does rapid aging occur on this planet?

RA: I am Ra. Rapid aging occurs upon this third-density planet due to an ongoing imbalance of receptor web complex in the etheric portion of the energy field of this planet. The thought-form distortions of your peoples have caused the energy streamings to enter the planetary magnetic atmosphere, if you would so term this web of energy patterns, in such a way that the proper streamings are not correctly imbued with balanced vibratory light/love from the, shall we say, cosmic level of this octave of existence.

QUESTIONER: Do I assume correctly that one of your attempts in service to this planet was to help the population more fully understand and practice the Law of One so that this rapid aging could be changed to normal aging?

RA: I am Ra. You assume correctly to a great degree.

QUESTIONER: What is the greatest service that our population on this planet could perform individually?

RA: I am Ra. There is but one service. The Law is One. The offering of self to Creator is the greatest service, the unity, the fountainhead. The entity who seeks the One Creator is with infinite intelligence. From this seeking, from this offering, a great multiplicity of opportunities will evolve depending upon the mind/body/spirit complexes' distortions with regard to the various illusory aspects or energy centers of the various complexes of your illusion.

Thus, some become healers, some workers, some teachers, and so forth.

QUESTIONER: If an entity were perfectly balanced with respect to the Law of One on this planet, would he undergo the aging process?

RA: I am Ra. A perfectly balanced entity would become tired rather than visibly aged. The lessons being learned, the entity would depart. However, this is appropriate and is a form of aging which your peoples do not experience. The understanding comes slowly, the body complex decomposing more rapidly.

QUESTIONER: Can you tell me a little more about the word "balancing," as we are using it?

RA: I am Ra. Picture, if you will, the One Infinite. You have no picture. Thus, the process begins. Love creating light, becoming love/light, streams into the planetary sphere according to the electromagnetic web of points or nexi of entrance. These streamings are then available to the individual who, like the planet, is a web of electromagnetic energy fields with points or nexi of entrance.

In a balanced individual each energy center is balanced and functioning brightly and fully. The blockages of your planetary sphere cause some distortion of intelligent energy. The blockages of the mind/body/spirit complex further distort or unbalance this energy. There is one energy. It may be understood as love/light or light/love or intelligent energy.

QUESTIONER: Am I correct to assume that one of the blockages of the mind/body/spirit complex might be, shall we say, ego, and this could be balanced using a worthiness/unworthiness balance. Am I correct?

RA: I am Ra. This is incorrect.

QUESTIONER: Can you tell me how you balance the ego?

RA: I am Ra. We cannot work with this concept, as it is misapplied and understanding cannot come from it.

QUESTIONER: How does an individual go about balancing himself? What is the first step?

RA: I am Ra. The steps are only one; that is, an understanding of the energy centers which make up the mind/body/spirit complex. This understanding may be briefly summarized as follows. The first balancing is of the Malkuth, or Earth, vibratory energy complex, called the red-ray complex. An understanding and acceptance of this energy is fundamental. The next energy complex which may be blocked is the emotional or personal complex, also known as the orange-ray complex. This blockage will often demonstrate itself as personal eccentricities or distortions with regard to self-conscious understanding or acceptance of self.

The third blockage resembles most closely that which you have called ego. It is the yellow-ray or solar-plexus center. Blockages in this center will often manifest as distortions toward power manipulation and other social behaviors concerning those close and those associated with the mind/body/spirit complex. Those with blockages in these first three energy centers, or nexi, will have continuing difficulties in ability to further their seeking of the Law of One.

The center of heart, or green ray, is the center from which third-density beings may springboard, shall we say, to infinite intelligence. Blockages in this area may manifest as difficulties in expressing what you may call universal love or compassion.

The blue-ray center of energy streaming is the center which, for the first time, is outgoing as well as inpouring. Those blocked in this area may have difficulty in grasping the spirit/mind complexes of its own entity and further difficulty in expressing such understandings of self. Entities blocked in this area may have difficulties in accepting communication from other mind/body/spirit complexes.

The next center is the pineal or indigo-ray center. Those blocked in this center may experience a lessening of the influx of intelligent energy due to manifestations which appear as unworthiness. This is that of which you spoke. As you can see, this is but one of many distortions due to the several points of energy influx into the mind/body/spirit complex. The indigo-ray balancing is quite central to the type of work which revolves about the spirit complex, which has its influx then into the transformation or transmutation of third density to fourth density, it being the energy center receiving the least distorted outpourings of love/light from intelligent energy and also the potential for the key to the gateway of intelligent infinity.

The remaining center of energy influx is simply the total expression of the entity's vibratory complex of mind, body, and spirit. It is as it will be; "balanced" or "imbalanced" has no meaning at this energy level, for it gives and takes in its own balance. Whatever the distortion may be, it cannot be manipulated as can the others and, therefore, has no particular importance in viewing the balancing of an entity.

QUESTIONER: You previously gave us information on what we should do in balancing. Is there any publishable information you can give us now about particular exercises or methods of balancing these energy centers?

RA: I am Ra. The exercises given for publication seen in comparison with the material now given are in total a good beginning. It is important to allow each seeker to enlighten itself rather than for any messenger to attempt in language to teach/learn for the entity, thus being teach/learner and learn/teacher. This is not in balance with your third density. We learn from you. We teach to you. Thus, we teach/learn. If we learned for you, this would cause imbalance in the direction of the distortion of free will. There are other items of information allowable. However, you have not yet reached these items in your line of questioning, and it is our belief/feeling complex that the questioner shall shape this material in such a way that your mind/body/spirit complexes shall have entry to it; thus we answer your queries as they arise in your mind complex.

QUESTIONER: Yesterday you stated that "the harvest is now. There is not at this time any reason to include efforts along this line of longevity, but rather to encourage efforts to seek the heart of self. This which resides clearly in the violet-ray energy field will determine the harvest of the mind/body/spirit complex." Could you tell us the best way to seek the heart of self?

RA: I am Ra. We have given you this information in several wordings. However, we can only say the material for your understanding is the self: the mind/body/spirit complex. You have been given information upon healing, as you call this distortion. This information may be seen in a more general context as ways to understand the self. The understanding, experiencing, accepting, and merging of self with self and other-self, and finally with the Creator, is the path to the heart of self. In each infinitesimal part of your self resides the One in all of Its power. Therefore, we can only encourage these lines of contemplation or prayer as a means of subjectively/objectively using or combining various understandings to enhance the seeking process. Without such a method of reversing the analytical process, one could not integrate into unity the many understandings gained in such seeking.

QUESTIONER: I don't mean to ask the same question twice, but there are some areas that I consider so important that possibly a greater understanding may be obtained if the answer is restated a number of times in other words. I thank you for your patience. Yesterday, you also mentioned that when there was no harvest at the end of the last 25,000-year period, "there were harvestable entities who shall choose the manner of their entrance into the fourth density." Could you tell me what you mean by "they shall choose the manner of their entry into the fourth density"?

RA: I am Ra. These shepherds, or, as some have called them, the "Elder Race," shall choose the time/space of their leaving. They are unlikely to leave until their other-selves are harvestable also.

QUESTIONER: What do you mean by their "other-selves" being harvestable?

RA: I am Ra. The other-selves with whom these beings are concerned are those which did not attain harvest during the second major cycle.

QUESTIONER: Could you tell me just a small amount of the history of what you call the Elder Race?

RA: I am Ra. The question is unclear. Please restate.

QUESTIONER: I ask this question because I have heard of the Elder Race before in a book, *Road in the Sky*, by George Hunt Williamson, and I was wondering if this Elder Race was the same that he talked about?

RA: I am Ra. The question now resolves itself, for we have spoken previously of the manner of decision-making which caused these entities to remain here upon the closing of the second major cycle of your current master cycle. There are some distortions in the descriptions of the one known as Michel; however, these distortions have to do primarily with the fact that these entities are not a social memory complex, but rather a group of mind/body/spirit complexes dedicated to service. These entities work together but are not completely unified; thus, they do not completely see each the other's thoughts, feelings, and motives. However, their desire to serve is the fourth-dimensional type of desire, thus melding them into what you may call a brotherhood.

QUESTIONER: Why do you call them the Elder Race?

RA: I am Ra. We called them thusly to acquaint you, the questioner, with their identity as is understood by your mind complex distortion.

QUESTIONER: Are there any Wanderers with this Elder Race?

RA: I am Ra. These are planetary entities harvested—Wanderers only in the sense that they chose, in fourth-density love, to immediately reincarnate in third density rather than proceeding towards fourth density. This causes them to be Wanderers of a type, Wanderers who have never left the Earth plane because of their free will rather than because of their vibrational level.

QUESTIONER: In yesterday's material you mentioned that the first distortion was the distortion of free will. Is there a sequence, a first, second, and third distortion of the Law of One?

RA: I am Ra. Only up to a very short point. After this point, the manyness of distortions are equal one to another. The first distortion, free will, finds focus. This is the second distortion known to you as Logos, the Creative Principle or Love. This intelligent energy thus creates a distortion known as Light. From these three distortions come many, many hierarchies of distortions, each having its own paradoxes to be synthesized, no one being more important than another.

QUESTIONER: You also said that you offered the Law of One, which is the balancing of love/light with light/love. Is there any difference between light/love and love/light?

RA: I am Ra. This will be the final question of this time/space.

There is the same difference between love/light and light/love as there is between teach/learning and learn/teaching. Love/light is the enabler, the power, the energy giver. Light/love is the manifestation which occurs when light has been impressed with love.

QUESTIONER: Is there anything we can do to make the instrument more comfortable? Can we have two sessions today?

RA: I am Ra. This instrument requires a certain amount of manipulation of the physical or body complex due to a stiffness. Other than this, all is well, the energies being balanced. There is a slight distortion in the mental energy of this instrument due to concern for a loved one, as you call it. This is only slightly lowering the vital energies of the instrument. Given a manipulation, this instrument will be well for another working.

QUESTIONER: By manipulation, do you mean that she should go for a walk or that we should rub her back?

RA: I am Ra. We meant the latter. The understanding must be added that this manipulation be done by one in harmony with the entity.

I am Ra. I leave you in the love and the light of the Infinite Creator. Go forth, then, rejoicing in the power and the peace of the One Infinite Creator. Adonai.

Session 16,
January 31, 1981

RA: I am Ra. I greet you in the love and the light of the Infinite Creator. We communicate now.

QUESTIONER: I would like to ask, considering the free-will distortion of the Law of One, how can the Guardians quarantine the Earth? Is this quarantine within free will?

RA: I am Ra. The Guardians guard the free-will distortion of the mind/body/spirit complexes of third density on this planetary sphere. The events which required activation of quarantine were interfering with the free-will distortion of mind/body/spirit complexes.

QUESTIONER: I may be wrong, but it seems to me that it would be the free will of, say, the Orion group, to interfere. How is this balanced with the information which you just gave?

RA: I am Ra. The balancing is from dimension to dimension. The attempts of the so-called Crusaders to interfere with free will are acceptable upon the dimension of their understanding. However, the mind/body/spirit complexes of this dimension you call third form a dimension of free will which is not able to, shall we say, recognize in full the distortions towards manipulation. Thus, in order to balance the dimensional variances in vibration, a quarantine, this being a balancing situation whereby the free will of the Orion group is not stopped but given a challenge. Meanwhile, the third group is not hindered from free choice.

QUESTIONER: Could these "windows" that occur to let the Orion group come through once in a while have anything to do with this free-will balancing?

RA: I am Ra. This is correct.

QUESTIONER: Could you tell me how that works?

RA: I am Ra. The closest analogy would be a random number generator within certain limits.

QUESTIONER: What is the source of this random number generator? Is it created by the Guardians to balance their guarding? Or is it a source other than the Guardians?

RA: I am Ra. All sources are one. However, we understand your query. The window phenomenon is an other-self phenomenon from the Guardians. It operates from the dimensions beyond space/time in what you may call the area of intelligent energy. Like your cycles, such balancing, such rhythms are as a clock striking. In the case of the windows, no entities have the clock. Therefore, it seems random. It is not random in the dimension which produces this balance. That is why we stated the analogy was within certain limits.

QUESTIONER: Then this window balancing prevents the Guardians from reducing their positive polarization by totally eliminating the Orion contact through shielding. Is this correct?

RA: I am Ra. This is partially correct. In effect, the balancing allows an equal amount of positive and negative influx, this balanced by the mind/body/spirit distortions of the social complex. Thus in your particular planetary sphere, less negative, as you would call it, information or stimulus is necessary than positive due to the somewhat negative orientation of your social complex distortion.

QUESTIONER: In this way, total free will is balanced so that individuals may have an equal opportunity to choose service to others or service to self. Is this correct?

RA: I am Ra. This is correct.

QUESTIONER: This is a profound revelation, I believe, in the Law of Free Will. Thank you.

This is a minor question further to make an example of this principle, but if the Confederation landed on Earth, they would be taken as gods, breaking the Law of Free Will and thus reducing their polarization of service to all. I assume that the same thing would happen if the Orion group landed. How would this affect their polarization of service to self if they were able to land and became known as gods?

RA: I am Ra. In the event of mass landing of the Orion group, the effect of polarization would be strongly toward an increase in the service to self, precisely the opposite of the former opportunity which you mentioned.

QUESTIONER: If the Orion group was able to land, would this increase their polarization? What I am trying to get at is, is it better for them to work behind the scenes to get recruits, shall we say, from our planet, the person from our planet going strictly on his own, using free will, or is it just as good for the Orion group to land on our planet and demonstrate remarkable powers and get people like that?

RA: I am Ra. This first instance is, in the long run, shall we put it, more salubrious for the Orion group in that it does not infringe upon the Law of One by landing and, thus, does its work through those of this planet. In the second circumstance, a mass landing would create a loss of polarization due to the infringement upon the free will of the planet. However, it would be a gamble. If the planet then were conquered and became part of the Empire, the free will would then be reestablished. This is restrained in action due to the desire of the Orion group to progress towards the One Creator. This desire to progress inhibits the group from breaking the Law of Confusion.

QUESTIONER: You mentioned the word "Empire" in relation to the Orion group. I have thought for some time that the movie *Star Wars* was somehow an allegory for what is actually happening. Is this correct?

RA: I am Ra. This is correct in the same way that a simple children's story is an allegory for physical/philosophical/social complex distortion/ understanding.

QUESTIONER: Is there a harvest of entities oriented toward service to self like there is a harvest of those oriented toward service to others?

RA: I am Ra. There is one harvest. Those able to enter fourth density through vibrational complex levels may choose the manner of their further seeking of the One Creator.

QUESTIONER: Then as we enter the fourth density there will be a split, shall we say, and part of the individuals who go into the fourth density will go into planets or places where there is service to others, and part will go into places where there is service to self. Is this correct?

RA: I am Ra. This is correct.

QUESTIONER: Can you tell me the origin of the Ten Commandments?

RA: I am Ra. The origin of these commandments follows the law of negative entities impressing information upon positively oriented mind/body/spirit complexes. The information attempted to copy or ape positivity while retaining negative characteristics.

QUESTIONER: Was this done by the Orion group?

RA: I am Ra. This is correct.

QUESTIONER: What was their purpose in doing this?

RA: I am Ra. The purpose of the Orion group, as mentioned before, is conquest and enslavement. This is done by finding and establishing an elite and causing others to serve the elite through various devices such as the laws you mentioned and others given by this entity.

QUESTIONER: Was the recipient of the commandments positively or negatively oriented?

RA: I am Ra. The recipient was one of extreme positivity, thus accounting for some of the pseudo-positive characteristics of the information received. As with contacts which are not successful, this entity, vibratory complex, Moishe, did not remain a credible influence among those who had first heard the philosophy of One, and this entity was removed from this third-density vibratory level in a lessened or saddened state, having lost, what you may call, the honor and faith with which he had begun the conceptualization of the Law of One and the freeing of those who were of his tribes, as they were called at that time/space.

QUESTIONER: If this entity was positively oriented, how was the Orion group able to contact him?

RA: I am Ra. This was an intensive, shall we say, battleground between positively oriented forces of Confederation origin and negatively oriented sources. The one called Moishe was open to impression and received the Law of One in its most simple form. However, the information became negatively oriented due to his people's pressure to do specific physical things in the third-density planes. This left the entity open for the type of information and philosophy of a self-service nature.

QUESTIONER: It would be wholly unlike an entity fully aware of the knowledge of the Law of One to ever say "Thou shalt not." Is this correct?

RA: I am Ra. This is correct.

QUESTIONER: Can you give me some kind of history of your social memory complex and how you became aware of the Law of One?

RA: I am Ra. The path of our learning is graven in the present moment. There is no history, as we understand your concept. Picture, if you will, a circle of being. We know the alpha and omega as infinite intelligence. The circle never ceases. It is present. The densities we have traversed at various points in the circle correspond to the characteristics of cycles: first, the cycle of awareness; second, the cycle of growth; third, the cycle of self-awareness; fourth, the cycle of love or understanding; fifth, the cycle of light or wisdom; sixth, the cycle of light/love, love/light, or unity; seventh, the gateway cycle; eighth, the octave which moves into a mystery we do not plumb.

QUESTIONER: Thank you very much. In previous material, before we communicated with you, it was stated by the Confederation that there is actually no past or future . . . that all is present. Would this be a good analogy?

RA: I am Ra. There is past, present, and future in third density. In an overview such as an entity may have, removed from the space/time continuum, it may be seen that in the cycle of completion there exists only the present. We, ourselves, seek to learn this understanding. At the seventh level or dimension, we shall, if our humble efforts are sufficient, become one with all, thus having no memory, no identity, no past or future, but existing in the all.

QUESTIONER: Does this mean that you would have awareness of all that is?

RA: I am Ra. This is partially correct. It is our understanding that it would not be our awareness, but simply awareness of the Creator. In the Creator is all that there is. Therefore, this knowledge would be available.

QUESTIONER: I was wondering how many inhabited planets there are in our galaxy, and if they all reach higher density by the Law of One? It doesn't seem that there would be any other way to reach higher density? Is this correct?

RA: I am Ra. Please restate your query.

QUESTIONER: How many inhabited planets are there in our galaxy?

RA: I am Ra. We are assuming that you intend all dimensions of consciousness or densities of awareness in this question. Approximately one-fifth of all planetary entities contain awareness of one or more densities. Some planets are hospitable only for certain densities. Your planet, for instance, is at this time hospitable for densities one, two, three, and four.

QUESTIONER: Roughly how many total planets in this galaxy of stars that we are in are aware regardless of density?

RA: I am Ra. Approximately sixty-seven million.

QUESTIONER: Can you tell me what percentage of those are third, fourth, fifth, sixth, etc. density?

RA: I am Ra. A percentage seventeen for first density, a percentage twenty for second density, a percentage twenty-seven for third density, a percentage sixteen for fourth density, a percentage six for fifth density. The other information must be withheld.

QUESTIONER: Of these first five densities, have all of the planets progressed from the third density by knowledge and application of the Law of One?

RA: I am Ra. This is correct.

QUESTIONER: Then the only way for a planet to get out of the situation that we are in is for the population to become aware of and start practicing the Law of One. Is this correct?

RA: I am Ra. This is correct.

QUESTIONER: Can you tell me what percentage of the third-, fourth-, and fifth-density planets which you have spoken of here are polarized negatively towards service to self?

RA: I am Ra. This is not a query to which we may speak, given the Law of Confusion.

We may say only that the negatively or self-service-oriented planetary spheres are much fewer. To give you exact numbers would not be appropriate.

QUESTIONER: I would like to make an analogy as to why there are fewer negatively oriented, and then ask you if the analogy is good. In a positively oriented society with service to others, it would be simple to move a large boulder by getting everyone to help move it. In a society oriented towards service to self, it would be much more difficult to get everyone to work for the good of all to move the boulder; therefore, it is much easier to get things done to create the service to others principle and to grow in positively oriented communities than in negatively oriented communities. Is this correct?

RA: I am Ra. This is correct.

QUESTIONER: Thank you very much.
Can you tell me how the Confederation of Planets was formed and why?

RA: I am Ra. The desire to serve begins, in the dimension of love or understanding, to be an overwhelming goal of the social memory complex. Thus, those percentiles of planetary entities, plus approximately 4 percent more of whose identity we cannot speak, found themselves long, long ago in your time seeking the same thing: service to others. The relationship between these entities as they entered an understanding of other beings, other planetary entities, and other concepts of service was to share and continue together these commonly held goals of service. Thus, each voluntarily placed the social memory complex data in what you may consider a central thought complex available to all. This then created a structure whereby each entity could work in its own service while calling upon any other understanding needed to enhance the service. This is the cause of the formation and the manner of the working of the Confederation.

QUESTIONER: With such a large number of planets in this galaxy, you say that there are approximately five hundred planets in the Confederation. There seems to be a relatively small number of Confederation planets around. Is there a reason for it?

RA: I am Ra. There are many Confederations. This Confederation works with the planetary spheres of seven of your galaxies, if you will, and is responsible for the callings of the densities of these galaxies.

QUESTIONER: Would you define the word "galaxy" as you just used it?

RA: I am Ra. We use that term in this sense as you would use star systems.

QUESTIONER: I'm a little bit confused as to how many total planets the Confederation that you are in serves?

RA: I am Ra. I see the confusion. We have difficulty with your language.

The galaxy term must be split. We call galaxy that vibrational complex that is local. Thus, your sun is what we would call the center of a galaxy. We see you have another meaning for this term.

QUESTIONER: Yes. In our science the term "galaxy" refers to the lenticular star system that contains millions and millions of stars. There was a confusion about this in one of our earlier communications, and I'm glad to get it cleared up.

Using the term "galaxy" in the sense that I just stated, using the lenticular star system that contains millions of stars, do you know of evolution in other galaxies besides this one?

RA: I am Ra. We are aware of life in infinite capacity. You are correct in this assumption.

QUESTIONER: Can you tell me if the progression of life in other galaxies is similar to the progression of life in our galaxy?

RA: I am Ra. The progression is somewhat close to the same, asymptotically approaching congruency throughout infinity. The free choosing of what you would call galactic systems causes variations of an extremely minor nature from one of your galaxies to another.

QUESTIONER: Then the Law of One is truly universal in creating a progression towards the eighth density in all galaxies. Is this correct?

RA: I am Ra. This is correct. There are infinite forms, infinite understandings, but the progression is one.

QUESTIONER: I am assuming that it is not necessary for an individual to understand the Law of One to go from the third to the fourth density. Is this correct?

RA: I am Ra. It is absolutely necessary that an entity consciously realize it does not understand in order for it to be harvestable. Understanding is not of this density.

QUESTIONER: That is a very important point. I used the wrong word. What I meant to say was that I believed that it was not necessary for an entity to be consciously aware of the Law of One to go from the third to the fourth density.

RA: I am Ra. This is correct.

QUESTIONER: At what point in the densities is it necessary for an entity to be consciously aware of the Law of One in order to progress?

RA: I am Ra. The fifth-density harvest is of those whose vibratory distortions consciously accept the honor/duty of the Law of One. This responsibility/honor is the foundation of this vibration.

QUESTIONER: Can you tell me a little more about this honor/responsibility concept?

RA: I am Ra. Each responsibility is an honor; each honor, a responsibility.

QUESTIONER: Thank you. Is it possible for you to give a short description of the conditions in the fourth density?

RA: I am Ra. We ask you to consider as we speak that there are not words for positively describing fourth density. We can only explain what is not and approximate what is. Beyond fourth density our ability grows more limited until we become without words.

That which fourth density is not: it is not of words, unless chosen. It is not of heavy chemical vehicles for body complex activities. It is not of disharmony within self. It is not of disharmony within peoples. It is not within limits of possibility to cause disharmony in any way.

Approximations of positive statements: it is a plane of type of bipedal vehicle which is much denser and more full of life; it is a plane wherein one is aware of the thought of other-selves; it is a plane wherein one is aware of vibrations of other-selves; it is a plane of compassion and understanding of the sorrows of third density; it is a plane striving towards wisdom or light; it is a plane wherein individual differences are pronounced although automatically harmonized by group consensus.

QUESTIONER: Could you define the word "density" as we have been using it?

RA: I am Ra. The term "density" is a, what you call, mathematical one. The closest analogy is that of music, whereby after seven notes on your Western type of scale, if you will, the eighth note begins a new octave. Within your great octave of existence, which we share with you, there are seven octaves or densities. Within each density there are seven sub-densities. Within each sub-density, are seven sub-sub-densities. Within each sub-sub-density, seven sub-sub-sub-densities, and so on infinitely.

QUESTIONER: I noticed that the time of this session has gone slightly over an hour. I would like to ask at this time if we should go on? What is the condition of the instrument?

RA: I am Ra. This instrument is in balance. It is well to continue if you desire.

QUESTIONER: I understand that each density has seven sub-densities which again have seven sub-densities and so on. This is expanding at a really large rate as each is increased by powers of seven. Does this mean that in any density level, anything that you can think of is happening?

RA: I am Ra. From your confusion we select the concept with which you struggle, that being infinity/opportunity. You may consider any possibility/probability complex as having an existence.

QUESTIONER: Do things like daydreams become real in other densities?

RA: I am Ra. This depends upon the nature of the daydream. This is a large subject. Perhaps the simplest thing we can say is if the daydream, as you call it, is one which attracts to self, this then becomes reality to self. If it is a contemplative general daydream, this may enter the infinity of possibility/probability complexes and occur elsewhere, having no particular attachment to the energy fields of the creator.

QUESTIONER: To make this a little more clear, if I were to daydream strongly about building a ship, would this occur in one of these other densities?

RA: I am Ra. This would/would have/or shall occur.

QUESTIONER: Then if an entity daydreams strongly about battling an entity, would this occur?

RA: I am Ra. In this case the entity's fantasy concerns the self and other-self, this binding the thought-form to the possibility/probability complex connected with the self which is the creator of this thought-form. This then would increase the possibility/probability of bringing this into third-density occurrence.

QUESTIONER: Does the Orion group use this principle to create conditions favorable to suit their purpose?

RA: I am Ra. We will answer more specifically than the question. The Orion group uses daydreams of hostile or other negative natures to feed back or strengthen these thought-forms.

QUESTIONER: Are the many Wanderers who have and are coming to our planet subject to the Orion thoughts?

RA: I am Ra. As we have said before, Wanderers become completely the creature of third density in mind/body complex. There is just as much chance of such influence to a Wanderer entity as to a mind/body/spirit complex of this planetary sphere. The only difference occurs in the spirit complex, which, if it wishes, has an armor of light, if you will, which enables it to recognize more clearly that which is not as it would appropriately be desired by the mind/body/spirit complex. This is not more than bias and cannot be called an understanding.

Furthermore, the Wanderer is, in its own mind/body/spirit, less distorted toward the, shall we say, deviousness of third-density positive/negative confusions. Thus, it often does not recognize as easily as a more negative individual the negative nature of thoughts or beings.

QUESTIONER: Then would the Wanderers, as they incarnate here, be high-priority targets of the Orion group?

RA: I am Ra. This is correct.

QUESTIONER: If a Wanderer should be successfully infringed upon, shall I say, by the Orion group, what would happen to this Wanderer when harvest came?

RA: I am Ra. If the Wanderer entity demonstrated through action a negative orientation towards other-selves it would be as we have said before, caught into the planetary vibration and, when harvested, possibly repeat again the master cycle of third density as a planetary entity. This shall be the last full question of this session.

Is there a short question we may answer before we close this session?

QUESTIONER: Can the instrument be made more comfortable?

RA: I am Ra. This instrument is as comfortable as it is possible for you to make it given the weakness distortions of its body complex. You are conscientious.

I am Ra. I leave you in the love and the light of the One Infinite Creator. Go forth, then, rejoicing in the power and the peace. Adonai.

Session 17,
February 3, 1981

RA: I am Ra. I greet you in the love and in the light of the Infinite Creator.

Before we communicate by answer, we shall correct an error which we have discovered in the transmission of our information to you. We have difficulty dealing with your time/space. There may again be errors of this type. Feel free to question us that we may recalculate in your time/space measurements.

The error we have discovered concerns one of the arrivals of both the Orion group into your planetary sphere of influence and the corresponding arrival of emissaries of the Confederation. We gave dates of 2,600 years for the Orion entry, 2,300 for Confederation entry. This is incorrect. The recalculation indicates numbers 3,600 for Orion entry, 3,300 for Confederation entry.

We communicate now.

QUESTIONER: Thank you very much. I would like to say again that we consider it a great honor, privilege, and duty to be able to do this particular work. I would like to reiterate that some of my questions may seem irrelevant at times, but I am trying to ask them in a manner so as to gain a foothold into the application of the Law of One.

We are now in the fourth density. Will the effects of the fourth density increase in the next thirty years? Will we see more changes in our environment and our effect upon our environment?

RA: I am Ra. The fourth density is a vibrational spectrum. Your time/

space continuum has spiraled your planetary sphere and your, what we would call galaxy, what you call star, into this vibration. This will cause the planetary sphere itself to electromagnetically realign its vortices of reception of the instreaming of cosmic forces expressing themselves as vibrational webs so that the Earth thus be fourth-density magnetized, as you may call it.

This is going to occur with some inconvenience, as we have said before, due to the energies of the thought-forms of your peoples which disturb the orderly constructs of energy patterns within your Earth spirals of energy, which increases entropy and unusable heat. This will cause your planetary sphere to have some ruptures in its outer garment while making itself appropriately magnetized for fourth density. This is the planetary adjustment.

You will find a sharp increase in the number of people, as you call mind/body/spirit complexes, whose vibrational potentials include the potential for fourth-vibrational distortions. Thus, there will seem to be, shall we say, a new breed. These are those incarnating for fourth-density work.

There will also be a sharp increase in the short run of negatively oriented or polarized mind/body/spirit complexes and social complexes, due to the polarizing conditions of the sharp delineation between fourth-density characteristics and third-density self-service orientation.

Those who remain in fourth density upon this plane will be of the so-called positive orientation. Many will come from elsewhere, for it would appear that with all the best efforts of the Confederation, which includes those from your people's inner planes, inner civilizations, and those from other dimensions, the harvest will still be much less than this planetary sphere is capable of comfortably supporting in service.

QUESTIONER: Is it possible by the use of some technique or other to help an entity to reach fourth-density level in these last days?

RA: I am Ra. It is impossible to help another being directly. It is only possible to make catalyst available in whatever form, the most important being the radiation of realization of oneness with the Creator from the self, less important being information such as we share with you.

We, ourselves, do not feel an urgency for this information to be widely disseminated. It is enough that we have made it available to three, four, or five. This is extremely ample reward, for if one of these obtains fourth-density understanding due to this catalyst, then we shall have fulfilled the Law of One in the distortion of service.

We encourage a dispassionate attempt to share information without concern for numbers or quick growth among others. That you attempt to make this information available is, in your terms, your service. The attempt, if it reaches one, reaches all.

We cannot offer shortcuts to enlightenment. Enlightenment is, of the moment, an opening to intelligent infinity. It can only be accomplished by the self, for the self. Another self cannot teach/learn enlightenment, but only teach/learn information, inspiration, or a sharing of love, of mystery, of the unknown that makes the other-self reach out and begin the seeking process that ends in a moment, but who can know when an entity will open the gate to the present?

QUESTIONER: Thank you. Can you tell me who was the entity, before his incarnation on Earth, known as Jesus of Nazareth?

RA: I am Ra. I have difficulty with this question as it is phrased. Can you discover another form for this query?

QUESTIONER: What I meant to say was can you tell me if Jesus of Nazareth came from the Confederation before incarnation here?

RA: I am Ra. The one known to you as Jesus of Nazareth did not have a name. This entity was a member of fifth density of the highest level of that sub-octave. This entity was desirous of entering this planetary sphere in order to share the love vibration in as pure a manner as possible. Thus, this entity received permission to perform this mission. This entity was then a Wanderer of no name, of Confederation origins, of fifth density, representing the fifth-density understanding of the vibration of understanding or love.

QUESTIONER: Did you say the fifth vibration was that of love?

RA: I am Ra. I have made an error. The fourth-density being is that which we intended to say, the highest level of fourth density going into the fifth. This entity could have gone on to the fifth but chose instead to return to third for this particular mission. This entity was of the highest sub-octave of the vibration of love. This is fourth density.

QUESTIONER: When I am communicating with you as Ra, are you at times individualized as an entity or am I speaking to an entire social memory complex?

RA: I am Ra. You speak with Ra. There is no separation. You would call it social memory complex, thus indicating manyness. To our understanding, you are speaking to an individualized portion of consciousness.

QUESTIONER: Am I always speaking to the same individualized portion of consciousness in each of the sessions?

RA: I am Ra. You speak to the same entity through a channel or instrument. This instrument is at times lower in vital energy. This will sometimes hamper our proceedings. However, this instrument has a great deal of faithfulness to the task and gives whatever it has to this task. Therefore, we may continue even when energy is low. This is why we usually speak to the ending of the session due to our estimation of the instrument's levels of vital energy.

QUESTIONER: I would like to make a point clear now that I am sure of myself. The people of this planet, following any religion or no religion at all, or having no intellectual knowledge at all of the Law of One, can still be harvested into the fourth density if they are of that vibration. Is that not correct?

RA: I am Ra. This is correct. However, you will find few who are harvestable whose radiance does not cause others to be aware of their, what you may call, spirituality, the quality of the mind/body/spirit complex distortion. Thus, it is not particularly probable that an entity would be completely unknown to his immediate acquaintances as an unusually radiant personality, even were this individual not caught up in any of the distortions of your so-called religious systems.

QUESTIONER: When Jesus of Nazareth incarnated, was there an attempt by the Orion group to discredit him in some way?

RA: I am Ra. This is correct.

QUESTIONER: Can you tell me what the Orion group did in order to try to cause his downfall?

RA: I am Ra. We may describe in general what occurred. The technique was that of building upon other negatively oriented information. This information had been given by the one whom your peoples called "Yahweh." This information involved many strictures upon behavior and promised power of the third-density, service to self nature. These two types of distortions were impressed upon those already oriented to think these thought-forms.

This eventually led to many challenges of the entity known as Jesus. It eventually led to one, sound vibration complex "Judas," as you call this entity, who believed that it was doing the appropriate thing in bringing about or forcing upon the one you call Jesus the necessity for bringing in the third-density planetary power distortion of third-density rule over others.

This entity, Judas, felt that if pushed into a corner, the entity you call Jesus would then be able to see the wisdom of using the power of intelligent infinity in order to rule others. The one you call Judas was mistaken in this estimation of the reaction of the entity Jesus, whose teach/learning was not oriented towards this distortion. This resulted in the destruction of the bodily complex of the one known as Jesus.

QUESTIONER: Then if the entity Jesus was fourth density and there are Wanderers on the planet today who came from fifth and sixth density, what was it that Jesus did that enabled him to be such a good healer, and could these fifth- and sixth-density beings here now do the same?

RA: I am Ra. Those who heal may be of any density which has the consciousness of the spirit. This includes third, fourth, fifth, sixth, and seventh. The third density can be one in which healing takes place just as the others. However, there is more illusory material to understand, to balance, to accept, and to move forward from.

The gate to intelligent infinity can only be opened when an understanding of the instreamings of intelligent energy are opened unto the healer. These are the so-called Natural Laws of your local space/time continuum and its web of electromagnetic sources or nexi of instreaming energy.

Know then, first, the mind and the body. Then as the spirit is integrated and synthesized, these are harmonized into a mind/body/spirit complex which can move among the dimensions and can open the gateway to intelligent infinity, thus healing self by light and sharing that light with others.

True healing is simply the radiance of the self causing an environment in which a catalyst may occur which initiates the recognition of self, by self, of the self-healing properties of the self.

QUESTIONER: How did Jesus learn this during his incarnation?

RA: I am Ra. This entity learned the ability by a natural kind of remembering at a very young age. Unfortunately, this entity first discovered his ability to penetrate intelligent infinity by becoming the distortion you call "angry" at a playmate. This entity was touched by the entity known as Jesus and was fatally wounded.

Thus the one known as Jesus became aware that there dwelt in him a terrible potential. This entity determined to discover how to use this energy for the good, not for the negative. This entity was extremely positively polarized and remembered more than most Wanderers do.

QUESTIONER: How did this aggressive action against a playmate affect Jesus in his spiritual growth? Where did he go after his physical death?

RA: I am Ra. The entity you call Jesus was galvanized by this experience and began a lifetime of seeking and searching. This entity studied first day and night in its own religious constructs which you call Judaism and was learned enough to be a rabbi, as you call teach/learners of this particular rhythm or distortion of understanding, at a very young age.

At the age of approximately thirteen and one-half of your years, this entity left the dwelling place of its earthly family, as you would call it, and walked into many other places seeking further information. This went on sporadically until the entity was approximately twenty-five, at which time it returned to its family dwelling and learned and practiced the art of its earthly father.

When the entity had become able to integrate or synthesize all experiences, the entity began to speak to other-selves and teach/learn what it had felt during the preceding years to be of an worthwhile nature. The entity was absolved karmically of the destruction of an other-self when it was in the last portion of lifetime and spoke upon what you would call a cross, saying, "Father, forgive them, for they know not what they do." In forgiveness lies the stoppage of the wheel of action, or what you call karma.

QUESTIONER: What density is the entity known as Jesus in now?

RA: I am Ra. This information is harmless though unimportant. This entity studies now the lessons of the wisdom vibration, the fifth density, also called the light vibration.

QUESTIONER: In our culture there is a saying that he will return. Can you tell me if this is planned?

RA: I am Ra. I will attempt to sort out this question. It is difficult.

This entity became aware that it was not an entity of itself but operated as a messenger of the One Creator, whom this entity saw as love. This entity was aware that this cycle was in its last portion, and spoke to the effect that those of its consciousness would return at the harvest.

The particular mind/body/spirit complex you call Jesus is, as what you would call an entity, not to return except as a member of the Confederation speaking through a channel. However, there are others of the identical congruency of consciousness that will welcome those to the fourth density. This is the meaning of the returning.

QUESTIONER: Can you tell me why you say that the Earth will be fourth density positive instead of fourth density negative, since there seems to be much negativity here now?

RA: I am Ra. The Earth seems to be negative. That is due to the quiet, shall we say, horror which is the common distortion which those good or positively oriented entities have towards the occurrences which are of your time/space present. However, those oriented and harvestable in the ways of service to others greatly outnumber those whose orientation towards service to self has become that of harvestable quality.

QUESTIONER: In other words, there will be fewer negative entities than positive entities harvested into the fourth density. Is this correct?

RA: I am Ra. This is correct. The great majority of your peoples will repeat third density.

QUESTIONER: How did Taras Bulba, Genghis Khan, and Rasputin get harvested prior to the harvest?

RA: I am Ra. It is the right/privilege/duty of those opening consciously the gate to intelligent infinity to choose the manner of their leaving of third density. Those of negative orientation who so achieve this right/duty most often choose to move forward in their learn/teaching of service to self.

QUESTIONER: Am I to understand that the harvest is to occur in the year 2011, or will it be spread out?

RA: I am Ra. This is an approximation. We have stated we have difficulty with your time/space. This is an appropriate probable/possible time/space nexus for harvest. Those who are not in incarnation at this time will be included in the harvest.

QUESTIONER: If an entity wants to be of service to others rather than service to self while he is in this third density, are there "best ways" of being of service to others, or is any way just as good as any other way?

RA: I am Ra. The best way to be of service to others has been explicitly covered in previous material. We will iterate briefly.

The best way of service to others is the constant attempt to seek to share the love of the Creator as it is known to the inner self. This involves self-knowledge and the ability to open the self to the other-self without hesitation. This involves, shall we say, radiating that which is the essence or the heart of the mind/body/spirit complex.

Speaking to the intention of your question, the best way for each seeker in third density to be of service to others is unique to that mind/body/spirit complex. This means that the mind/body/spirit complex must then seek within itself the intelligence of its own discernment as to the way it may best serve other-selves. This will be different for each. There is no best. There is no generalization. Nothing is known.

QUESTIONER: I don't wish to take up extra time asking questions over again. Some areas I consider important enough in relation to the Law of One to ask questions in a different way in order to get another perspective in the answer.

In the book *Oahspe* it states that if an entity goes over 51 percent service to others and is less than 50 percent service to self, then that entity is harvestable. Is this correct?

RA: I am Ra. This is correct if the harvesting is to be for the positive fourth-dimensional level.

QUESTIONER: What is to be the entity's percentage if he is to be harvested for the negative?

RA: I am Ra. The entity who wishes to pursue the path of service to self must attain a grade of five; that is, 5 percent service to others, 95 percent service to self. It must approach totality. The negative path is quite difficult to attain harvestability upon and requires great dedication.

QUESTIONER: Why is the negative path so much more difficult to attain harvestability upon than the positive?

RA: I am Ra. This is due to a distortion of the Law of One which indicates that the gateway to intelligent infinity be a gateway at the end of a straight and narrow path, as you may call it. To attain 51 percent dedication to the welfare of other-selves is as difficult as attaining a grade of 5 percent dedication to other-selves. The, shall we say, sinkhole of indifference is between those two.

QUESTIONER: Then if an entity is harvested into the fourth density with a grade of 51 percent for others and 49 percent for self, what level of the fourth density would he go into? I am assuming that there are different levels of the fourth density.

RA: I am Ra. This is correct. Each enters that sub-density which vibrates in accordance with the entity's understanding.

QUESTIONER: How many levels do we have here in the third density at this time?

RA: I am Ra. The third density has an infinite number of levels.

QUESTIONER: I've heard that there are seven astral and seven devachanic levels. Is this correct?

RA: I am Ra. You speak of some of the more large distinctions in levels in your inner planes. That is correct.

QUESTIONER: Who inhabits the astral and devachanic planes?

RA: I am Ra. Entities inhabit the various planes due to their vibration/nature. The astral plane varies from thought-forms in the lower extremities to enlightened beings who become dedicated to teach/learning in the higher astral planes.

In the devachanic planes, as you call them, are those whose vibrations are even more close to the primal distortions of love/light.

Beyond these planes there are others.

QUESTIONER: Are there seven sub-planes to what we call our physical plane here?

RA: I am Ra. You are correct. This is difficult to understand. There are an infinite number of planes. In your particular space/time continuum distortion, there are seven sub-planes of mind/body/spirit complexes. You will discover the vibrational nature of these seven planes as you pass through your experiential distortions, meeting other-selves of the various levels which correspond to the energy influx centers of the physical vehicle.

The invisible, or inner, third-density planes are inhabited by those who are not of body complex natures such as yours; that is, they do not collect about their spirit/mind complexes a chemical body. Nevertheless these entities are divided in what you may call an artificial dream within a dream into various levels. In the upper levels, desire to communicate knowledge back down to the outer planes of existence becomes less, due to the intensive learn/teaching which occurs upon these levels.

QUESTIONER: Is it necessary to penetrate one level at a time as we move through these planes?

RA: I am Ra. It has been our experience that some penetrate several planes at one time. Others penetrate them slowly. Some in eagerness attempt to penetrate the higher planes before penetrating the energies of the so-called more fundamental planes. This causes energy imbalance.

You will find ill health, as you call this distortion, to frequently be the result of a subtle mismatch of energies in which some of the higher energy levels are being activated by the conscious attempts of the entity while the entity has not penetrated the lower energy centers or sub-densities of this density.

QUESTIONER: Is there a "best way" to meditate?

RA: I am Ra. No.

QUESTIONER: At this time, near the end of the cycle, how are reincarnations into the physical allocated, shall we say, on this planet?

RA: I am Ra. Entities wishing to obtain critically needed experience in order to become harvestable are incarnated with priority over those who will, without too much probable/possible doubt, need to re-experience this density.

QUESTIONER: How long has this type of allocation been going on?

RA: I am Ra. This has been going on since the first individual entity became conscious of its need to learn the lessons of this density. This was the beginning of what you may call a seniority by vibration.

QUESTIONER: Can you explain what you mean by a seniority by vibration?

RA: I am Ra. This will be the final question of this session of working.

The seniority by vibration is the preferential treatment, shall we say, which follows the ways of the Law of One which encourages harvestable individuals, each individual becoming aware of the time of harvest and the need on a self-level to bend mind/body/spirit towards the learn/teaching of these lessons, by giving them priority in order that an entity may have the best possible chance, shall we say, in succeeding in this attempt.

May we ask at this time if there are any brief questions?

QUESTIONER: My only question is, what can we do to make the instrument more comfortable?

RA: I am Ra. This instrument is not wearing the appropriate apparel for this work. As inpourings occur in the regions of the, what you may call, seventh chakra as you speak of these energy centers, filtering through the sixth and so forth, the entity's other or base chakras become somewhat de-energized. Thus, this entity should be more careful in its selection of warm apparel for the part of the body complex you call the feet.

May we answer any other brief questions?

QUESTIONER: Then we want to put heavier clothing on the feet. Is this correct?

RA: I am Ra. This is correct.

I will leave this instrument now. I leave you in the love and the light of the One Infinite Creator. Adonai.

Session 18,
February 4, 1981

RA: I am Ra. I greet you in the love and the light of the Infinite Creator. We communicate now.

QUESTIONER: I was thinking last night that if I were in the place of Ra right now, the first distortion of the Law of One might cause me to mix some erroneous data with the true information that I was transmitting to this group. Do you do this?

RA: I am Ra. We do not intentionally do this. However, there will be confusion. It is not our intent in this particular project to create erroneous information, but to express in this confining ambiance of your language system the feeling of the Infinite Mystery of the One Creation in its infinite and intelligent unity.

QUESTIONER: Thank you. I have a question here that I will read: "Much of the mystic tradition of seeking on Earth holds the belief that the individual self must be erased or obliterated and the material world ignored for the individual to reach 'nirvana,' as it is called, or enlightenment. What is the proper role of the individual self and its worldly activities to aid an individual to grow more into the Law of One?"

RA: I am Ra. The proper role of the entity is in this density to experience all things desired, to then analyze, understand, and accept these experiences, distilling from them the love/light within them. Nothing shall be overcome. That which is not needed falls away.

The orientation develops due to analysis of desire. These desires become more and more distorted towards conscious application of love/light as the entity furnishes itself with distilled experience. We have found it to be inappropriate in the extreme to encourage the overcoming of any desires, except to suggest the imagination rather than the carrying out in the physical plane, as you call it, of those desires not consonant with the Law of One, thus preserving the primal distortion of free will.

The reason it is unwise to overcome is that overcoming is an unbalanced action creating difficulties in balancing in the time/space continuum. Overcoming thus creates the further environment for holding on to that which apparently has been overcome.

All things are acceptable in the proper time for each entity, and in experiencing, in understanding, in accepting, in then sharing with other-selves, the appropriate distortion shall be moving away from distortions of one kind to distortions of another which may be more consonant with the Law of One.

It is, shall we say, a shortcut to simply ignore or overcome any desire. It must instead be understood and accepted. This takes patience and experience which can be analyzed with care, with compassion for self and for other-self.

QUESTIONER: Basically I would say that to infringe upon the free will of another entity would be the basic thing never to do under the Law of One. Can you state any other breaking of the Law of One than this basic rule?

RA: I am Ra. As one proceeds from the primal distortion of free will, one proceeds to the understanding of the focal points of intelligent energy which have created the intelligences or the ways of a particular mind/body/spirit complex in its environment, both what you would call natural and what you would call man-made. Thus, the distortions to be avoided are those which do not take into consideration the distortions of the focus of energy of love/light, or shall we say, the Logos of this particular sphere or density. These include the lack of understanding of the needs of the natural environment, the needs of other-selves' mind/body/spirit complexes. These are many due to the various distortions of man-made complexes in which the intelligence and awareness of entities themselves have chosen a way of using the energies available.

Thus, what would be an improper distortion with one entity is proper with another. We can suggest an attempt to become aware of the other-self as self and thus do that action which is needed by other-self, understanding from the other-self's intelligence and awareness. In many cases this does not involve the breaking of the distortion of free will into a distortion or fragmentation called infringement. However, it is a delicate matter to be of service, and compassion, sensitivity, and an ability to empathize are helpful in avoiding the distortions of man-made intelligence and awareness.

The area or arena called the societal complex is an arena in which there are no particular needs for care, for it is the prerogative/honor/duty of those in the particular planetary sphere to act according to their free will for the attempted aid of the social complex.

Thus, you have two simple directives: awareness of the intelligent energy expressed in nature, awareness of the intelligent energy expressed in self to be shared when it seems appropriate by the entity with the social complex, and you have one infinitely subtle and various set of distortions of which you may be aware; that is, distortions with respect to self and other-selves not concerning free will but concerning harmonious relationships and service to others as other-selves would most benefit.

QUESTIONER: As an entity in this density grows from childhood, he becomes more aware of his responsibilities. Is there an age below which an entity is not responsible for his actions, or is he responsible from the time of his birth?

RA: I am Ra. An entity incarnating upon the Earth plane becomes conscious of self at a varying point in its time/space progress through the continuum. This may have a median, shall we say, of approximately fifteen of your months. Some entities become conscious of self at a period closer to incarnation, some at a period farther from this event. In all cases responsibility becomes retroactive from that point backward in the continuum so that distortions are to be understood by the entity and dissolved as the entity learns.

QUESTIONER: Then an entity four years old would be totally responsible for any actions that were against or inharmonious with the Law of One. Is this correct?

RA: I am Ra. This is correct. It may be noted that it has been arranged by your social complex structures that the newer entities to incarnation are to be provided with guides of a physical mind/body/spirit complex, thus being able to learn quickly what is consonant with the Law of One.

QUESTIONER: Who are these guides?

RA: I am Ra. These guides are what you call parents, teachers, and friends.

QUESTIONER: You stated yesterday that forgiveness is the eradicator of karma. I am assuming that balanced forgiveness for the full eradication of karma would require forgiveness not only of other-selves but also the forgiveness of self. Am I correct?

RA: I am Ra. You are correct. We will briefly expand upon this understanding in order to clarify.

Forgiveness of other-self is forgiveness of self. An understanding of this insists upon full forgiveness upon the conscious level of self and other-self, for they are one. A full forgiveness is thus impossible without the inclusion of self.

QUESTIONER: Thank you—a most important point.

You mentioned that there were a number of Confederations. Do all serve the Infinite Creator in basically the same way, or do some specialize in some particular types of service?

RA: I am Ra. All serve the One Creator. There is nothing else to serve, for the Creator is all that there is. It is impossible not to serve the Creator. There are simply various distortions of this service.

As in the Confederation which works with your peoples, each Confederation is a group of specialized individual social memory complexes, each doing that which it expresses to bring into manifestation.

QUESTIONER: Can you tell me how Yahweh communicated to Earth's people?

RA: I am Ra. This is a somewhat complex question.

The first communication was what you would call genetic. The second communication was the walking among your peoples to produce further genetic changes in consciousness. The third was a series of dialogues with chosen channels.

QUESTIONER: Can you tell me what these genetic changes were and how they were brought about?

RA: I am Ra. Some of these genetic changes were in a form similar to what you call the cloning process. Thus, entities incarnated in the image of the Yahweh entities. The second was a contact of the nature you know as sexual, changing the mind/body/spirit complex through the natural means of the patterns of reproduction devised by the intelligent energy of your physical complex.

QUESTIONER: Can you tell me specifically what they did in this case?

RA: I am Ra. We have answered this question. Please restate for further information.

QUESTIONER: Can you tell me the difference between the sexual programming prior to Yahweh's intervention and after intervention?

RA: I am Ra. This is a question which we can only answer by stating that intervention by genetic means is the same no matter what the source of this change.

QUESTIONER: Can you tell me Yahweh's purpose in making the genetic sexual changes?

RA: I am Ra. The purpose 75,000 years ago, as you measure time, was of one purpose only: that to express in the mind/body complex those characteristics which would lead to further and more speedy development of the spiritual complex.

QUESTIONER: How did these characteristics go about leading to the more spiritual development?

RA: I am Ra. The characteristics which were encouraged included sensitivity of all the physical senses to sharpen the experiences, and the strengthening of the mind complex in order to promote the ability to analyze these experiences.

QUESTIONER: When did Yahweh act to perform the genetic changes?

RA: I am Ra. The Yahweh group worked with those of the planet you call Mars 75,000 years ago in what you would call the cloning process. There are differences, but they lie in the future of your time/space continuum, and we cannot break the free-will Law of Confusion.

The 2,600, approximately, time was the second time—we correct ourselves: 3,600—approximately, the time of attempts by those of the Orion group during this cultural complex; this was a series of encounters in which the ones called Anak were impregnated with the new genetic coding by your physical complex means so that the organisms would be larger and stronger.

QUESTIONER: Why did they want larger and stronger organisms?

RA: I am Ra. The ones of Yahweh were attempting to create an understanding of the Law of One by creating mind/body complexes capable of grasping the Law of One. The experiment was a decided failure from the view of the desired distortions due to the fact that rather than assimilating the Law of One, it was a great temptation to consider the so-called social complex or subcomplex elite or different and better than other-selves, this one of the techniques of service to self.

QUESTIONER: Then the Orion group produced this larger body complex to create an elite so that the Law of One could be applied in what we call the negative sense?

RA: I am Ra. This is incorrect. The entities of Yahweh were responsible for this procedure in isolated cases as experiments in combating the Orion group.

However, the Orion group were able to use this distortion of mind/body complex to inculcate the thoughts of the elite rather than concentrations upon the learning/teaching of oneness.

QUESTIONER: Was Yahweh then of the Confederation?

RA: I am Ra. Yahweh was of the Confederation but was mistaken in its attempts to aid.

QUESTIONER: Then Yahweh's communications did not help or create what Yahweh wished for them to create. Is this correct?

RA: I am Ra. The results of this interaction were quite mixed. Where the entities were of a vibrational sum characteristic which embraced oneness, the manipulations of Yahweh were very useful. Wherein the entities of free will had chosen a less positively oriented configuration of sum total vibratory complex, those of the Orion group were able for the first time to make serious inroads upon the consciousness of the planetary complex.

QUESTIONER: Can you tell me specifically what allowed the most serious of these inroads to be made by the Orion group?

RA: I am Ra. This will be the final full question.
Specifically those who are strong, intelligent, etc., have a temptation to feel different from those who are less intelligent and less strong. This is a distorted perception of oneness with other-selves. It allowed the Orion group to form the concept of the holy war, as you may call it. This is a seriously distorted perception. There were many of these wars of a destructive nature.

QUESTIONER: Thank you very much. As you probably know, I will be working for the next three days, so we will possibly have another session tonight if you think it is possible. The next session after that would not be until four days from now. Do you believe another session tonight is possible?

RA: I am Ra. This instrument is somewhat weak. This is a distortion caused by lack of vital energy. Thus, nurturing the instrument in physical balancing will allow another session. Do you understand?

QUESTIONER: Not completely. What specifically shall we do for physical balancing?

RA: I am Ra. One—take care with the foodstuffs. Two—manipulate the physical complex to alleviate the distortion toward pain. Three—encourage a certain amount of what you would call your exercise. The final injunction: to take special care with the alignments this second session so that the entity may gain as much aid as possible from the various symbols. We suggest you check these symbols most carefully. This entity is slightly misplaced from the proper configuration. Not important at this time. More important when a second session is to be scheduled.
I am Ra. I leave you in the love and the light of the One Infinite Creator. Go forth, therefore, rejoicing in the power and the peace of the One Creator. Adonai.

Session 19,
February 8, 1981

RA: I am Ra. I greet you in the love and the light of the Infinite Creator. We communicate now.

QUESTIONER: We are concerned in this communication with the evolution of mind, body, and spirit. It seems to me that a good place to start would be the transition from the second to the third density, then to investigate in detail the evolution of third-density entities of Earth, paying particular attention to the mechanisms which help or hinder that evolution.

Do all entities make a transition from second to third density, or are there some entities who have never gone through this transition?

RA: I am Ra. Your question presumes the space/time continuum understandings of the intelligent energy which animates your illusion. Within the context of this illusion, we may say that there are some that do not transfer from one particular density to another, for the continuum is finite.

In the understanding which we have of the universe or creation as one infinite being, its heart beating as alive in its own intelligent energy, it merely is one beat of the heart of this intelligence from creation to creation. In this context, each and every entity of consciousness has/is/will experienced/experiencing/experience each and every density.

QUESTIONER: Let's take the point at which an individualized entity of second density is ready for transition to third. Is this second-density being what we would call animal?

RA: I am Ra. There are three types of second-density entities which become, shall we say, enspirited. The first is the animal. This is the most predominant. The second is the vegetable, most especially that which you call, sound vibration complex, "tree." These entities are capable of giving and receiving enough love to become individualized. The third is mineral. Occasionally a certain location/place, as you may call it, becomes energized to individuality through the love it receives and gives in relationship to a third-density entity which is in relationship to it. This is the least common transition.

QUESTIONER: When this transition from second to third density takes place, how does the entity, whether it be animal, [vegetable] tree, or mineral, become enspirited?

RA: I am Ra. Entities do not become enspirited. They become aware of the intelligent energy within each portion, cell, or atom, as you may call it, of its beingness.

This awareness is that which is awareness of that already given. From the infinite come all densities. The self-awareness comes from within, given the catalyst of certain experiences understanding, as we may call this particular energy, the upward spiraling of the cell or atom or consciousness.

You may then see that there is an inevitable pull toward the, what you may call, eventual realization of self.

QUESTIONER: Then after the transition into the third density, am I correct in assuming—we'll take Earth as an example—the entities would then look like us? They would be in human form? Is this correct?

RA: I am Ra. This is correct, taking your planetary sphere as an example.

QUESTIONER: When the first second-density entities became third density on this planet, was this with the help of the transfer of beings from Mars, or were there second-density beings who transferred into third density with no outside influence?

RA: I am Ra. There were some second-density entities which made the graduation into third density with no outside stimulus, but only the efficient use of experience.

Others of your planetary second density joined the third-density cycle due to harvesting efforts by the same sort of sending of vibratory aid as those of the Confederation send you now. This communication was, however, telepathic rather than telepathic/vocal or telepathic/written due to the nature of second-density beings.

QUESTIONER: Who sent the aid to the second-density beings?

RA: I am Ra. We call ourselves the Confederation of Planets in the Service of the Infinite Creator. This is a simplification in order to ease the difficulty of understanding among your people. We hesitate to use the term, sound vibration "understanding," but it is closest to our meaning.

QUESTIONER: Then did this second-density to third-density transition take place 75,000 years ago? Approximately?

RA: I am Ra. This is correct.

QUESTIONER: Where did the second-density beings get physical vehicles of third-density type to incarnate into?

RA: I am Ra. There were among those upon this second-density plane those forms which when exposed to third-density vibrations became the third density, as you would call the sound vibration, human entities.

That is, there was loss of body hair, as you would call it; the clothing of the body to protect it; the changing of the structure of the neck, jaw, and forehead in order to allow the easier vocalization; and the larger cranial development characteristic of third-density needs. This was a normal transfiguration.

QUESTIONER: Over how long a period of time was this transfiguration? It must have been very short.

RA: I am Ra. The assumption is correct, in our terms at least—within a generation and one-half, as you know these things. Those who had been harvested of this planet were able to use the newly created physical complex of chemical elements suitable for third-density lessons.

QUESTIONER: Can you tell me how this newly created physical complex was suited to third-density lessons, and what those lessons were?

RA: I am Ra. There is one necessity for third density. That necessity is self-awareness, or self-consciousness. In order to be capable of such, this chemical complex of body must be capable of abstract thought. Thus, the fundamental necessity is the combination of rational and intuitive thinking. This was transitory in the second-density forms operating largely upon intuition, which proved through practice to yield results.

The third-density mind was capable of processing information in such a way as to think abstractly and in what could be termed "useless" ways, in the sense of survival. This is the primary requisite.

There are other important ingredients: the necessity for a weaker physical vehicle to encourage the use of the mind, the development of the already present awareness of the social complex. These also being necessary: the further development of physical dexterity in the sense of the hand, as you call this portion of your body complex.

QUESTIONER: This seems to be a carefully planned or engineered stage of development. Can you tell me anything of the origin of this plan or its development?

RA: I am Ra. We go back to previous information. Consider and remember the discussion of the Logos. With the primal distortion of free will, each galaxy developed its own Logos. This Logos has complete free will in determining the paths of intelligent energy which promote the lessons of each of the densities given the conditions of the planetary spheres and the sun bodies.

QUESTIONER: I will make a statement then of my understanding and ask you if I am correct. There is a, what I would call, physical catalyst operating at all times upon the entities in third density. I assume this operates approximately the same way in second density. It is a catalyst which acts through what we call pain and emotion. Is the primary reason for the weakening of the physical body and the elimination of body hair etc. so that this catalyst would act more strongly upon the mind and therefore create the evolutionary process?

RA: I am Ra. This is not entirely correct, although closely associated with the distortions of our understanding. Consider, if you will, the tree for instance. It is self-sufficient. Consider, if you will, the third-density entity. It is self-sufficient only through difficulty and deprivation. It is difficult to learn alone, for there is a built-in handicap, at once the great virtue and the great handicap of third density. That is the rational/intuitive mind.

Thus, the weakening of the physical vehicle, as you call it, was designed to distort entities towards a predisposition to deal with each other. Thus, the lessons which approach a knowing of love can be begun.

This catalyst then is shared between peoples as an important part of each self's development as well as the experiences of the self in solitude and the synthesis of all experience through meditation. The quickest way to learn is to deal with other-selves. This is a much greater catalyst than dealing with the self. Dealing with the self without other-selves is akin to living without what you would call mirrors. Thus, the self cannot see the fruits of its beingness. Thus, each may aid each by reflection. This is also a primary reason for the weakening of the physical vehicle, as you call the physical complex.

QUESTIONER: Then we have second-density beings who have primarily motivation towards self and possibly a little motivation towards service to others with respect to their immediate family going into third density and carrying this bias with them but being in a position now where this bias will slowly be modified to one which is aimed toward a social complex and ultimately towards union with the all. Am I correct?

RA: I am Ra. You are correct.

QUESTIONER: Then the newest third-density beings who have just made the transition from second are still strongly biased towards self-service. There must be many other mechanisms to create an awareness of the possibility of service to others.

I am wondering, first, about the mechanism, and I am wondering when the split takes place where the entity is able to continue on the road to service to self that will eventually take him on to fourth density.

I'm assuming that an entity can start, say, in second density with service to self and continue right on through and just stay on what we would call the path of service to self and never be pulled over. Is this correct?

RA: I am Ra. This is incorrect. The second-density concept of serving self includes the serving of those associated with tribe or pack. This is not seen in second density as separation of self and other-self. All is seen as self since in some forms of second-density entities, if the tribe or pack becomes weakened, so does the entity within the tribe or pack.

The new or initial third density has this innocent, shall we say, bias or distortion towards viewing those in the family, the society, as you would call, perhaps, country, as self. Thus, though a distortion not helpful for progress in third density, it is without polarity.

The break becomes apparent when the entity perceives other-selves as other-selves and consciously determines to manipulate other-selves for the benefit of the self. This is the beginning of the road of which you speak.

QUESTIONER: Then, through free will, sometime within the third-density experience, the path splits and the entity consciously chooses—or he probably doesn't consciously choose. Does the entity consciously choose this path of the initial splitting point?

RA: I am Ra. We speak in generalities, which is dangerous for always inaccurate. However, we realize you look for the overview, so we will eliminate anomalies and speak of majorities.

The majority of third-density beings is far along the chosen path before realization of that path is conscious.

QUESTIONER: Can you tell me what bias creates the momentum towards the chosen path of service to self?

RA: I am Ra. We can speak only in metaphor. Some love the light. Some love the darkness. It is a matter of the unique and infinitely various Creator choosing and playing among its experiences as a child upon a picnic. Some enjoy the picnic and find the sun beautiful, the food delicious, the games refreshing, and glow with the joy of creation. Some find the night delicious, their picnic being pain, difficulty, sufferings of others, and the examination of the perversities of nature. These enjoy a different picnic.

All these experiences are available. It is the free will of each entity which chooses the form of play, the form of pleasure.

QUESTIONER: I assume that an entity on either path can decide to change paths at any time and possibly retrace steps, the path-changing being more difficult the farther along the path the change is made. Is this correct?

RA: I am Ra. This is incorrect. The further an entity has, what you would call, polarized, the more easily this entity may change polarity, for the more power and awareness the entity will have.

Those truly helpless are those who have not consciously chosen but who repeat patterns without knowledge of the repetition or the meaning of the pattern.

QUESTIONER: I believe we have a very important point here. It then seems that there is an extreme potential in this polarization, the same as there is in electricity. We have a positive and negative pole. The more you build the charge on either of these, the more the potential difference and the greater the ability to do work, as we call it in the physical.

This would seem to me to be the same analogy that we have in consciousness. Is this correct?

RA: I am Ra. This is precisely correct.

QUESTIONER: Then it would seem that there is a relationship between what we perceive as a physical phenomenon, say the electrical phenomenon, and the phenomenon of consciousness in that they, having stemmed from the One Creator, are practically identical but have different actions. Is this correct?

RA: I am Ra. Again we oversimplify to answer your query.

The physical complex alone is created of many, many energy or electromagnetic fields interacting due to intelligent energy, the mental configurations or distortions of each complex further adding fields of electromagnetic energy and distorting the physical complex patterns of energy, the spiritual aspect serving as a further complexity of fields which is of itself perfect but which can be realized in many distorted and unintegrated ways by the mind and body complexes of energy fields.

Thus, instead of one, shall we say, magnet with one polarity, you have in the body/mind/spirit complex one basic polarity expressed in what you would call violet-ray energy, the sum of the energy fields, but which is affected by thought of all kinds generated by the mind complex, by distortions of the body complex, and by the numerous relationships between the microcosm which is the entity and the macrocosm in many forms which you may represent by viewing the stars, as you call them, each with a contributing energy ray which enters the electromagnetic web of the entity due to its individual distortions.

QUESTIONER: Is this then the root of what we call astrology?

RA: I am Ra. This will be the last full question of this session.

The root of astrology, as you speak it, is one way of perceiving the primal distortions which may be predicted along probability/possibility lines given, shall we say, cosmic orientations and configurations at the time of the entrance into the physical/mental complex of the spirit and at the time of the physical/mental/spiritual complex into the illusion.

This then has the possibility of suggesting basic areas of distortion. There is no more than this. The part astrology plays is likened unto that of one root among many.

QUESTIONER: Is there anything that we can do to make the instrument more comfortable?

RA: I am Ra. This instrument is well aligned. You are being very conscientious. We request you take more care in being assured that this instrument is wearing footwear of what you would call vibratory sound complex "shoes."

I am Ra. I leave you in the love and the light of the One Infinite Creator. Go forth, therefore, rejoicing in the power and the peace of the One Creator. Adonai.

Session 20,
February 9, 1981

RA: I am Ra. I greet you in the love and the light of the Infinite Creator. I communicate now.

QUESTIONER: To go back a bit, what happened to the second-density entities who were unharvestable when the third density began? I assume that there were some that did not make it into third density.

RA: I am Ra. The second density is able to repeat during third density a portion of its cycle.

QUESTIONER: Then the second-density entities who did not get harvested at the beginning of this 75,000-year period, some are still on this planet. Were any of these second-density entities harvested into the third density within the past 75,000 years?

RA: I am Ra. This has been increasingly true.

QUESTIONER: So more and more second-density entities are making it into third density. Can you give me an example of a second-density entity coming into the third density in the recent past?

RA: I am Ra. Perhaps the most common occurrence of second-density graduation during third-density cycle is the so-called pet.

For the animal which is exposed to the individualizing influences of the bond between animal and third-density entity, this individuation causes a sharp rise in the potential of the second-density entity so that upon the cessation of physical complex, the mind/body complex does not return into the undifferentiated consciousness of that species, if you will.

QUESTIONER: Then can you give me an example of an entity in third density that was just previously a second-density entity? What type of entity do they become here?

RA: I am Ra. As a second-density entity returns as third density for the beginning of this process of learning, the entity is equipped with the lowest, if you will so call these vibrational distortions, forms of third-density consciousness; that is, equipped with self-consciousness.

QUESTIONER: This would be a human in our form, then, who would be beginning the understandings of third density. Is this correct?

RA: I am Ra. This is correct.

QUESTIONER: Speaking of the rapid change that occurred in the physical vehicle from second to third density: this occurred, you said, in approximately a generation and a half. Body hair was lost and there were structural changes.

I am aware of the physics of Dewey B. Larson, who states that all is motion or vibration. Am I correct in assuming that the basic vibration that makes up the physical world changes, thus creating a different set of parameters, shall I say, in this short period of time between density changes allowing for the new type of being? Am I correct?

RA: I am Ra. This is correct.

QUESTIONER: Is the physics of Dewey Larson correct?

RA: I am Ra. The physics of sound vibrational complex, Dewey, is a correct system as far as it is able to go. There are those things which are not included in this system. However, those coming after this particular entity, using the basic concepts of vibration and the study of vibrational distortions, will begin to understand that which you know as gravity and those things you consider as "n" dimensions. These things are necessary to be included in a more universal, shall we say, physical theory.

QUESTIONER: Did this entity, Dewey, then bring this material through for use primarily in the fourth density?

RA: I am Ra. This is correct.

QUESTIONER: Yesterday we were talking about the split that occurs when an entity either consciously or unconsciously chooses the path that leads to either service to others or service to self. The philosophical question of why such a split even exists came up. It was my impression that just as it is in electricity, if we have no polarity in electricity we have no electricity; we have no action. Therefore, I am assuming that it is the same in consciousness. If we have no polarity in consciousness, we also have no action or experience. Is this correct?

RA: I am Ra. This is correct. You may use the general term "work."

QUESTIONER: Then the concept of service to self and service to others is mandatory if we wish to have work, whether it be work in consciousness or work of a mechanical nature in the Newtonian concept in the physical. Is this correct?

RA: I am Ra. This is correct with one addendum. The coil, as you may understand this term, is wound, is potential, is ready. The thing that is missing without polarizing is the charge.

QUESTIONER: Then the charge is provided by individualized consciousness. Is this correct?

RA: I am Ra. The charge is provided by the individualized entity using the inpourings and instreamings of energy by the choices of free will.

QUESTIONER: Thank you. As soon as the third density started 75,000 years ago and we have incarnate third-density entities, what was the average human life span at that time?

RA: I am Ra. At the beginning of this particular portion of your space/time continuum, the average life span was approximately nine hundred of your years.

QUESTIONER: Did the average life span grow longer or shorter as we progressed into third-density experience?

RA: I am Ra. There is a particular use for the span of life in this density, and, given the harmonious development of the learning/teachings of this density, the life span of the physical complex would remain the same throughout the cycle. However, your particular planetary sphere developed vibrations by the second major cycle, which shortened the life span dramatically.

QUESTIONER: Assuming a major cycle is 25,000 years, at the end of the first major cycle, what was the life span?

RA: I am Ra. The life span at the end of the first cycle which you call major was approximately seven hundred of your years.

QUESTIONER: Then in 25,000 years we lost two hundred years of life span. Is this correct?

RA: I am Ra. This is correct.

QUESTIONER: Can you tell me the reason for this shortening of life span?

RA: I am Ra. The causes of this shortening are always an ineuphonious or inharmonious relational vibration between other-selves. In the first cycle this was not severe due to the dispersion of peoples, but there was the growing feeling complex/distortion towards separateness from other-selves.

QUESTIONER: I am assuming that at the start of one of these cycles there could have been either a positive polarization that would generally occur over the 25,000 years or a negative polarization. Is the reason for the negative polarization and the shortening of the life span the influx of entities from Mars who had already polarized somewhat negatively?

RA: I am Ra. This is incorrect. There was not a strong negative polarization due to this influx. The lessening of the life span was due primarily to the lack of the building of positive orientation. When there is no progress, those conditions which grant progress are gradually lost. This is one of the difficulties of remaining unpolarized. The chances, shall we say, of progress become steadily less.

QUESTIONER: The way I understand it, at the beginning of this 75,000-year cycle, then, we had a mixture of entities—those who had graduated from second density on Earth to become third density and then a group of entities transferred from the planet Mars to continue third density here. Is this correct?

RA: I am Ra. This is correct. You must remember that those transferred to this sphere were in the middle of their third density, so that this third density was an adaptation rather than a beginning.

QUESTIONER: What percentage of the entities who were here in third density at that time were Martian, and what percentage were harvested from Earth's second density?

RA: I am Ra. There were perhaps one-half of the third-density population being entities from the Red Planet, Mars, as you call it. Perhaps one-quarter from second density of your planetary sphere. Approximately one-quarter from other sources, other planetary spheres whose entities chose this planetary sphere for third-density work.

QUESTIONER: When they incarnated here, did all three of these types mix together in societies or groups or were they separated by groups and society?

RA: I am Ra. They remained largely unmixed.

QUESTIONER: Then did this unmixing lend to a possibility of warlike energy between groups?

RA: I am Ra. This is correct.

QUESTIONER: Did this help to reduce the life span?

RA: I am Ra. This did reduce the life span, as you call it.

QUESTIONER: Can you tell me why 900 years is the optimum life span?

RA: I am Ra. The mind/body/spirit complex of third density has perhaps one hundred times as intensive a program of catalytic action from which to distill distortions and learn/teachings than any other of the densities. Thus the learn/teachings are most confusing to the mind/body/spirit complex, which is, shall we say, inundated by the ocean of experience.

During the first, shall we say, perhaps 150 to 200 of your years as you measure time, a mind/body/spirit complex is going through the process of a spiritual childhood. The mind and the body are not enough in a disciplined configuration to lend clarity to the spiritual influxes. Thus, the remaining time span is given to optimize the understandings which result from experience itself.

QUESTIONER: Then at present it would seem that our current life span is much too short for those who are new to third-density lessons. Is this correct?

RA: I am Ra. This is correct. Those entities which have, in some way, learned/taught themselves the appropriate distortions for rapid growth can now work within the confines of the shorter life span. However, the greater preponderance of your entities find themselves in what may be considered a perpetual childhood.

QUESTIONER: Back in the first 25,000-year period, or major cycle, what type of aid was given by the Confederation to the entities who were in this 25,000-year period so that they would have the opportunity to grow?

RA: I am Ra. The Confederation members which dwell in inner-plane existence within the planetary complex of vibratory densities worked with these entities. There was also the aid of one of the Confederation which worked with those of Mars in making the transition.

For the most part, the participation was limited, as it was appropriate to allow the full travel of the workings of the confusion mechanism to operate in order for the planetary entities to develop that which they wished in, shall we say, freedom within their own thinking.

It is often the case that a third-density planetary cycle will take place in such a way that there need be no outside, shall we say, or other-self aid in the form of information. Rather, the entities themselves are able to work themselves towards the appropriate polarizations and goals of third-density learn/teachings.

QUESTIONER: I make the assumption that if maximum efficiency had been achieved in this 25,000-year period, the entities would have polarized either toward service to self or toward service to others, one or the other. This would have made them harvestable at the end of that 25,000-year period, in which case they would have had to move to another planet because this one would have been third density for 50,000 more years. Is this correct?

RA: I am Ra. Let us untangle your assumption, which is complex and correct in part.

The original desire is that entities seek and become one. If entities can do this in a moment, they may go forward in a moment, and, thus, were this to occur in a major cycle, indeed, the third-density planet would be vacated at the end of that cycle.

It is, however, more towards the median or mean, shall we say, of third-density developments throughout the one infinite universe that there be a small harvest after the first cycle; the remainder having significantly polarized, the second cycle having a much larger harvest; the remainder being even more significantly polarized, the third cycle culminating the process and the harvest being completed.

QUESTIONER: Was the Confederation watching to see and expecting to see a harvest at the end of the 25,000-year period in which a percentage would be harvestable fourth-density positive and a percentage harvestable fourth-density negative?

RA: I am Ra. That is correct. You may see our role in the first major cycle as that of the gardener who, knowing the season, is content to wait for the spring. When the springtime does not occur, the seeds do not sprout; then it is that the gardener must work in the garden.

QUESTIONER: Am I to understand, then, that there was neither a harvest of positive or negative entities at the end of that 25,000 years?

RA: I am Ra. This is correct. Those whom you call the Orion group made one attempt to offer information to those of third density during that cycle. However, the information did not fall upon the ears of any who were concerned to follow this path to polarity.

QUESTIONER: What technique did the Orion group use to give this information?

RA: I am Ra. The technique used was of two kinds: one, the thought transfer or what you may call "telepathy"; two, the arrangement of certain stones in order to suggest strong influences of power, this being those of statues and of rock formations in your Pacific areas, as you now call them, and to an extent in your Central American regions, as you now understand them.

QUESTIONER: Were you speaking in part of the stone heads of Easter Island?

RA: I am Ra. This is correct.

QUESTIONER: How would such stone heads influence the people to take the path of service to self?

RA: I am Ra. Picture, if you will, the entities living in such a way that their mind/body/spirit complexes are at what seems to be the mercy of forces which they cannot control. Given a charged entity such as a statue or a rock formation charged with nothing but power, it is possible for the free will of those viewing this particular structure or formation to ascribe to this power, power over those things which cannot be controlled. This, then, has the potential for the further distortion to power over others.

QUESTIONER: How were these stone heads constructed?

RA: I am Ra. These were constructed by thought after a scanning of the deep mind, the trunk of mind tree, looking at the images most likely to cause the experience of awe in the viewer.

QUESTIONER: Did the Orion entities do this themselves? Did they do this in the physical? Did they land, or did they do it from mental planes?

RA: I am Ra. Nearly all of these structures and formations were constructed at a distance by thought. A very few were created in later times in imitation of original constructs by entities upon your Earth plane/density.

QUESTIONER: What density Orion entity did the construction of these heads?

RA: I am Ra. The fourth density, the density of love or understanding, was the density of the particular entity which offered this possibility to those of your first major cycle.

QUESTIONER: You use the same nomenclature for the fourth-density negative as for the fourth-density positive. Both are called the dimension of love or of understanding. Is this correct?

RA: I am Ra. This is correct. Love and understanding, whether it be of self or of self toward other-self, is one.

QUESTIONER: What was the approximate date in years past of the construction of these heads?

RA: I am Ra. This approximately was 60,000 of your years in the past time/space of your continuum.

QUESTIONER: What structures were built in South America?

RA: I am Ra. In this location were fashioned some characteristic statues, some formations of what you call rock and some formations involving rock and earth.

QUESTIONER: Were the lines at Nazca included in this?

RA: I am Ra. This is correct.

QUESTIONER: Since these can only be seen from an altitude, of what benefit were they?

RA: I am Ra. The formations were of benefit because charged with energy of power.

QUESTIONER: I'm a little confused. These lines at Nazca are hardly understandable for an entity walking on the surface. He cannot see anything but disruption of the surface. However, if you go up to a high altitude you can see the patterns. How was it of benefit to the entities walking on the surface?

RA: I am Ra. At the remove of the amount of time/space which is now your present, it is difficult to perceive that at the time/space 60,000 years ago, the Earth was formed in such a way as to be visibly arranged in powerful structural designs, from the vantage point of distant hills.

QUESTIONER: In other words, at that time there were hills overlooking these lines?

RA: I am Ra. This will be the last full question of this session.

The entire smoothness, as you see this area now, was built up in many places in hills. The time/space continuum has proceeded with wind and weather, as you would say, to erode to a great extent both the somewhat formidable structures of earth designed at that time and the nature of the surrounding countryside.

QUESTIONER: I think I understand then that these lines are just the faint traces of what used to be there?

RA: I am Ra. This is correct.

QUESTIONER: Thank you. We need to know whether or not it is possible to continue with another session today and whether there is anything that we can do to make the instrument more comfortable?

RA: I am Ra. It is possible. We ask that you observe carefully the alignment of the instrument. Otherwise, you are conscientious.

Is there any short query before we close?

QUESTIONER: I intend in the next session to focus upon the development of the positively oriented entities in the first 25,000 years. I know you can't make suggestions. Can you give me any comment on this at all?

RA: I am Ra. The choices are yours according to your discernment.

I am Ra. I leave you in the love and the light of the One Infinite Creator. Adonai.

Session 21,
February 10, 1981

RA: I am Ra. I greet you in the love and the light of the Infinite Creator. I communicate now.

QUESTIONER: I have a couple of questions that I don't want to forget to ask in this period, so I will ask them first.

The first question is: Would the future content of this book be affected in any way if the instrument reads the material that we have already obtained?

RA: I am Ra. The future, as you measure in time/space, communications which we offer through this instrument have no connection with the instrument's mind complex. This is due to two things: first, the fidelity of the instrument in dedicating its will to the service of the Infinite Creator; secondly, the distortion/understanding of our social memory complex that the most efficient way to communicate material with as little distortion as possible, given the necessity of the use of sound vibration complexes, is to remove the conscious mind complex from the spirit/mind/body complex so that we may communicate without reference to any instrument's orientation.

QUESTIONER: Do you use the instrument's vocabulary or your own vocabulary to communicate with us?

RA: I am Ra. We use the vocabulary of the language with which you are familiar. This is not the instrument's vocabulary. However, this particular mind/body/spirit complex retains the use of a sufficiently large number of sound vibration complexes that the distinction is often without any importance.

QUESTIONER: So at the start of this 75,000-year cycle, we know that the quarantine was fully set up. I am assuming then that the Guardians were aware of the infringements on the free will that would occur if they didn't set this up at that time, and therefore did it. Is this correct?

RA: I am Ra. This is partially incorrect. The incorrectness is as follows: those entities whose third-density experience upon your Red Planet was brought to a close prematurely were aided genetically while being transferred to this third density. This, although done in a desire to aid, was seen as infringement upon free will. The light quarantine which consists of the Guardians, or gardeners as you may call them, which would have been in effect was intensified.

QUESTIONER: When the 75,000-year cycle started, the life span was approximately nine hundred years, average. What was the process and scheduling mechanism, shall I say, of reincarnation at that time, and how did the time in between incarnations into third-density physical apply to the growth of the mind/body/spirit complex?

RA: I am Ra. This query is more complex than most. We shall begin. The incarnation pattern of the beginning third-density mind/body/spirit complex begins in darkness, for you may think or consider of your density as one of, as you may say, a sleep and a forgetting. This is the only plane of forgetting. It is necessary for the third-density entity to forget so that the mechanisms of confusion or free will may operate upon the newly individuated consciousness complex.

Thus, the beginning entity is one in all innocence oriented towards animalistic behavior using other-selves only as extensions of self for the preservation of the all-self. The entity becomes slowly aware that it has needs, shall we say, that are not animalistic; that is, that are useless for survival. These needs include the need for companionship, the need for laughter, the need for beauty, the need to know the universe about it. These are the beginning needs.

As the incarnations begin to accumulate, further needs are discovered: the need to trade, the need to love, the need to be loved, the need to elevate animalistic behaviors to a more universal perspective.

During the first portion of third-density cycles, incarnations are automatic and occur rapidly upon the cessation of energy complex of the physical vehicle. There is small need to review or to heal the experiences of the incarnation. As, what you would call, the energy centers begin to be activated to a higher extent, more of the content of experience during incarnation deals with the lessons of love.

Thus the time, as you may understand it, between incarnations is lengthened to give appropriate attention to the review and the healing of experiences of the previous incarnation. At some point in third density, the green-ray energy center becomes activated and at that point incarnation ceases to be automatic.

QUESTIONER: When incarnation ceases to be automatic I am assuming that the entity can decide when he needs to incarnate for the benefit of his own learning. Does he also select his parents?

RA: I am Ra. This is correct.

QUESTIONER: At this time in our cycle, near the end, what percentage of the entities incarnating are making their own choices?

RA: I am Ra. The approximate percentage is 54 percent.

QUESTIONER: Thank you. During this first 25,000-year cycle was there any industrial development at all, any machinery available to the people?

RA: I am Ra. Using the term "machine" to the meaning which you ascribe, the answer is no. However, there were, shall we say, various implements of wood and rock which were used in order to obtain food and for use in aggression.

QUESTIONER: At the end of this first 25,000-year cycle was there any physical change that occurred rapidly like that which occurs at the end of a 75,000-year cycle, or is this just an indexing time for harvesting period?

RA: I am Ra. There was no change except that which according to intelligent energy, or what you may term physical evolution, suited physical complexes to their environment, this being of the color of the skin due to the area of the sphere upon which entities lived; the gradual growth of peoples due to improved intake of foodstuffs.

QUESTIONER: Then, at the end of the first 25,000-year period, I am guessing that the Guardians discovered that there was no harvest of either positively or negatively oriented entities. Tell me then what happened. What action was taken?

RA: I am Ra. There was no action taken except to remain aware of the possibility of a calling for help or understanding among the entities of this density. The Confederation is concerned with the preservation of the conditions conducive to learning. This, for the most part, revolves about the primal distortion of free will.

QUESTIONER: Then the Confederation gardeners did nothing until some of the plants in their garden called them for help. Is this correct?

RA: I am Ra. This is correct.

QUESTIONER: When did the first call occur, and how did it occur?

RA: I am Ra. The first calling was approximately 46,000 of your years ago. This calling was of those of Maldek. These entities were aware of their need for rectifying the consequences of their action and were in some confusion in an incarnate state as to the circumstances of their incarnation; the unconscious being aware, the conscious being quite confused. This created a calling. The Confederation sent love and light to these entities.

QUESTIONER: How did the Confederation send this love and light? What did they do?

RA: I am Ra. There dwell within the Confederation planetary entities who from their planetary spheres do nothing but send love and light as pure streamings to those who call. This is not in the form of conceptual thought but of pure and undifferentiated love.

QUESTIONER: Did the first distortion of the Law of One then require that equal time, shall I say, be given to the self-service-oriented group?

RA: I am Ra. In this case this was not necessary for some of your time due to the orientation of the entities.

QUESTIONER: What was their orientation?

RA: I am Ra. The orientation of these entities was such that the aid of the Confederation was not perceived.

QUESTIONER: Since it was not perceived, it was not necessary to balance this. Is that correct?

RA: I am Ra. This is correct. What is necessary to balance is opportunity. When there is ignorance, there is no opportunity. When there exists a potential, then each opportunity shall be balanced, this balancing caused by not only the positive and negative orientations of those offering aid but also the orientation of those requesting aid.

QUESTIONER: Thank you very much. I apologize in being so stupid in stating my questions, but this has cleared up my understanding nicely.

Then in the second 25,000-year major cycle, was there any great civilization that developed?

RA: I am Ra. In the sense of greatness of technology there were no great societies during this cycle. There was some advancement among those of Deneb who had chosen to incarnate as a body in what you would call China.

There were appropriately positive steps in activating the green-ray energy complex in many portions of your planetary sphere, including the Americas, the continent which you call Africa, the island which you call Australia, and that which you know as India, as well as various scattered peoples.

None of these became what you would name great as the greatness of Lemuria or Atlantis is known to you due to the formation of strong social complexes and, in the case of Atlantis, very great technological understandings.

However, in the South American area of your planetary sphere as you know it, there grew to be a great vibratory distortion towards love. These entities were harvestable at the end of the second major cycle without ever having formed strong social or technological complexes.

This will be the final question in completion of this session. Is there a query we may answer quickly before we close, as this instrument is somewhat depleted?

QUESTIONER: I would just like to apologize for the confusion on my part in carrying on to this second 25,000 years.

I would like to ask if there is anything that we can do to make the instrument more comfortable? We would like to have a second session today.

RA: I am Ra. You may observe a slight misalignment between book, candle, and perpendicularity of censer. This is not significant, but as we have said, the cumulative effects upon this instrument are not well. You are conscientious. It is well to have a second session given the appropriate exercising and manipulation of this instrument's physical complex.

I am Ra. I leave you in the love and the light of the One Infinite Creator. Go forth, therefore, rejoicing in the power and the peace of the One Creator. Adonai.

Session 22,
February 10, 1981

RA: I am Ra. I greet you in the love and in the light of the One Infinite Creator. I communicate now.

QUESTIONER: I will ask a couple of questions to clear up the end of the second major cycle. Then we will go on to the third and last of the major cycles.

Can you tell me what was the average life span at the end of the second major cycle?

RA: I am Ra. By the end of the second major cycle the life span was as you know it, with certain variations among geographically isolated peoples more in harmony with intelligent energy and less bellicose.

QUESTIONER: Can you tell me the length of the average life span in years at the end of the second major cycle?

RA: I am Ra. The average is perhaps misleading. To be precise, many spent approximately thirty-five to forty of your years in one incarnation, with the possibility not considered abnormal of a life span approaching one hundred of your years.

QUESTIONER: Can I assume then that this drastic drop in average life span from seven hundred years to less than one hundred years in length during this second 25,000 years was caused by an intensification of a lack of service to others?

RA: I am Ra. This is in part correct. By the end of the second cycle, the Law of Responsibility had begun to be effectuated by the increasing ability of entities to grasp those lessons which there are to be learned in this density. Thus, entities had discovered many ways to indicate a bellicose nature, not only as tribes or what you call nations but in personal relationships, each with the other, the concept of barter having given way to the concept of money; also, the concept of ownership having won ascendancy over the concept of nonownership on an individual or group basis.

Each entity then was offered many more subtle ways of demonstrating either service toward others or service to self with the distortion of the manipulation of others. As each lesson was understood, those lessons of sharing, of giving, of receiving in free gratitude—each lesson could be rejected in practice.

Without demonstrating the fruits of such learn/teaching, the life span became greatly reduced, for the ways of honor/duty were not being accepted.

QUESTIONER: Would this shortened life span help the entity in any way in that he would have more time in between incarnations to review his mistakes, or would this shortened life span hinder him?

RA: I am Ra. Both are correct. The shortening of the life span is a distortion of the Law of One which suggests that an entity not receive more experience in more intensity than it may bear. This is only in effect upon an individual level and does not hold sway over planetary or social complexes.

Thus the shortened life span is due to the necessity for removing an entity from the intensity of experience which ensues when wisdom and love are, having been rejected, reflected back into the consciousness of the Creator without being accepted as part of the self, this then causing the entity to have the need for healing and for much evaluation of the incarnation.

The incorrectness lies in the truth that, given appropriate circumstances, a much longer incarnation in your space/time continuum is very helpful for continuing this intensive work until conclusions have been reached through the catalytic process.

QUESTIONER: You spoke of the South American group which was harvestable at the end of the second cycle. How long was their average life span at the end of the second cycle?

RA: I am Ra. This isolated group had achieved life spans stretching upwards towards the 900-year life span appropriate to this density.

QUESTIONER: I am assuming that the planetary action that we are experiencing now, which it seems shortens all life spans here, was not strong enough then to affect them and shorten their life span. Is this correct?

RA: I am Ra. This is correct. It is well to remember that at that nexus in space/time, great isolation was possible.

QUESTIONER: How many people populated the Earth totally at that time; that is, were incarnate in the physical at any one time?

RA: I am Ra. I am assuming that you intend to query regarding the number of incarnate mind/body/spirit complexes at the end of the second major cycle, this number being approximately 345,000 entities.

QUESTIONER: Approximately how many were harvestable out of that total number at the end of the cycle?

RA: I am Ra. There were approximately 150 entities harvestable.

QUESTIONER: Then as the next cycle started, were these the entities who stayed to work on the planet?

RA: I am Ra. These entities were visited by the Confederation and became desirous of remaining in order to aid the planetary consciousness. This is correct.

QUESTIONER: What type of visit did the Confederation make to this group of 150 entities?

RA: I am Ra. A light being appeared bearing that which may be called a shield of light. It spoke of the oneness and infinity of all creation and of those things which await those ready for harvest. It described in golden words the beauties of love as lived. It then allowed a telepathic linkage to progressively show those who were interested the plight of third density when seen as a planetary complex. It then left.

QUESTIONER: Did all of these entities then decide to stay and help during the next 25,000-year cycle?

RA: I am Ra. This is correct. As a group they stayed. There were those peripherally associated with this culture which did not stay. However, they were not able to be harvested either and so, beginning at the very highest, shall we say, of the sub-octaves of third density, repeated this density. Many of those who have been of the loving nature are not Wanderers but those of this particular origin of second cycle.

QUESTIONER: Are all of these entities still with us in this cycle?

RA: I am Ra. The entities repeating the third-density major cycle have, in some few cases, been able to leave. These entities have chosen to join their brothers and sisters, as you would call these entities.

QUESTIONER: Are any of these entities names that we would know from our historical past?

RA: I am Ra. The one known as sound vibration complex, Saint Augustine, is of such a nature. The one known as Saint Teresa of such a nature. The one known as Saint Francis of Assisi of such nature. These entities, being of monastic background, as you would call it, found incarnation in the same type of ambiance appropriate for further learning.

QUESTIONER: As the cycle terminated 25,000 years ago, what was the reaction of the Confederation to the lack of harvest?

RA: I am Ra. We became concerned.

QUESTIONER: Was any action taken immediately, or did you wait for a call?

RA: I am Ra. The Council of Saturn acted only in allowing the entry into third density of other mind/body/spirit complexes of third density, not Wanderers, but those who sought further third-density experience. This was done randomly so that free will would not be violated, for there was not yet a call.

QUESTIONER: Was the next action taken by the Confederation when a call occurred?

RA: I am Ra. This is correct.

QUESTIONER: Who or what group produced this call, and what action was taken by the Confederation?

RA: I am Ra. The calling was that of Atlanteans. This calling was for what you would call understanding with the distortion towards helping other-selves. The action taken is that which you take part in at this time: the impression of information through channels, as you would call them.

QUESTIONER: Was this first calling then at a time before Atlantis became technologically advanced?

RA: I am Ra. This is basically correct.

QUESTIONER: Then did the technological advancement of Atlantis come because of this call? I am assuming that the call was answered to bring them the Law of One, and the Law of Love as a distortion of the Law of One, but did they also then get technological information that caused them to grow into such a highly advanced technological society?

RA: I am Ra. Not at first. At about the same time as we first appeared in the skies over Egypt and continuing thereafter, other entities of the Confederation appeared unto Atlanteans who had reached a level of philosophical understanding, shall we misuse this word, which was consonant with communication, to encourage and inspire studies in the mystery of unity.

However, requests being made for healing and other understanding, information was passed having to do with crystals and the building of pyramids as well as temples, as you would call them, which were associated with training.

QUESTIONER: Was this training the same sort of initiatory training that was done with Egyptians?

RA: I am Ra. This training was different in that the social complex was more, shall we say, sophisticated and less contradictory and barbarous in its ways of thinking. Therefore the temples were temples of learning rather than the attempt being made to totally separate and put upon a pedestal the healers.

QUESTIONER: Then were there what we call priests trained in these temples?

RA: I am Ra. You would not call them priests in the sense of celibacy, of obedience, and of poverty. They were priests in the sense of those devoted to learning.

The difficulties became apparent as those trained in this learning began to attempt to use crystal powers for those things other than healing, as they were involved not only with learning but became involved with what you would call the governmental structure.

QUESTIONER: Was all of their information given to them in the same way that we are getting our information now, through an instrument such as this instrument?

RA: I am Ra. There were visitations from time to time, but none of importance in the, shall we say, historical passage of events in your space/time continuum.

QUESTIONER: Was it necessary for them to have a unified social complex for these visitations to occur? What conditions were necessary for these visitations to occur?

RA: I am Ra. The conditions were two: the calling of a group of people whose square overcame the integrated resistance of those unwilling to search or learn; the second requirement, the relative naiveté of those members of the Confederation who felt that direct transfer of information would necessarily be as helpful for Atlanteans as it had been for the Confederation entity.

QUESTIONER: I see, then. What you are saying is that these naive Confederation entities had had the same thing happen to them in the past, so they were doing the same thing for the Atlantean entities. Is this correct?

RA: I am Ra. This is correct. We remind you that we are one of the naive members of that Confederation and are still attempting to recoup the damage for which we feel responsibility. It is our duty as well as honor to continue with your peoples, therefore, until all traces of the distortions of our teach/learnings have been embraced by their opposite distortions, and balance achieved.

QUESTIONER: I see. Then I will state the picture I have of Atlantis, and you tell me if I am correct.

We have a condition where a large enough percentage of the people of Atlantis had started at least going in the direction of the Law of One and living the Law of One for their call to be heard by the Confederation. This call was heard because, using the Law of Squares, it overrode the opposition of the Atlantean entities who were not calling. The Confederation then used channels such as we use now in communication and also made contact directly, but this turned out to be a mistake because it was perverted by the entities of Atlantis. Is this correct?

RA: I am Ra. This is correct with one exception. There is only one law. That is the Law of One. Other so-called laws are distortions of this law, some of them primal and most important for progress to be understood. However, it is well that each so-called law, which we also call "way," be understood as a distortion rather than a law. There is no multiplicity to the Law of One.

This will be the final question in length of this working. Please ask it now.

QUESTIONER: Can you give me the average life span of the Atlantean population?

RA: I am Ra. The average life span, as we have said, is misleading. The Atlanteans were, in the early part of their cultural experience, used to life spans from 70 to 140 years, this being, of course, approximate. Due to increasing desire for power, the lifetime decreased rapidly in the later stages of the civilization, and, thus, the healing and rejuvenating information was requested.

Do you have any brief queries before we close?

QUESTIONER: Is there anything that we can do to make the instrument more comfortable? Is there anything that we can do for her?

RA: I am Ra. The instrument is well. It is somewhat less easy to maintain clear contact during a time when some or one of the entities in the circle of working is or are not fully conscious. We request that entities in the circle be aware that their energy is helpful for increasing the vitality of this contact. We thank you for being conscientious in the asking.

I am Ra. It is a great joy to leave you in the love and the light of the One Infinite Creator. Go forth, therefore, rejoicing in the power and the peace of the One Creator. Adonai.

Session 23,
February 11, 1981

RA: I am Ra. I greet you in the love and the light of the Infinite Creator. We communicate now.

QUESTIONER: You were speaking yesterday of the first contact made by the Confederation which occurred during our third major cycle. You stated that you appeared in the skies over Egypt at approximately the same time that aid was given to Atlantis. Can you tell me why you went to Egypt, and your orientation of attitude and thinking when you first went to Egypt?

RA: I am Ra. At the time of which you speak there were those who chose to worship the hawk-headed sun god, which you know as vibrational sound complex, "Horus." This vibrational sound complex has taken other vibrational sound complexes, the object of worship being the sun disc represented in some distortion.

We were drawn to spend some time, as you would call it, scanning the peoples for a serious interest amounting to a seeking with which we might help without infringement. We found that at that time the social complex was quite self-contradictory in its so-called religious beliefs, and, therefore, there was not an appropriate calling for our vibration. Thus, at that time, which you know of as approximately 18,000 of your years in the past, we departed without taking action.

QUESTIONER: You stated yesterday that you appeared in the skies over Egypt at that time. Were the Egyptian entities able to see you in their skies?

RA: I am Ra. This is correct.

QUESTIONER: What did they see, and how did this affect their attitudes?

RA: I am Ra. They saw what you would speak of as crystal-powered, bell-shaped craft.

This did not affect them due to their firm conviction that many wondrous things occurred as a normal part of a world, as you would call it, in which many, many deities had powerful control over supernatural events.

QUESTIONER: Did you have a reason for being visible to them rather than being invisible?

RA: I am Ra. This is correct.

QUESTIONER: Can you tell me your reason for being visible to them?

RA: I am Ra. We allowed visibility because it did not make any difference.

QUESTIONER: Then at this time you did not contact them. Can you answer the same question that I just asked with respect to your next attempt to contact the Egyptians?

RA: I am Ra. The next attempt was prolonged. It occurred over a period of time. The nexus, or center, of our efforts was a decision upon our parts that there was a sufficient calling to attempt to walk among your peoples as brothers.

We laid this plan before the Council of Saturn, offering ourselves as service-oriented Wanderers of the type which land directly upon the inner planes without incarnative processes. Thus we emerged, or materialized, in physical-chemical complexes representing as closely as possible our natures, this effort being to appear as brothers and spend a limited amount of time as teachers of the Law of One, for there was an ever-stronger interest in the sun body, and this vibrates in concordance with our particular distortions.

We discovered that for each word we could utter, there were thirty impressions we gave by our very being, which confused those entities we had come to serve. After a short period we removed ourselves from these entities and spent much time attempting to understand how best to serve those to whom we had offered ourselves in love/light.

The ones who were in contact with that geographical entity, which you know of as Atlantis, had conceived of the potentials for healing by use of the pyramid-shape entities. In considering this and making adjustments for the difference as in the distortion complexes of the two geographical cultures, as you would call them, we went before the Council again, offering this plan to the Council as an aid to the healing and the longevity of those in the area you know of as Egypt. In this way we hoped to facilitate the learning process as well as offer philosophy articulating the Law of One. Again the Council approved.

Approximately 11,000 of your years ago we entered, by thought-form, your—we correct this instrument. We sometimes have difficulty due to low vitality. Approximately 8,500 years ago, having considered these concepts carefully, we returned, never having left in thought, to the thought-form areas of your vibrational planetary complex and considered for some of your years, as you measure time, how to appropriately build these structures.

The first, the Great Pyramid, was formed approximately 6,000 of your years ago. Then, in sequence, after this performing by thought of the building or architecture of the Great Pyramid using the more, shall we say, local or earthly material rather than thought-form material to build other pyramidal structures.

This continued for approximately 1,500 of your years.

Meanwhile, the information concerning initiation and healing by crystal was being given. The one known as "Ikhnaton" was able to perceive this information without significant distortion and, for a time, moved, shall we say, heaven and earth in order to invoke the Law of One and to order the priesthood of these structures in accordance with the distortions of initiation and true compassionate healing. This was not to be long lasting.

At this entity's physical dissolution from your third-density physical plane, as we have said before, our teachings became quickly perverted; our structures once again went to the use of the so-called "royal" or those with distortions towards power.

QUESTIONER: When you spoke of pyramid healing, I am assuming that the primary healing was for the mind. Is this correct?

RA: I am Ra. This is partially correct. The healing, if it is to be effectuated, must be a funneling without significant distortion of the instreamings through the spiritual complex into the tree of mind. There are parts of this mind which block energies flowing to the body complex. In each case, in each entity, the blockage may well differ.

However, it is necessary to activate the sense of the spiritual channel or shuttle. Then whether the blockage is from spiritual to mental or from mental to physical, or whether it may simply be a random and purely physical trauma, healing may then be carried out.

QUESTIONER: When you started building the pyramid at Giza using thought, were you at that time in contact with incarnate Egyptians and did they observe this building?

RA: I am Ra. At that time we were not in close contact with incarnate entities upon your plane. We were responding to a general calling of sufficient energy in that particular location to merit action. We sent thoughts to all who were seeking our information.

The appearance of the pyramid was a matter of tremendous surprise. However, it was carefully designed to coincide with the incarnation of one known as a great architect. This entity was later made into a deity, in part due to this occurrence.

QUESTIONER: What name did they give this deity?

RA: I am Ra. This deity had the sound vibration complex, "Imhotep."

QUESTIONER: What can you tell me about the overall success of the pyramid? I understand that the pyramids were not successful in producing a rise in consciousness that was hoped for, but there must have been some success that came from them.

RA: I am Ra. We ask you to remember that we are of the Brothers and Sisters of Sorrow. When one has been rescued from that sorrow to a vision of the One Creator, then there is no concept of failure.

Our difficulty lay in the honor/responsibility of correcting the distortions of the Law of One which occurred during our attempts to aid these entities. The distortions are seen as responsibilities rather than failures; the few who were inspired to seek, our only reason for the attempt.

Thus, we would perhaps be in the position of paradox in that as one saw an illumination, we were what you call successful, and as others became more sorrowful and confused, we were failures. These are your terms. We persist in seeking to serve.

QUESTIONER: Can you tell me what happened to Ikhnaton after his physical death?

RA: I am Ra. This entity was then put through the series of healing and review of incarnational experiences which is appropriate for third-density experience. This entity had been somewhat in the distortions of power ameliorated by the great devotion to the Law of One. This entity thus resolved to enter a series of incarnations in which it had no distortions towards power.

QUESTIONER: Can you tell me what the average life span was for the Egyptians at the time of Ikhnaton?

RA: I am Ra. The average life span of these people was approximately thirty-five to fifty of your years. There was much, what you would call, disease of a physical complex nature.

QUESTIONER: Can you tell me of the reasons for the disease? I think I already know, but I think it might be good for the book to state this at this time.

RA: I am Ra. This is, as we have mentioned before, not particularly informative with regard to the Law of One. However, the land you know of as Egypt at that time was highly barbarous in its living conditions, as you would call them. The river which you call Nile was allowed to flood and to recede, thus providing the fertile grounds for the breeding of diseases which may be carried by insects. Also, the preparation of foodstuffs allowed diseases to form. Also, there was difficulty in many cases with sources of water, and water which was taken caused disease due to the organisms therein.

QUESTIONER: I was really questioning about the more basic cause of disease rather than the mechanism of its transmission. I was going back to the root of thought that created the possibility of disease. Could you briefly tell me if I am correct in assuming the general reduction of thought over the long time on planet Earth with respect to the Law of One created a condition whereby what we call disease could develop? Is this correct?

RA: I am Ra. This is correct and perceptive. You, as questioner, begin now to penetrate the outer teachings.

The root cause in this particular society was not so much a bellicose action, although there were, shall we say, tendencies, but rather the formation of a money system and a very active trading and development of those tendencies towards greed and power; thus, the enslaving of entities by other entities and the misapprehension of the Creator within each entity.

QUESTIONER: I understand, if I am correct, that a South American contact was also made. Can you tell me of the nature of your contact with respect to the attitude about the contact, its ramifications, the plan for the contact, and why the people were contacted in South America?

RA: I am Ra. This will be the final full question of this session.

The entities who walked among those in your South American continent were called by a similar desire upon the part of the entities therein to learn of the manifestations of the sun. They worshipped this source of light and life.

Thus, these entities were visited by light beings not unlike ourselves. Instructions were given and they were more accepted and less distorted than ours. The entities themselves began to construct a series of underground and hidden cities including pyramid structures.

These pyramids were somewhat at variance from the design that we had promulgated. However, the original ideas were the same with the addition of a desire or intention of creating places of meditation and rest, a feeling of the presence of the One Creator; these pyramids then being for all people, not only initiates and those to be healed.

They left this density when it was discovered that their plans were solidly in motion and, in fact, had been recorded. During the next approximately 3,500 years these plans became, though somewhat distorted, in a state of near completion in many aspects.

Therefore, as is the case of the breakings of the quarantine, the entity who was helping the South American entities along the South American ways you call in part the Amazon River went before the Council of Saturn to request a second attempt to correct in person the distortions which had occurred in their plans. This having been granted, this entity or social memory complex returned, and the entity chosen as messenger came among the peoples once more to correct the errors.

Again, all was recorded and the entity rejoined its social memory complex and left your skies.

As in our experience, the teachings were, for the most part, greatly and grossly perverted to the extent in later times of actual human sacrifice rather than healing of humans. Thus, this social memory complex is also given the honor/duty of remaining until those distortions are worked out of the distortion complexes of your peoples.

May we ask if there are any questions of a brief nature before we close?

QUESTIONER: Is there anything we can do to make the instrument more comfortable? Since you stated that she seems to be low on energy, is it possible to have another session later on today?

RA: I am Ra. All is well with alignments. However, this instrument would benefit from rest from the trance state for this diurnal period.

I am Ra. I leave this instrument now. I leave each of you in the love and the light of the One Infinite Creator. Go forth, therefore, rejoicing in the power and the peace of the One Creator. Adonai.

Session 24,
February 15, 1981

RA: I am Ra. I greet you in the love and in the light of the Infinite Creator. We communicate now.

QUESTIONER: We are a little concerned about the physical condition of the instrument. She has a slight congestion. If you can tell me of the advisability of the session, I would appreciate it.

RA: I am Ra. This instrument's vital energies of the physical complex are low. The session will be appropriately shortened.

QUESTIONER: In the last session you mentioned that in this last 25,000-year cycle the Atlanteans, Egyptians, and those in South America were contacted and then the Confederation departed. I understand that the Confederation did not come back for some time. Could you tell me of the reasons, consequences, and attitudes with respect to the next contact with those here on planet Earth?

RA: I am Ra. In the case of the Atlanteans, enlargements upon the information given resulted in those activities distorted towards bellicosity, which resulted in the final second Atlantean catastrophe 10,821 of your years in the past, as you measure time.

Many, many were displaced due to societal actions both upon Atlantis and upon those areas of what you would call North African deserts, to which some Atlanteans had gone after the first conflict. Earth changes continued due to these, what you would call, nuclear bombs and other crystal weapons, sinking the last great land masses approximately 9,600 of your years ago.

In the Egyptian and the South American experiments, results, though not as widely devastating, were as far from the original intention of the Confederation. It was clear to not only us but also to the Council and the Guardians that our methods were not appropriate for this particular sphere.

Our attitude thus was one of caution, observation, and continuing attempts to creatively discover methods whereby contact from our entities could be of service with the least distortion and, above all, with the least possibility of becoming perversions or antitheses of our intention in sharing information.

QUESTIONER: Thank you. Then I assume that the Confederation stayed away from Earth for a period of time. What condition created the next contact that the Confederation made?

RA: I am Ra. In approximately 3,600 of your years in the past, as you measure time, there was an influx of those of the Orion group, as you call them. Due to the increasing negative influences upon thinking and acting distortions, they were able to begin working with those whose impression from olden times, as you may say, was that they were special and different.

An entity of the Confederation, many, many thousands of your years in the past, the one you may call "Yahweh," had, by genetic cloning, set up these particular biases among these peoples who had come gradually to dwell in the vicinity of Egypt, as well as in many, many other places, by dispersion after the down-sinking of the land mass Mu. Here the Orion group found fertile soil in which to plant the seeds of negativity, these seeds, as always, being those of the elite, the different, those who manipulate or enslave others.

The one known as Yahweh felt a great responsibility to these entities. However, the Orion group had been able to impress upon the peoples the name Yahweh as the one responsible for this elitism. Yahweh then was able to take what you would call stock of its vibratory patterns and became, in effect, a more eloquently effective sound vibration complex.

In this complex the old Yahweh, now unnamed but meaning "He comes," began to send positively oriented philosophy. This was approximately in your past of 3,300 years. Thus, the intense portion of what has become known as Armageddon was joined.

QUESTIONER: How did the Orion group get through the quarantine 3,600 years ago? The random window effect?

RA: I am Ra. At that time this was not entirely so, as there was a proper calling for this information. When there is a mixed calling, the window effect is much more put into motion by the ways of the densities.

The quarantine in this case was, shall we say, not patrolled so closely, due to the lack of strong polarity, the windows thus needing to be very weak in order for penetration. As your harvest approaches, those forces of what you would call light work according to their call. The ones of Orion have the working only according to their call. This calling is in actuality not nearly as great.

Thus, due to the way of empowering or squares, there is much resistance to penetration. Yet, free will must be maintained and those desiring negatively oriented information, as you would call it, must then be satisfied by those moving through by the window effect.

QUESTIONER: Then Yahweh, in an attempt to correct what I might call

Session 25,
February 16, 1981

RA: I am Ra. I greet you in the love and the light of the Infinite Creator. We communicate now.

QUESTIONER: We shall now continue with the material from yesterday. You stated that about 3,000 years ago the Orion group left due to Diaspora. Was the Confederation then able to make any progress after the Orion group left?

RA: I am Ra. For many of your centuries, both the Confederation and the Orion Confederation busied themselves with each other upon planes above your own, shall we say, planes in time/space whereby machinations were conceived and the armor of light girded. Battles have been and are continuing to be fought upon these levels.

Upon the Earth plane, energies had been set in motion which did not cause a great deal of call. There were isolated instances of callings, one such taking place beginning approximately 2,600 of your years in the past in what you would call Greece (at this time) and resulting in writings and understandings of some facets of the Law of One. We especially note the one known as Thales and the one known as Heraclitus, those being of the philosopher career, as you may call it, teaching their students. We also point out the understandings of the one known as Pericles.

At this time there was a limited amount of visionary information which the Confederation was allowed to telepathically impress. However, for the most part, during this time empires died and rose according to the attitudes and energies set in motion long ago, not resulting in strong polarization but rather in that mixture of the positive and the warlike or negative which has been characteristic of this final minor cycle of your beingness.

QUESTIONER: You spoke of an Orion Confederation and of a battle being fought between the Confederation and the Orion Confederation. Is it possible to convey any concept of how this battle is fought?

RA: I am Ra. Picture, if you will, your mind. Picture it then in total unity with all other minds of your society. You are then single-minded, and that which is a weak electrical charge in your physical illusion is now an enormously powerful machine whereby thoughts may be projected as things.

In this endeavor the Orion group charges or attacks the Confederation armed with light. The result, a standoff, as you would call it, both energies being somewhat depleted by this and needing to regroup; the negative depleted through failure to manipulate, the positive depleted through failure to accept that which is given.

QUESTIONER: Could you amplify the meaning of what you mean by the "failure to accept that which is given"?

RA: I am Ra. At the level of time/space at which this takes place in the form of what you may call thought war, the most accepting and loving energy would be to so love those who wished to manipulate that those entities were surrounded and engulfed, transformed by positive energies.

This, however, being a battle of equals, the Confederation is aware that it cannot, on equal footing, allow itself to be manipulated in order to remain purely positive, for then though pure it would not be of any consequence, having been placed by the so-called powers of darkness under the heel, as you may say.

It is thus that those who deal with this thought war must be defensive rather than accepting in order to preserve their usefulness in service to others. Thusly, they cannot accept fully what the Orion Confederation wishes to give, that being enslavement. Thusly, some polarity is lost due to this friction, and both sides, if you will, must then regroup.

It has not been fruitful for either side. The only consequence which has been helpful is a balancing of the energies available to this planet so that these energies have less necessity to be balanced in this space/time, thus lessening the chances of planetary annihilation.

QUESTIONER: Does a portion of the Confederation then engage in this thought battle? What percent engages?

RA: I am Ra. This is the most difficult work of the Confederation. Only four planetary entities at any one time are asked to partake in this conflict.

QUESTIONER: What density are these four planetary entities?

RA: I am Ra. These entities are of the density of love, numbering four.

QUESTIONER: Would an entity of this density be more effective for this work than an entity of density five or six?

RA: I am Ra. The fourth density is the only density besides your own which, lacking the wisdom to refrain from battle, sees the necessity of the battle. Thus it is necessary that fourth-density social memory complexes be used.

QUESTIONER: Am I correct in assuming that both the Confederation and the Orion group utilize only their fourth densities in this battle, and that the fifth and sixth densities of the Orion group do not engage in this?

RA: I am Ra. This will be the last full question, as this entity's energies are low.

It is partially correct. Fifth- and sixth-density entities positive would not take part in this battle. Fifth-density negative would not take part in this battle. Thus, the fourth density of both orientations join in this conflict.

May we ask for a few short questions before we close?

QUESTIONER: I will first ask if there is anything that we can do to make the instrument more comfortable. I would also really like to know the orientation of the fifth-density negative for not participating in this battle.

RA: I am Ra. The fifth density is the density of light or wisdom. The so-called negative service to self entity in this density is at a high level of awareness and wisdom and has ceased activity except by thought. The fifth-density negative is extraordinarily compacted and separated from all else.

QUESTIONER: Thank you very much. We do not wish to deplete the instrument. Is there anything that we can do to make the instrument more comfortable?

RA: I am Ra. You are very conscientious. As we requested previously, it would be well to observe the angles taken by the more upright posture of the entity. It is causing some nerve blockage in the portion of the body complex called the elbows.

I am Ra. I leave you in the love and in the light of the One Infinite Creator. Go forth, then, rejoicing in the power and the peace of the One Creator. Adonai.

Session 26,
February 17, 1981

RA: I am Ra. I greet you in the love and the light of the Infinite Creator. I communicate now.

QUESTIONER: Is any of the changing that we have done here going to affect communication with the instrument in any way?
    Is what we've set up here all right?

RA: I am Ra. This is correct.

QUESTIONER: Do you mean that everything is satisfactory for continued communication?

RA: I am Ra. We meant that the changes affect this communication.

QUESTIONER: Should we discontinue communication because of these changes, or should we continue?

RA: I am Ra. You may do as you wish. However, we would be unable to use this instrument at this space/time nexus without these modifications.

QUESTIONER: Assuming that it is all right to continue, we're down to the last 3,000 years of this present cycle, and I was wondering if the Law of One in its written or spoken form has been made available within this last 3,000 years in any complete way such as we are doing now? Is it available in any other source?

RA: I am Ra. There is no possibility of a complete source of information of the Law of One in this density. However, certain of your writings passed on to you as your so-called holy works have portions of this law.

QUESTIONER: Does the Bible that we know have portions of this law in it?

RA: I am Ra. This is correct.

QUESTIONER: Can you tell me if any of the Old Testament has any of the Law of One?

RA: I am Ra. This is correct.

QUESTIONER: Which has more of the Law of One in it, the Old Testament or the New Testament?

RA: I am Ra. Withdrawing from each of the collections of which you speak the portions having to do with the Law of One, the content is approximately equal. However, the so-called Old Testament has a larger amount of negatively influenced material, as you would call it.

QUESTIONER: Can you tell me about what percentage is of Orion influence in both the Old and New Testaments?

RA: I am Ra. We prefer that this be left to the discretion of those who seek the Law of One. We are not speaking in order to judge. Such statements would be construed by some of those who may read this material as judgmental. We can only suggest a careful reading and inward digestion of the contents. The understandings will become obvious.

QUESTIONER: Thank you. Have you communicated with any of our population in the third-density incarnate state in recent times?

RA: I am Ra. Please restate, specifying "recent times" and the pronoun "you."

QUESTIONER: Has Ra communicated with any of our population in this century, in the last, say, eighty years?

RA: I am Ra. We have not.

QUESTIONER: Has the Law of One been communicated in the last eighty years by any other source to an entity in our population?

RA: I am Ra. The ways of One have seldom been communicated, although there are rare instances in the previous eighty of your years, as you measure time.

There have been many communications from fourth density due to the drawing towards the harvest to fourth density. These are the ways of universal love and understanding. The other teachings are reserved for those whose depth of understanding, if you will excuse this misnomer, recommend and attract such further communication.

QUESTIONER: Then did the Confederation step up its program of helping planet Earth sometime late in this last major cycle? It seems that they did from previous data, especially with the Industrial Revolution. Can you tell me the attitudes and the reasonings behind this?

Is there any reason other than they just wanted to produce more leisure time in the last, say, one hundred years of the cycle? Is this the total reason?

RA: I am Ra. This is not the total reason. Approximately two hundred of your years in the past, as you measure time, there began to be a significant amount of entities who by seniority were incarnating for learn/teaching purposes rather than for the lesser of the learn/teachings of those less aware of the process. This was our signal to enable communication to take place.

The Wanderers which came among you began to make themselves felt at approximately this time, firstly offering ideas or thoughts containing the distortion of free will. This was the prerequisite for further Wanderers which had information of a more specific nature to offer. The thought must precede the action.

QUESTIONER: I was wondering if the one, Abraham Lincoln, could have been a Wanderer?

RA: I am Ra. This is incorrect. This entity was a normal, shall we say, Earth being which chose to leave the vehicle and allow an entity to use it on a permanent basis. This is relatively rare compared to the phenomenon of Wanderers.

You would do better considering the incarnations of Wanderers such as the one known as "Thomas," the one known as "Benjamin."

QUESTIONER: I am assuming that you mean Thomas Edison and Benjamin Franklin?

RA: I am Ra. This is incorrect. We were intending to convey the sound vibration complex, Thomas Jefferson. The other, correct.

QUESTIONER: Thank you. Can you tell me where the entity who used Abraham Lincoln's body—what density he came from and where?

RA: I am Ra. This entity was fourth vibration.

QUESTIONER: I assume positive?

RA: I am Ra. That is correct.

QUESTIONER: Was his assassination in any way influenced by Orion or any other negative force?

RA: I am Ra. This is correct.

QUESTIONER: Thank you. In the recent past of the last thirty to forty years, the UFO phenomena have become known to our population. What was the original reason for the increase in what we call UFO activity in the past forty years?

RA: I am Ra. Information which Confederation sources had offered to your entity, Albert [Einstein], became perverted, and instruments of destruction began to be created, examples of this being the Manhattan Project and its product.

Information offered through Wanderer, sound vibration, Nikola, also was experimented with for potential destruction: example, your so-called Philadelphia Experiment.

Thus, we felt a strong need to involve our thought-forms in whatever way we of the Confederation could be of service in order to balance these distortions of information meant to aid your planetary sphere.

QUESTIONER: Then what you did, I am assuming, is to create an air of mystery with the UFO phenomenon, as we call it, and then by telepathy send many messages which could be accepted or rejected under the Law of One so that the population would start thinking seriously about the consequences of what it was doing. Is this correct?

RA: I am Ra. This is partially correct. There are other services we may perform. Firstly, the integration of souls or spirits, if you will, in the event of use of these nuclear devices in your space/time continuum. This the Confederation has already done.

QUESTIONER: I don't fully understand what you mean by that. Could you expand on that a little bit?

RA: I am Ra. The use of intelligent energy transforming matter into energy is of such a nature among these weapons that the transition from space/time third density to time/space third density or what you may call your heaven worlds is interrupted in many cases.

Therefore, we are offering ourselves as those who continue the integration of soul or spirit complex during transition from space/time to time/space.

QUESTIONER: Could you give us an example from Hiroshima or Nagasaki of how this is done?

RA: I am Ra. Those who were destroyed, not by radiation but by the trauma of the energy release, found not only the body/mind/spirit complex made unviable, but also a disarrangement of that unique vibratory complex you have called the spirit complex, which we understand as a mind/body/spirit complex, to be completely disarranged without possibility of reintegration. This would be the loss to the Creator of part of the Creator, and thus we were given permission not to stop the events, but to ensure the survival of the, shall we say, disembodied mind/body/spirit complex. This we did in those events which you mention, losing no spirit or portion or holograph or microcosm of the macrocosmic Infinite One.

QUESTIONER: Could you tell me just vaguely how you accomplished this?

RA: I am Ra. This is accomplished through our understanding of dimensional fields of energy. The higher or more dense energy field will control the less dense.

QUESTIONER: Then you are saying that in general, you will allow the population of this planet to have a nuclear war and many deaths from that war, but you will be able to create a condition where these deaths will be no more traumatic than entrance to what we call the heaven worlds or the astral world due to death by a bullet or by the normal means of dying by old age. Is this correct?

RA: I am Ra. This is incorrect. It would be more traumatic. However, the entity would remain an entity.

QUESTIONER: Can you tell me the condition of the entities who were killed in Nagasaki and Hiroshima at this time?

RA: I am Ra. They of this trauma have not yet fully begun the healing process. They are being helped as much as is possible.

QUESTIONER: When the healing process is complete with these entities, will this experience of death due to nuclear bomb cause them to be regressed in their climb towards fourth density?

RA: I am Ra. Such actions as nuclear destruction affect the entire planet. There are no differences at this level of destruction, and the planet will need to be healed.

QUESTIONER: I was thinking specifically if an entity was in Hiroshima or Nagasaki at that time, and he was reaching harvestability at the end of our cycle, would this death by nuclear bomb create such trauma that he would not be harvestable at the end of the cycle?

RA: I am Ra. This is incorrect. Once the healing has taken place the harvest may go forth unimpeded. However, the entire planet will undergo healing for this action, no distinction being made betwixt victim and aggressor, this due to damage done to the planet.

QUESTIONER: Can you describe the mechanism of the planetary healing?

RA: I am Ra. Healing is a process of acceptance, forgiveness, and, if possible, restitution. The restitution not being available in time/space, there are many among your peoples now attempting restitution while in the physical.

QUESTIONER: How do these people attempt this restitution in the physical?

RA: I am Ra. These attempt feelings of love towards the planetary sphere and comfort and healing of the scars and the imbalances of these actions.

QUESTIONER: Then as the UFO phenomenon was made obvious to many of the population, many groups of people were reporting contact and telepathic contact with UFO entities and recorded the results of what they considered telepathic communication. Was the Confederation oriented to impressing telepathic communication on groups that were interested in UFOs?

RA: I am Ra. This is correct, although some of our members have removed themselves from the time/space using thought-form projections into your space/time and have chosen, from time to time, with permission of the Council, to appear in your skies without landing.

QUESTIONER: Then are all of the landings that have occurred with the exception of the landing that occurred when [name] was contacted of the Orion group or similar groups?

RA: I am Ra. Except for isolated instances of those of, shall we say, no affiliation, this is correct.

QUESTIONER: Is it necessary in each case of these landings for the entities involved to be calling the Orion group, or do some of these entities come in contact with the Orion group even though they are not calling that group?

RA: I am Ra. You must plumb the depths of fourth-density negative understanding. This is difficult for you. Once having reached third-density space/time continuum through your so-called windows, these crusaders may plunder as they will, the results completely a function of the polarity of the, shall we say, witness/subject or victim.

This is due to the sincere belief of fourth-density negative that to love self is to love all. Each other-self which is thus either taught or enslaved thus has a teacher which teaches love of self. Exposed to this teaching, it is intended there be brought to fruition an harvest of fourth-density negative or self-serving mind/body/spirit complexes.

*3QUESTIONER: Can you tell me of the various techniques used by the service to others positively oriented Confederation contacts with the people of this planet, the various forms and techniques of making contact?

RA: I am Ra. We could.

QUESTIONER: Would you do this, please?

RA: I am Ra. The most efficient mode of contact is that which you experience at this space/time. The infringement upon free will is greatly undesired. Therefore, those entities which are Wanderers upon your plane of illusion will be the only subjects for the thought projections which make up the so-called "Close Encounters" and meetings between positively oriented social memory complexes and Wanderers.

QUESTIONER: Could you give me an example of one of these meetings between a social memory complex and a Wanderer as to what the Wanderer would experience?

RA: I am Ra. One such example of which you are familiar is that of the one known as Morris.**4 In this case the previous contact which other entities in this entity's circle of friends experienced was negatively

*3. The following material, from Session 53, May 25, 1981, was added for clarity.
**4. This refers to CASE #1 in Secrets of the UFO by D. T. Elkins with Carla L. Rueckert, Louisville, L/L Research, 1976, pp 10–11

oriented. However, you will recall that the entity, Morris, was impervious to this contact and could not see with the physical optical apparatus, this contact.

However, the inner voice alerted the one known as Morris to go by itself to another place, and there an entity with the thought-form shape and appearance of the other contact appeared and gazed at this entity, thus awakening in it the desire to seek the truth of this occurrence and of the experiences of its incarnation in general.

The feeling of being awakened or activated is the goal of this type of contact. The duration and imagery used varies depending upon the subconscious expectations of the Wanderer which is experiencing this opportunity for activation.

QUESTIONER: In a "Close Encounter" by a Confederation type of craft, I am assuming that this "Close Encounter" is with a thought-form type of craft. Do Wanderers within the past few years have "Close Encounters" with landed thought-form type of craft?

RA: I am Ra. This has occurred, although it is much less common than the Orion type of so-called "Close Encounter."

We may note that in a universe of unending unity, the concept of a "Close Encounter" is humorous, for are not all encounters of a nature of self with self? Therefore, how can any encounter be less than very, very close?

QUESTIONER: Well, talking about this type of encounter of self to self, do any Wanderers of a positive polarization ever have a so-called "Close Encounter" with the Orion or negatively oriented polarization?

RA: I am Ra. This is correct.

QUESTIONER: Why does this occur?

RA: I am Ra. When it occurs it is quite rare and occurs either due to the Orion entities' lack of perception of the depth of positivity to be encountered or due to the Orion entities' desire to, shall we say, attempt to remove this positivity from this plane of existence. Orion tactics normally are those which choose the simple distortions of mind which indicate less mental and spiritual complex activity.

QUESTIONER: I have become aware of a very large variation in the contact with individuals. Could you give me general examples of the methods used by the Confederation to awaken or partially awaken the Wanderers they contact?

RA: I am Ra. The methods used to awaken Wanderers are varied. The center of each approach is the entrance into the conscious and subconscious in such a way as to avoid causing fear and to maximize the potential for an understandable subjective experience which has meaning for the entity. Many such occur in sleep, others in the midst of many activities during the waking hours. The approach is flexible and does not necessarily include the "Close Encounter" syndrome, as you are aware.

QUESTIONER: What about the physical examination syndrome? How does that relate to Wanderers and Confederation and Orion contacts?

RA: I am Ra. The subconscious expectations of entities cause the nature and detail of thought-form experience offered by Confederation thought-form entities. Thus, if a Wanderer expects a physical examination, it will, perforce, be experienced with as little distortion towards alarm or discomfort as is allowable by the nature of the expectations of the subconscious distortions of the Wanderer.

QUESTIONER: Well, are those who are taken on both Confederation and Orion craft then experiencing a seeming physical examination?

RA: I am Ra. Your query indicates incorrect thinking. The Orion group uses the physical examination as a means of terrifying the individual and causing it to feel the feelings of an advanced second-density being such as a laboratory animal. The sexual experiences of some are a subtype of this experience. The intent is to demonstrate the control of the Orion entities over the Terran inhabitant.

The thought-form experiences are subjective and, for the most part, do not occur in this density.

QUESTIONER: Then both Confederation and Orion contacts are being made, and "Close Encounters" are of a dual nature as I understand it. They can either be of the Confederation or of the Orion type of contact. Is this correct?

RA: I am Ra. This is correct, although the preponderance of contacts is Orion oriented.

QUESTIONER: Well, we have a large spectrum of entities on Earth with respect to harvestability, both positively oriented and negatively oriented. Would the Orion group target in on the ends of this spectrum, both positively and negatively oriented, for contact with Earth entities?

RA: I am Ra. This query is somewhat difficult to accurately answer. However, we shall attempt to do so.

The most typical approach of Orion entities is to choose what you might call the weaker-minded entity that it might suggest a greater amount of Orion philosophy to be disseminated.

Some few Orion entities are called by more highly polarized negative entities of your space/time nexus. In this case they share information just as we are now doing. However, this is a risk for the Orion entities due to the frequency with which the harvestable negative planetary entities then attempt to bid and order the Orion contact, just as these entities bid planetary negative contacts. The resulting struggle for mastery, if lost, is damaging to the polarity of the Orion group.

Similarly, a mistaken Orion contact with highly polarized positive entities can wreak havoc with Orion troops unless these crusaders are able to depolarize the entity mistakenly contacted. This occurrence is almost unheard of. Therefore, the Orion group prefers to make physical contact only with the weaker-minded entity.

QUESTIONER: Then in general we could say that if an individual has a "Close Encounter" with a UFO or any other type of experience that seems to be UFO related, he must look to the heart of the encounter and the effect upon him to determine whether it was Orion or Confederation contact. Is this correct?

RA: I am Ra. This is correct. If there is fear and doom, the contact was quite likely of a negative nature. If the result is hope, friendly feelings, and the awakening of a positive feeling of purposeful service to others, the marks of Confederation contact are evident.*5

QUESTIONER: Then I am assuming all of the groups getting telepathic contact from the Confederation are high-priority targets for the Orion crusaders, and I would assume that a large percentage of them are having their messages polluted by the Orion group. Can you tell me what percentage of them had their information polluted by the Orion group, and if any of them were able to remain purely a Confederation channel?

RA: I am Ra. To give you this information would be to infringe upon the free will or confusion of some living. We can only ask each group to consider the relative effect of philosophy and your so-called specific information. It is not the specificity of the information which attracts negative influences. It is the importance placed upon it.

---

*5. End of material from Session 53, May 25, 1981.

This is why we iterate quite often, when asked for specific information, that it pales to insignificance, just as the grass withers and dies while the love and the light of the One Infinite Creator redounds to the very infinite realms of creation forever and ever, creating and creating itself in perpetuity.

Why then be concerned with the grass that blooms, withers, and dies in its season only to grow once again due to the infinite love and light of the One Creator? This is the message we bring. Each entity is only superficially that which blooms and dies. In the deeper sense there is no end to beingness.

QUESTIONER: As you have stated, it is a straight and narrow path. There are many distractions.

We have created an introduction to the Law of One, traveling through and hitting the high points of this 75,000-year cycle. After this introduction, I would like to get directly to the main work, which is an investigation of evolution. I am very appreciative and feel a great honor and privilege to be doing this, and hope that we can accomplish this next phase.

RA: I am Ra. I leave you, my friends, in the love and the light of the One Infinite Creator. Go forth, then, merry and glad and rejoicing in the power and the peace of the One Creator. Adonai.

INDEX

ABOUT THE AUTHORS

DON ELKINS was born in Louisville, Kentucky, in 1930. He held a BS and MS in mechanical engineering from the University of Louisville, as well as an MS in general engineering from Speed Scientific School. He was professor of physics and engineering at the University of Louisville for twelve years from 1953 to 1965. In 1965 he left his tenured position and became a Boeing 727 pilot for a major airline to devote himself more fully to UFO and paranormal research. He also served with distinction in the US Army as a master sergeant during the Korean War.

Don Elkins began his research into the paranormal in 1955. In 1962, Don started an experiment in channeling, using the protocols he had learned from a contactee group in Detroit, Michigan. That experiment blossomed into a channeling practice that led eventually to the Law of One material 19 years later. Don passed away on November 7, 1984.

CARLA L. RUECKERT (McCarty) was born in 1943 in Lake Forest, Illinois. She completed undergraduate studies in English literature at the University of Louisville in 1966 and earned her master's degree in library service in 1971.

Carla became partners with Don in 1968. In 1970, they formed L/L Research. In 1974, she began channeling and continued in that effort until she was stopped in 2011 by a spinal fusion surgery. During four of those thirty-seven years of channeling (1981–1984), Carla served as the instrument for the Law of One material.

In 1987, she married Jim McCarty, and together they continued the mission of L/L Research. Carla passed into larger life on April 1, 2015.

JAMES MCCARTY was born in 1947 in Kearney, Nebraska. After receiving an undergraduate degrees from the University of Nebraska at Kearney and a master of science in early childhood education from the University of Florida, Jim moved to a piece of wilderness in Marion County, Kentucky, in 1974 to build his own log cabin in the woods, and to develop a self-sufficient lifestyle. For the next six years, he was in almost complete retreat.

He founded the Rock Creek Research and Development Laboratories in 1977 to further his teaching efforts. After experimenting, Jim decided that he preferred the methods and directions he had found in studying with L/L Research in 1978. In 1980, he joined his research with Don's and Carla's.

Jim and Carla were married in 1987. Jim has a wide L/L correspondence and creates wonderful gardens and stonework. He enjoys beauty, nature, dance, and silence.

NOTE: The Ra contact continued until session number 106. There are five volumes total in The Law of One series, Book I–Book V. There is also other material available from our research group on our archive website, www.llre- search.org.

You may reach us by email at contact@llresearch.org, or by mail at: L/L Research, P.O. Box 5195, Louisville, KY 40255-0195

NOTES